Does your husband mumble to you behind the news-paper as you ask for his input on your upcoming dinner party?

Does your wife wear a bored expression as you excitedly tell her all about your new computer system at work?

It wasn't always that way. When you were dating and in the first months of marriage, you two used to be so attentive and talked for hours on end. What happened? Does it have to be this way? Author Nancy Van Pelt answers emphatically, "No!"

In *How to Talk So Your Mate Will Listen and Listen So Your Mate Will Talk* you will learn to communicate the way you did when you were going out — no, even better! This intriguing book will enable you to become more aware of your communication patterns and your partner's needs. You will come to understand the mysterious differences between male and female communication patterns, while sharpening your awareness of the communication process.

In these pages, you'll find out how to get your loved one to talk and listen once again, so you can experience the God-given joy of an exciting, growing marriage.

How to Talk
So Your Mate
Will Listen

and Listen
So Your Mate
Will Talk

How to Talk So Your Mate Will Listen

and Listen So Your Mate Will Talk

Nancy L. Van Pelt

Power Books

Fleming H. Revell Company
Old Tappan, New Jersey

Library of Congress Cataloging-in-Publication Data

Van Pelt, Nancy L.
  How to talk so your mate will listen and listen so your mate will talk: compleat communication / Nancy L. Van Pelt.
     p.   cm.
  Bibliography: p.
  ISBN 0-8007-5330-5
  1. Communication in marriage. I. Title.
HQ734.V344   1989
646.7'8—dc20   89-34278
                                                            CIP

Copyright © 1989 by Nancy L. Van Pelt
Published by the Fleming H. Revell Company
Old Tappan, New Jersey 07675
Printed in the United States of America

TO my husband, Harry, who has worked tirelessly with me to prove beyond a shadow of a doubt that communication patterns can always be changed and deeper intimacy achieved.

And to YOU—because if we did it, you can too!

Contents

Acknowledgments

This book was not produced by me alone. *How to Talk So Your Mate Will Listen and Listen So Your Mate Will Talk* has come to be, not through my ideas alone, but from many people who have touched my life during the nineteen years I have specialized in family life education. It is a result of attending seminars and workshops on communication, researching a multitude of books written by professionals, and getting feedback from the couples who have attended the hundreds of Compleat Marriage, Compleat Parent, and Compleat Courtship Seminars my husband, Harry, and I have taught over the years. It also draws from the Communication Inventory I personally conducted on several hundred seminar participants.

Specifically, I am indebted to Harry, who has patiently been trying out many of the ideas and skills presented in this book so I could prove they do work, for acting as my research assistant in locating articles and books as well as for valuable insights obtained as he processed my ideas through his powerful left hemisphere, ensuring that I maintained a balanced perspective; for the many hours he spent editing this manuscript in our independent-minded computer; and most of all for his patience with my preoccupation during the preparation of this manuscript.

Special appreciation is also given to Alberta Mazat, M.F.C.C., and my son Rodney S. Van Pelt, M.D., who provided technical advice for the chapter dealing with sexual communication; to my daughter, Carlene, and her husband, Brian Will, M.D., who tirelessly fed the Communication Inventory into their computer and organized the results into readable information. To Judy Coulston, Ph.D., who painstakingly edited this work and suggested valuable insights. Her creative ideas and profound perceptions have made her an indispensable powerhouse of ideas.

Thanks also to the thousands of couples who have attended our Compleat Marriage seminars over the years and testified by their improved lives that the communication skills taught have profoundly changed their relationships for the better when they were consistently practiced . . . but who also plead with us for another seminar that slows the pace and deals solely with communication. This one's for you!

And to the hundreds of couples in attendance at our seminars who willingly participated in the Communication Inventory so I might have anonymous but firsthand, candid information regarding their personal communication patterns. Their forthright responses have provided support for many of the ideas presented.

And to God be the glory!

An Invitation to Readers

This book is an outgrowth of nineteen years of specialization in teaching family life seminars and ten years in the pastoral ministry. Harry and I have personally talked with hundreds of married couples over the years—enough to convince us that an enormous number were not enjoying their marriages to the fullest simply because they lacked basic communication skills. Some refused to communicate out of anger or fear. Others were completely indifferent. Some were willing but didn't know how or where to begin. These relationships frequently soured.

As a result of this early discovery, we began to include basic communication skills in each of our family life seminars. Several principles were taught that helped couples in a relatively short period of time.

In our Compleat Marriage seminar, for instance, in one two-hour session on communication we covered the levels of communication; basic male and female communication differences; nonverbal communication; active listening and the use of I-messages. People were literally breathless by the time we heaped so much information on them in such a short period of time, and there was little time to practice or integrate all of this into daily living. Within the hour we were off and running with the next vital marriage topic.

During the tightly packed weekend, we found a real longing on the part of the couples present for another weekend seminar, similar to the Compleat Marriage, but one in which they could focus just on communication. A new fire was kindled within me . . . was it possible that Harry and I could design another seminar as successful as Compleat Marriage where couples could learn these skills in a comfortable atmosphere which would not be threatening or embarrassing to them?

This book is my attempt to fill the need so keenly pressed upon me by the thousands of couples who have attended our Compleat Marriage seminars over the years. It is our plan to teach this seminar, using this book, over a weekend and cover the material at a slow enough pace that participants have time to practice and integrate the information into daily living. Each chapter will form a lesson of study. During each session of the seminar, the previous lesson's skills will be reviewed and new skills added. The additional review and practice will greatly assist participants in moving from the awkward stage of learning toward being more intentional and competent when putting new skills to work.

Within the covers of this book are some of the most powerful techniques and strategies ever accumulated for communicating with a partner in an easy-to-read, simple-to-apply format. Here lies an endless range of possibilities for people who may have given up on ever getting through to a partner. This book is designed to be a real breakthrough in combating the number-one marriage problem: communication.

The material is derived from such varied fields as linguistics and psychology as well as sales and management, but it is applied to couple communication. Research into the social and behavioral sciences reports many exciting discoveries about human relationships. Now we can understand why one person responds while another resists; how to deal effectively with resistance to change; and how to communicate so others will understand what is being said.

The word *communication* means a transferring, imparting, or sharing of information, ideas, messages, or signals. Originally the word had religious overtones as it was derived from the word *communion*—the sharing of a significant experience. *Compleat communication* combines both the old and new meaning. My definition is this: *Communication is the sharing of thoughts, feelings, or experience between a couple, or a couple is communicating to the extent they are sharing common information and/or experience.* A couple may or may not consciously be aware of the sharing.

Since so many messages filter in and out daily, much of

the communication process takes place at an unconscious level. Since we are all creatures of habit, a couple may or may not be responding from habit—unconsciously. Good habits are necessary and desirable; bad habits need to be monitored. Within our relationships we need to become aware of which habits are enhancing our ability to communicate and which are destructive.

A major objective of this book, then, is to help you become more aware of your communication patterns. By becoming aware of the patterns which serve you well, you can build on them and use them to your advantage. Becoming more aware of destructive habits allows you to choose a new way of relating to your partner. You are free to choose new patterns that will no longer interfere with your relationship.

Some habits are easy to change because it is simply a matter of greater awareness of something you are inadvertently doing or not doing that irritates your spouse. Sometimes it takes a major effort, willpower, and concentrated practice to change firmly established habits. Habits we have lived for years tend to die hard, but change is possible. Harry and I changed our communication habits after thirty years of marriage—and if we did it, you can too! The first step is awareness.

Another major objective is to present the information and skills necessary to change long-established negative patterns. Awareness is useful, but we must progress toward actual change. As you become aware of negative patterns, you need new skills to replace the old, destructive ones. Presented here is an exciting array of alternatives with which to experiment.

A third objective of this book is to help you become more aware of your partner's needs. Your new awareness will assist you in understanding your partner's communication patterns, and you can begin to predict responses in almost any given situation. You will be better able to adjust your patterns to influence a more positive interaction between the two of you. Being able to predict this, and having a wide range of skills to use, will give you a powerful advantage.

A fourth objective is to assist you in understanding the differences between male and female communication. Males and females tend to follow certain ingrained patterns often misinterpreted by the opposite sex. Becoming aware of and

understanding the different patterns will allow you to interpret conversations more accurately from your partner's point
of view. This ability could drastically reduce the number of
misunderstandings between the two of you.

To put into use all of the information and skills in this book
will take time and require a lot of you. There may be moments
when you may wish to throw in the towel when your partner
won't respond, misinterprets, or breaks the rules. Even those
who rate their communication a "ten" occasionally find
themselves out of sync. Even our best efforts will sometimes
be misinterpreted and met with hostility and resentment and
result in chaos. Meaningful communication always has been
and always will be difficult and risky at times.

Yet the need for intimacy, to connect with the one you love,
constantly reemerges. With consistent effort you will notice a
gradual change taking place between you and your mate.
Your communication will take on purpose. A closeness will
replace the more shallow manner in which you used to
communicate. You will find your partner opening up more.
You can communicate on a deeper level about topics previously discussed only on a superficial level as fear and anger
are reduced. Since negative communication patterns sap our
strength and make us irritable, you will experience more
energy and joyful living.

Yes, the rewards of consistent effort will begin to outweigh
the risks for anyone who practices the principles presented.
It's worth the risk . . . and the effort.

My communication with Harry is not yet perfect. To be
brutally frank, it isn't even close. We are still learning
. . . growing . . . and working on it. But I can assure you of one
thing: We are growing closer and improving the quality of our
communication as well as deepening the intimacy between us.

Won't you join us in the search for compleat communication? It is my prayer that reading and sharing these concepts
will bond you more closely with your partner and with the
God who created us all.

How to Talk
So Your Mate
Will Listen

and Listen
So Your Mate
Will Talk

1 Communication: The Number-One Marriage Problem

The happiness of a couple can be measured to a large degree by the effectiveness of their communication. How a couple communicates is one of the most powerful factors affecting the success or failure of their relationship.

A group of 730 marriage counselors was asked by *Redbook* magazine to list the most common marriage problems that divide and push apart couples. From this survey, a list of the ten most common marital problems was formulated. Listed in order of frequency they were as follows:

1. breakdown in communication
2. loss of shared goals and interests
3. sexual incompatibility
4. infidelity
5. excitement and fun gone from relationship
6. money
7. conflicts over children
8. alcohol and drug abuse
9. women's rights issues
10. in-laws[1]

"Breakdown in communication" as number one is no surprise. But numbers two through five also relate to a breakdown in communication. Where there is a lessening of desire to share each other's goals and interests, a natural diminishing of communication results. We prefer spending time with those who enjoy the activities we enjoy. We gravitate to those of like interests, those who speak our language and with whom we feel a kinship through shared activities.

"Sexual incompatibility," listed as number three, doesn't pinpoint the heart of the problem. Any two adults can be sexually compatible, provided they possess the desired equipment. What prompts sexual incompatibility, then? Numbers one and two—a breakdown in communication and a lack of shared interests and goals.

"Infidelity," in the number four spot, follows on the heels of the previous three, as does number five, "excitement and fun gone from relationship." Partners caught in these binds have multiple problems; they can't talk about them due to a breakdown in communication, so they often turn to others for comfort and solace. Infidelity isn't the problem. It is the *result* of other problems between a couple that commence with a communication breakdown.

A mere twenty years ago, communication was hardly mentioned in books dealing with marriage. Family specialist David R. Mace says that prior to 1970, there was very little understanding of the communication process and how it affects the marriage relationship. To check this point, I reviewed a number of books published before that time and noted that not one even mentioned communication, but all contained chapters on building sexual intimacy!

Why does communication now top the list when it wasn't even on the charts just a few years ago?

Yesteryear's marriage was held together by the struggle for survival. Couples were concerned with providing shelter, food, and clothing for the family. Little time or thought was given to building a relationship. Today's marriage is totally relational. The pendulum has swung in the other direction. We think more in terms of wanting emotional rather than physical needs met. We want to be valued for what we are, not because we bring home a paycheck or perform household tasks. Affluence and leisure-time pursuits have freed the vast majority from worries about staying alive.

Thus, communication tops everyone's list nowadays because it is basic to intimate relationships. Communication is what sparks caring, giving, sharing, and affirming. Unless we understand and utilize properly the principles of listening and speaking, we can't really know or understand each other. We remain closed to one another.

Why Couples Can't Communicate

Many reasons exist for a lack of proficiency in the area of communication. The most prevalent is that skills have never been taught or learned. The husband who walks in the door and says, "Hi, honey," which pretty well sums up the evening's conversation, is not demonstrating that he has mastered many communication skills. A wife who sinks into the silent treatment because her husband said something that hurt her feelings is doing likewise. What each is really showing is that he or she doesn't care enough to risk telling the other who he/she is or what he/she is experiencing each day. Nor does either one care enough to find a more productive method of relating to one another. If each is that disinterested in the relationship, we can't expect much to happen. Many couples keep their communication on such a superficial level because they lack basic skills.

Another reason husband and wife fail to communicate adequately is they are afraid to share real thoughts and feelings with their mates. Fear of experiencing the ultimate hurt—rejection—blocks open sharing of thoughts and feelings.

There is justification for such fear. Who hasn't opened up to a partner and been rebuffed? Some people get hurt so badly they refuse to come back for more. Instead, they crawl inside a shell and stay there, maintaining the appearance of a functioning marriage partner but denying the reality.

A third reason couples fail to communicate is it is easier to avoid and repress ideas and feelings than it is to learn how to process them properly. This reason is closely connected to how we feel about ourselves. If you think you or your opinions are worthless, why attempt to share them? Who wants to hear what you have to say? When a partner shoots you down, the picture is complete. You conclude that it is easier to withdraw than be hurt.

Connie was going through her third divorce by age thirty-one. Connie's first husband turned out to be an alcoholic who mistreated her. Fred, husband number two, showed much potential but also had a problem with alcohol, lost his job, and couldn't support the family. Husband number three was repeatedly unfaithful. How could one woman turn up three losers in ten years?

The answer is she asked for it—not verbally, but Connie's low feelings of worth projected to her partners that she did not consider herself worthy to be treated with respect. Deliberately but unknowingly, Connie selected men who would mistreat and relate to her in distant, unloving ways. Connie's life won't change until she changes how she views herself.

The fourth reason couples can't communicate is they never have experienced success at it. Whenever they attempted to open up, they were tuned out or shot down. Such experiences begin early in life. Has your child ever run to you with an exciting discovery to have you respond with a disinterested, "That's nice, dear." A message came through: "What you have just shared with me is not important and I am not interested in what interests you."

Early lessons in protecting our feelings teach us to measure carefully what can and cannot be shared with those we love. As a result, many people live much like turtles: They stick out their heads cautiously for air, only to have them lopped off by predators. Eventually, they spend more time inside than outside their shells. Dark it may be, but at least it's safe.

In any series of conversations between marrieds, each conversation has present implications as well as implications from the past. The present is influenced by current attempts to communicate and understand, but present conversations are also very much influenced by the misunderstandings and disappointments from past encounters. The greater the hurt and anger from the past, the less likely the couple can change without professional help.

Why We Communicate the Way We Do

Learned patterns from the past   Supposedly Sigmund Freud's favorite question was, "And vat did your mother do to you that made you this vay?" This implies that your mother or father made you the way you are.

How you communicate today was influenced by the home you grew up in. While growing up, you carefully observed how family members spoke and responded to one another. This became your model for how people talk, listen, and respond. Positive patterns of respect, cheerfulness, and openness in asking for what you wanted were learned—if you were lucky enough to have such behavior modeled. Destructive patterns of hostility, mind reading, silent treatment, and yelling were also, to a large extent, learned in childhood.

As such patterns were observed, you began to experiment with various methods of getting what you wanted, and you eventually settled on patterns you found most effective. Most likely you have carried many of these patterns into your marriage.

You may assume your communication patterns are the correct and possibly the only way to communicate. After all, this is what you learned as you grew up. However, your communication patterns may conflict sharply with your partner's. Your family may have settled differences of opinion through quiet discussion. In your partner's family, they may have been settled through loud arguments.

Social conditioning   All of our speech patterns are not learned from parents. Between the years of five and fifteen, a child spends much time with peers of his or her own sex, learning to converse much the same way they do. Since boys and girls communicate differently, such differences will be reinforced through social conditioning.

According to anthropologists Daniel Maltz and Ruth Borker, boys and girls socialize differently. Little girls play most frequently in pairs. As they grow up, their lives center mostly on a "best friend" or a series of best friends. These best-friend relationships are made and broken by what the girls discuss. Much of what is shared could be classified as private talk or secrets. If any of this information is divulged to others, the relationship is likely to be broken; each finds a new and sympathetic friend to whom they can confide more secrets. The information shared is usually unimportant; it is the experience of sharing that is important to girls. They infrequently play in groups, but if a newcomer is admitted she is treated equally until trouble occurs. Girls prefer cooperative play and when it becomes otherwise, the friendship is probably broken.

Little boys, on the other hand, play more frequently in larger groups, often outdoors. Studies show that boys are not as verbal as girls, and there is less talking and more doing when boys get together. A new boy is easily admitted to the group but once in must jockey for position and status within the group. This takes place in various ways but is easily recognized by wisecracking, challenges, joking, and competitive talk about who is best. Each seeks his place in life through the group.

Boys and girls carry these attitudes, reinforced through their growing-up years, into adult life. After she gets married, a woman expects intimate and meaningful heart-to-heart talks. Most men don't need heart-to-heart talks but may miss doing things with male friends where activities play a major role.

Furthermore, these heart-to-heart talks may mean different things to each when and if they do occur. The woman often feels tremendous emotional satisfaction and the man may sense real trouble since they have to keep discussing things! Their relationship can weaken as she pushes for more intimate talks about what she feels is wrong and he tries to prevent them.

Men and women come from totally different past experiences from the time they are born. A little boy is talked to and treated differently from a little girl. As each grows up, these patterns are reinforced and each brings to marriage differing expectations about the place talk fills in relationships. Each tends to listen differently, discuss differing topics, solve problems differently, have differing intimacy needs, and search for closeness in a different manner.[2]

Whether these differences are the result of social conditioning may be debatable. But one thing is known for sure: Males and females have very different ideas on how to be friends. More of these differences and ways of combating misunderstandings as a result of them will be discussed later.

Brain sex differences   Another reason males and females communicate the way they do has to do with genetics. Literally thousands of studies prove that significant sex differences exist, but it is genetic psychological differences that affect communication between the sexes.

"Until recently," writes science and medical writer Tim Hackler, "it was widely assumed that male and female behavior was determined by socialization. Environment was considered the most dominant factor. To suggest that male and female behavior could even remotely be genetically determined was barbaric. This notion has all but collapsed as researchers in both the social and natural sciences uncover evidence in favor of genetically based sex difference."[3]

It is now known, for instance, that the brain is differentiated during fetal development. During the sixteenth to twenty-sixth week, the left hemisphere of the male fetus's brain is bathed with androgens released from the mother. The corpus callosum—the connecting links between the two hemispheres of the brain—also receives this bath, which reduces the size and number of connections between the hemispheres. The brain actually changes color, which is visible under scientific examination. In some cases, it is noted that the size of the left hemisphere shrinks for a time while the right hemisphere flourishes.[4]

This means that males don't have as easy access to both hemispheres as females do. However, the hormonal bath gives a specialization to the male brain that might be called logical linear isolation, which females don't tend to get. Left brain is more logical and right brain is more intuitive or emotional. This explains what is called "woman's intuition." A woman can more readily scan both hemispheres, leap to a conclusion, and come up with a solution. A man tends to plod through the logistics of the situation item by item, more slowly arriving at a conclusion—but he can verify his conclusions, which the woman can't do.

It is not being implied here that a woman can't think logically or a man emotionally. But a man's brain is wired to be more analytical and a female's to be more intuitive or emotional. Women complain that their husbands won't talk to them and men complain about how emotional their wives are. It is more than societal in nature. There is a physiological root, which means God planned it this way![5]

Healthy adults must use both sides of their brains to live full and complete lives. They must combine both logic and feeling. But how incredibly creative of God to put dominance of logic in the male and dominance of feeling in the female. Each of these perspectives is needed in order to be whole or *complete*.

It is difficult to lump all males and females into one basket and assume each will always respond in accordance with their sex. Everyone of the same sex will not always have identical emotional needs, duplicate behavior patterns, or precisely corresponding ways of thinking. But recognizing that brain-sex differences affect the communication process provides insights into how the other half will often think and respond.

Temperament type   Nothing may have a more profound influence on your style of communication than your temperament. Temperament is a combination of inherited traits that subconsciously affect your behavior. These traits are passed on through the genes. Some studies suggest that more genes are passed on from grandparents than parents. This combination of traits is largely responsible for your actions, reactions, and emotional responses and to a large extent determines how you communicate.

The temperament theory was conceived by Hippocrates and divides people into four basic categories: sanguine, choleric, melancholy, and phlegmatic. The following brief description of the four temperaments introduces you to the communication patterns most likely used by each.[6]

Sanguine.   The sanguine person is an outgoing, exuberant conversationalist. Talking is the name of the game for him and he can easily dominate conversations. A compulsiveness compels him to talk, to take center stage, and to tell long, dramatic stories. This compulsion to talk makes him a poor listener. A short attention span and the fact that he is easily distracted further complicates his ability to listen. The sanguine often speaks before thinking. His decisions are based more on feelings of the moment than on analytic thought. He tends to be a loud person or even a screamer. Anger is rarely repressed since he is so emotionally expressive. He explodes easily but rarely carries a grudge. Sanguines are a cheerful, noisy, blustery bunch with lovable dispositions. Since they are never at a loss for words, they are frequently the envy of the more timid types.

Choleric.   The choleric is another extrovert who also speaks freely but much more deliberately than the sanguine. The choleric dislikes the long, detailed stories of the sanguine. He might tell the same story but would skip insignificant details, press his point home, and move to the punch line. Unlike the sanguine, he does not sympathize easily and can be insensitive to the needs of others. His strengths lie with leadership, where he finds it easy to make decisions for himself and others. He often appears opinionated, domineering, and bossy. The choleric is not given to analytical thought but rather to quick intuitive appraisal of a situation. Cholerics usually think they are right, and because of their keen and very practical minds, they usually are! Cholerics make good debaters but they are argumentative and can be sarcastic. They tend to ask many *why* questions.

Melancholy.   The melancholy, the first of the two introverts, is given to exceptional analytical thinking. His inquisitive mind has the ability to take a situation and dissect and examine each part. After thought and careful analysis, he'll speak. Whereas the choleric finds details boring, the melancholy thrives on detail. He is dominated by a variety of moods and vacillates between highs and lows. Sometimes the melancholy is withdrawn, depressed, and irritable, and other times he is outgoing, friendly, and extroverted. Because he is dominated by his emotional nature, the melancholy frequently has a difficult time making emotional adjustments to life. He is a gifted perfectionist with an extremely sensitive nature. Of all the temperaments, he will probably have the most difficulty expressing his true feelings.

Phlegmatic.   The phlegmatic is a quiet, slower, and more deliberate, noncombative speaker. His calm manner rarely allows him to become angry; instead he'll go to any length to avoid unpleasant confrontations. "Peace at any cost" is his motto. Whereas he rarely appears agitated, he feels more emotion than he shows. He never laughs very loud or cries very hard. His facial expressions will be the most difficult to decipher, for he can appear as a "stoneface." He gives the appearance of being distant and unemotional. He remains uninvolved in his surroundings and rarely volunteers information without prodding. The phlegmatic has an orderly mind and is capable of analysis and deduction. Unlike the melancholy temperament, which is always changing, the phlegmatic is always the same: steady and dependable. His natural dry sense of humor can be a joy—except to a partner. He makes a dependable mate who is easy to live with unless his slow and methodical manner becomes a real source of irritation to a more aggressive partner.

The sanguine does not communicate in a manner superior to the choleric, melancholy, or phlegmatic. Each communicates in a different and distinct manner. One is not "right" and the others "wrong." Each is different from the others, and this affects communication.

None of us are all one temperament; we are blends of all four. Usually one predominates and another is secondary.[7] Since temperament is determined by inherited genes, it cannot be changed. I am a chlor-san and nothing can change that. But I can praise God for the strengths and pray that my weaknesses can be transformed. This also helps me understand my mel-san husband's style and why he goes on and on about things. Our inherent temperaments play a big part in determining communication styles.

Achieving More Effective Communication Patterns

The happiness of a couple can be measured, to a large degree, by the effectiveness of their communication. How a couple communicates is one of the most powerful factors affecting the success or failure of their relationship. Effective patterns of communication will allow the couple to negotiate problem areas, fulfill needs, avoid misunderstandings, and develop intimacy over the years. Through ineffective patterns, the couple will misinterpret motives, needs will go unfulfilled, problems will go unsolved, and hostility will increase. As the years roll on, the chance for solving these problems lessens due to ingrained habit patterns and deep-seated resentment.

Many people get so caught in a web of inadequate communication habits that they give up trying. Multitudes communicate through ineffective, shallow, and hollow methods, never thinking of changing their own patterns of communication. Yet 50 percent of the women and 38 percent of the men in my Communication Inventory (CI) said they were always searching for ways to improve communication.[8] The desire is there, but the methods and commitment to break negative habit patterns and establish new ones is lacking.

Now the real questions come into play: *What specific changes do you need to make in order to achieve your goal of more effective communication? What changes are you willing to make?* You may or may not be aware of what you should or should not be doing. But that is what compleat communication is all about: sharpening your awareness of the communication process. By becoming more aware of the patterns you and your partner are using, you can avoid typical pitfalls that trap thousands, greatly improve your chances for learning to communicate at new and deeper levels, and understand your mate better.

The chapters that follow describe the elements, attitudes, and skills necessary to achieve this goal. But this book needs more than surface reading. It will require practice for all the skills, information, and suggestions to become a part of your everyday life. Only when your new habit patterns become instinctual and habitual will you see a change take place in your relationship. Then you will begin to experience change and growth as never before.

Give improving your communication all you've got. No conditional commitments; no exceptions; no fine print; no ifs, ands, or buts; no time limits. Work at it whether or not you feel like it—even when your partner breaks all the rules. Resist the inclination to pout, run, or punish your spouse when your attempts fail. Simply resolve to work at improving your communication, regardless of any distractions.

Unless you are really committed, not much is going to happen. If you want good communication badly enough, you will be motivated to learn, make changes, and practice. This will take precedence over other things. When it is given priority, you are much more likely to succeed.

Once upon a time a frog tried to hop across a dirt road. He landed instead in a deep rut made by many passing vehicles. In vain he leaped this way and that, attempting to scale the steep walls which fenced him in. Eventually a group of his froggy friends happened along and encouraged him to get out of the rut.

"I can't," he cried despondently. "I've tried and tried, but I just can't make it." His bulgy-eyed friends begged him to reconsider and try again. The frog refused.

Eventually, the frog's friends left him to his misery and doom. Later in the day, they found him leaping about at the river's edge. "We thought you were stuck in the rut forever. How did you get out?" they queried with obvious interest.

"I had to," replied the frog. "A truck was coming."

Why wait until a truck threatens your relationship with obliteration before you make a change. You may be in a rut, but you *can* get out if you are motivated. And there's no better time to try than *now!*

2 Pair Bonding: Pathway to Intimacy

Almost any small crisis can separate and divide an improperly bonded couple, yet a strongly bonded couple can survive any crisis.

"Dearly Beloved," Harry began. "We are gathered together to unite this man and this woman in holy matrimony." From the second pew, I could sense my husband was having trouble getting the words past the heavy lump in his throat, but he bravely swallowed and continued the wedding ceremony.

"Carlene, I remember the first glimpse I had of you in the hospital, your first tooth, and the first time you said 'Dada.' I treasure the memory of your first hug and watching you take your first step."

Even though I was not able to communicate verbally with my husband at that moment, I knew his thoughts were the same as mine. *Have we adequately prepared you for the adventure of marriage? Your eyes shine with a new and amazing confidence. But you are so young! Have you made the right choice? Is Brian the right one? How can any of us be sure? Will Brian be as good to you five, ten, twenty, thirty years down the line as he has been in the last three years?*

The radiant bride and groom now turned to face each other while Harry recited a "pledge of love" Brian had written for the occasion:

My beloved companion. This day we share is the beginning of a new and thrilling dimension of the love relationship we have shared and built over the last three years. . . . I'm afraid of the unknown before us . . . yet confident our love will endure . . . it is my desire to live with you just as you are. . . . I have chosen you above all others. . . . Therefore, I take you as my

31

life partner. . . . I pledge to share my life openly with you, to
disclose to you the innermost thoughts of my heart and to
speak the truth to you in love. . . .

Confidence radiated from them—assurance of the future—
hearts united.

"So, Brian, do you now take Carlene to be your wife, to
love her as Christ loves His bride, to comfort, honor, and
cherish her in sickness and in health, in prosperity or
adversity, and forsaking all others, keep thee only unto her so
long as you both shall live? Do you so declare?"

Brian had had other opportunities to marry, but Carlene
was different. She had that special quality that made him
resist all others and select her.

"And now, Carlene, do you take Brian to be your husband,
to join your lives together in a living union, to love, honor,
and cherish him in prosperity. . . ."

When they began dating, she was only a junior in high
school and he was a senior in college. We didn't think the
romance would last. But it had, and three years later. . . .

After the prayer came the kiss. Both felt the blessing of
heaven on their union. Harry continued, "I, as a minister of
the Gospel, do now pronounce that they are husband and
wife. What God hath joined together, let no man put asun-
der."

When Harry performed the service for Carlene and Brian,
we thought he was the one who married them. We now
know that the wedding was only a legal ceremony to protect
a relationship or the "pair bond" that had developed between
them.

Being "bonded" and married are not the same thing. Many
couples are bonded but not married; others are married but
suffering from weak, damaged, or disintegrating bonds. Dr.
Donald Joy, author of *Bonding: Relationships in the Image of God*,
likens the bond to an expensive automobile—long, sleek, and
shiny.[1] If you were lucky enough to own such a car, you
wouldn't leave it on the street to suffer the effects of severe
weather conditions, vandalism, or theft. You would want
your investment protected inside a well-secured garage. The
car represents the bond that is already formed; the garage

represents the ceremony to protect the already-formed bond.

This chapter is devoted to exploring the "glue" which mysteriously bonds male to female. It is clear there is a definite developmental pattern in romantic relationships. The pattern revolves around various forms of communication: verbal, nonverbal, touching, and eye contact. To a large degree, communication is determined by how well pair bonded a couple is. Their basis for communication and intimacy is laid as they progress through the twelve-step sequence of pair bonding. But first let us take a brief look at birth bonding.

Birth Bonding: Magnificent Moments Between Parent and Child

It has been known for some time that animals will bond to their young soon after birth. After a young duckling hatches from its shell, it bonds itself to the first object it sees moving. Ordinarily, of course, the duckling attaches itself to its mother, but if the mother is removed, it will settle for any moving object. In fact, researchers tell us that the duckling will become bonded most easily to a blue football bladder dragged in front of it on a string. A week after this process is begun, it will fall in line behind the bladder whenever it scoots by in order to stay close to "mom."

It was many years before we were willing to accept the idea it might be possible that similar bonding procedures were evident among humans. The best medical and scientific information available today points to the following birth bonding information:

1. Timing   There is a critical time period in which bonding can take place. In human birth bonding this period can last two-and-one-half to three hours immediately following birth.

M. H. Klaus and J. H. Kennell reported in *Parent-Infant Bonding* that parent and child needed more than fifteen minutes of skin-to-skin contact within the first three-and-one-half hours in order for maximum bonding to be achieved. When traditional-birth babies were compared with birth-bonded babies, it was found that at the end of three months,

traditional-delivery babies spent 540 percent more time cry-
ing!

Traditional-delivery babies experienced much more anxiety. Traditional-delivery mothers also spent 550 percent
more time in an almost endless activity of poking, wiping,
cleaning noses and ears, changing diapers, etc., than did
birth-bonded mothers, signaling dissatisfaction with the
baby. Birth-bonded babies tended to be more peaceful, it was
concluded.[2]

2. Eye bonding   Immediately following birth, a baby is
equipped with sharp visual acuteness—a zoom lens that
allows him to focus on any object close or distant. This visual
acuteness allows the baby to search for objects with which to
bond. Newborns can turn their heads and follow with their
eyes someone who is entering or leaving the room and can
mimic facial expressions such as sticking out the tongue.
Within a few hours this ability lessens and will not reappear
for weeks. Newborns whose mothers do not spend time eye
bonding with them tend not to thrive.[3]

3. Voice bonding   Mothers are equipped with special high
voices which they tend to use instinctively when viewing and
talking with their children. It is more than "baby talk." It is an
elevated tone to which babies are particularly responsive.
Voice bonding in the animal kingdom is a well-documented
fact. Parent and child quickly become voice-bonded.[4]

4. Tactile bonding   The rituals of touch—hugging, patting, hand holding, and kissing—are important throughout
life but never more important than during the birth-bonding
process. As early as 1915, Dr. Henry Chapin gave a report
regarding ten orphanages in the United States, where every
infant under the age of two years had died! The orphanages
were understaffed with overworked employees. Without the
gestures of prolonged eye contact, voice bonding, and human
touch, the babies regressed. A regulated diet and hygienic
conditions were not enough.[5]

Experts highly recommend that fathers remove their shirts
while bonding to their infants to maximize the amount of skin

contact, warmth, and affection. Mothers instinctively do this when putting baby to breast.

The power of bonding through the avenue of touch is now so evident that it is possible to say you become attached to those you touch.

5. Mouth-to-mouth bonding   Yes, mouth-to-mouth contact or kissing is a necessary step in the birth-bonding process. It is critical that mother and father kiss their baby, because in so doing they exchange harmless bacteria which provides the base for healthy digestion of food. It also prepares the baby to live in their home without getting sick. Without the nuzzling or kissing and exchanging of bacteria, the baby is likely to be colicky. This bonding is universal in the animal kingdom with the mother licking her young to activate the digestive juices. Kissing an infant is an instinctual love response during the bonding process.[6]

6. Odor bonding   Odor is another powerful bonding agent. The lanolin-laced lining of the placenta covers the infant with a unique odor which apparently motivates mother to touch, hold, and embrace her child. Not only has this odor been known to motivate mothers but similar responses have been noted in women present in the delivery room as well.[7]

Each mother and father possesses a distinct odor which binds them to their child and prepares the child to be "at peace" at home. In-the-know baby-sitters can comfort a restless child by securing a piece of clothing from mom or dad's closet. The familiarity of the odor relieves anxiety and produces feelings of security.

The *American Scientific Affiliation Journal* cites reasons newborns are so ready to bond. It is due at least in part to a chemical released in their systems while they are passing through the birth canal. This chemical prepares them to withstand the compression and squeezing. Newborns are very flexible and plastic while going through the birth canal, and there can be intermittent oxygen deprivation as the umbilical cord is cut. The release of this chemical could explain why some of the babies survived the Mexico City earthquake in 1985 for up to nine days without care after the collapse of the hospital.

The chemical is released only during delivery and the babies are born with a natural "high"—wide-awake, kicking, and very alert. Within several hours, almost all of these responses fade and do not return until weeks later.

The end result of proper birth bonding is a profound attachment between parent and child. A solid foundation has been laid for mutual affection and respect. The greatest gift any parent can give to his or her child upon birth is the gift of oneself and time to develop the special attachment birth-bonded babies have for their parents.

Pair Bonding: The Search for Intimacy Begins

Just as early contact links parent to child through eye and skin contact along with verbal intonations, so do male and female form a true bond of attachment. The process is a gradual one, progressing through a twelve-step sequence. Pair bonding was first reported by secular zoologist Desmond Morris in *Intimate Behaviour*. However, it was Dr. Donald Joy's book *Bonding* that opened my mind to the importance and relevance of bonding occurring between men and women for healthy marriages.

The Reader's Digest Great Encyclopedic Dictionary gives several clear definitions regarding what the word *bonding* means: "That which binds or holds together; a uniting force; a substance that cements or unites." Pair bonding, then, refers to the emotional attachment that grows between male and female as their affections for each other deepen. As the relationship develops, an almost predictable pattern of intimacy unfolds.

The term *bonding* describes the mysterious romantic attraction between two lovers, and it goes far beyond physical appeal. Included would be the emotional, physical, spiritual, and intellectual components. *Pair bonding* is a term to describe a relationship between a couple who are mutually attracted and joined together for an exclusive lifetime journey. Even without the benefits of marriage, they have become as one because they have become one in purpose and identity.

Bonding is more than a matter of "falling in love" with the heart or emotions. It is both an emotional and physical response between lovers which attaches them to each other in ways that may appear mysterious to the casual observer. Bonding describes the fusing not only of two separate and distinct individual lives but also a blending of their minds, ideas, and personalities. Two previously separate and distinct persons now blend their values, goals, and beliefs. Their hopes, dreams, and futures merge to form one unit. And note, all of this occurs without a formal contractual agreement.

The gift of bonding is not reserved for the young and beautiful. A person of any age can lay claim to the development of a bond. Whenever two persons begin to "fall in love," as we put it, the process of bonding is under way. The couple enters each other's world and begins to view life through another pair of eyes. As the attraction solidifies and if it is mutual between the pair, the relationship is not easily broken. Time and distance cannot disrupt the developing pair bond.

Desmond Morris notes that the twelve-step bonding process tends to be present in all human cultures. Although odor bonding does not appear among the twelve steps, many couples attest to the fact that they are powerfully attached to the smell of a home, body odors, or even the sexual secretions of a partner.

Pair bonding is a gradual process, although at times it appears to happen rapidly. Couples frequently tell me, "It was love at first sight with us." What occurs is not love but a powerful attraction upon which they later reflect and interpret as love. The process of falling in love and forming a bond of attachment is a long, drawn-out one.

We simply cannot, in the true sense of the word, "bond" ourselves to a member of the opposite sex instantly. The initial contact may spark interest and the bonding process may be set in motion. From there begins a gradually increasing series of intimate encounters which lead the couple to the formation of a pair bond.

Although there really is no typical love relationship, since each pair of lovers tends to think theirs is unique, human love affairs do tend to follow a pattern.

The Twelve Steps to Pair Bonding

Let's explore the first stage of human bonding:

1. Eye to body   The first glance at a person reveals much. This look notes the physical qualities of the other: size, shape, coloring, age, and personality. Immediately, an almost unconscious grading process begins, rating the person on a scale of low to high interest and/or desirability. Whether or not the person is viewed as an attractive possibility determines whether or not the relationship progresses to higher levels.

2. Eye to eye   While looking each other over, the eyes occasionally meet. A quickening of the heartbeat frequently follows, along with the flush of embarrassment. The usual response at this point is to break the gaze and glance away, since we usually reserve direct eye contact for those we know and trust.

When eye contact occurs between two persons who have already developed bonds of friendship, their eyes will often lock and lead to further gestures of recognition and greeting—a sudden smile, a handshake, lift of the eyebrows, or wave of the hand. When locking eyes with a stranger, we tend to break the gaze so as not to invade privacy or personal space. To stare at someone whom you do not know well would make the person extremely uncomfortable or wary.

Therefore, two persons who are looking each other over usually do so taking turns rather than simultaneously. If one likes what he sees, he might add a smile to the next meeting of the eyes. Unless the eyes convey a message during future glances, the relationship will probably not proceed.

Note that eye contact at level two is brief. At step seven, eye contact dominates the scene. This correlates with the fact that when a couple is experiencing serious marriage problems, they rarely look into one another's faces when talking.

3. Voice to voice   Now the couple makes verbal contact. At first their conversation centers on trivia such as name, where you live, what you do for a living, the weather—small talk. The exchange of small talk, however, permits further observations and analysis regarding a whole new field of information—tone of voice, rate of speech, accent, use of vocabulary, and mode of thinking.

During this stage, the couple can learn much about each other—opinions, pastimes, hobbies, ideas, likes and dislikes, hopes and dreams for the future. A couple should spend hundreds of hours at this level. It is during this phase that a couple learns if they are compatible and if the relationship should continue.

These first three steps often occur rapidly, frequently, and innocently between male and female, and we tend not to attach much importance to them. But many bonds are broken by ignoring these three steps, and many bonds are formed in innocence under such circumstances. When comparing them to what takes place in deteriorating relationships, the steps should assume more significance. Where a bond has been broken or is deteriorating there is limited eye contact. The magic of discovery has faded into oblivion. Furthermore, there is little communication between the two people. All that remains are lovemaking episodes in which two bodies meet without emotional satisfaction.

Touch begins during the second stage of bonding, but none of it is directly sexual. The couple spends much time talking, but eye contact is still limited. Some light hugging and kissing may take place during the next three steps, but it should be light conventional contact only. Prolonged periods of face-to-face embracing or deep kissing would rush the bonding process and awaken sexual responses ahead of schedule.

4. Hand to hand   First touch is now encountered. It is almost always innocent and nonsexual—a handshake, accidentally touching hands while reaching for something, or assisting a woman with a coat or into a car. If she pulls away from his touch, he will know he cannot proceed further with such contact. If his efforts at support or protection are received warmly, the relationship may move into first occa-

sional and then constant hand-holding, which is evidence of
a growing attachment between the two. Even though two
hands represent only four inches of skin applied to four
inches of skin, the first touch along with continued touch
causes a quickening of the heart and an increased indication
of interest. Hand-holding is also a social statement which
says, "I am no longer alone. I have someone who enjoys
being with me."

5. Arm to shoulder   Until now the bodies have not been
close, but the arm-to-shoulder embrace pulls the trunks of the
bodies into close contact. Another boundary has been
crossed. Whether the couple is sitting or standing, physical
contact in the side-to-side position is maintained.

This is an easy step up from the hand-to-hand position.
The shoulder embrace is a gesture of ownership. It says more
than holding hands does. In effect it states, "This relationship
is going someplace." The relationship continues with limited
eye contact and verbals but closer body contact.

6. Arm to waist   A transition occurs at this step. Arm to
waist displays ownership of more of the body. Frequently the
smaller of the two will slip under the armpit of the larger,
their arms crisscrossing in back, forming an X. Often, the
trunks of their bodies appear "glued" together.

This position reveals a slight but important shift in the
position of the hands. The arm rests around the waist and the
gesture clearly signals romantic interest, since a man would
rarely do that to another man. Football players in a huddle
may put arms around others' shoulders but never around the
waist, as it has a different connotation. Notice that the hands
are much closer to the genital region than at any previous
time—a slight but important variation.

Frequently, you will see couples at this stage of bonding on
a school campus, at a park, or walking down the street. Their
bodies are close but there is still limited eye contact. Often it
might appear they are conversing with their feet as they seem
to be looking down, picking grass, studying their feet, or
playing with something in their hands, which keeps their
eyes busy but their bodies close.

Real and genuine communication develops at this stage. Personal disclosures are made and elaborated upon. The topics for discussion are endless, but basic issues of life are being discussed and evaluated. Many personal secrets are shared, and a couple really get to know each other intimately.

Values, goals, and beliefs must be scrutinized closely now. Do your life goals and personal beliefs blend well? Do you each bring out the best in the other, motivating one another to better and higher challenges and accomplishments? Do you know your partner's expectations of you for the future? Can you fulfill them? Will your partner allow you to develop your talents and be yourself?

These and many other questions must be considered seriously at this point because it is now that a decision about the future of the relationship must be made. Enough personal disclosures have been shared so that compatibility can be evaluated. If serious doubts or questions regarding any facet of the relationship exist, now is the time to say good-bye to further involvement. Proceeding can leave deep scars of grief and pain on one or both parties unless the relationship is truly compatible and the couple genuinely cares for each other. The bond is well under way.

Several changes occur during the third stage of bonding. The couple now face one another. Although no direct sexual contact occurs, it appears on a hidden agenda that both are mildly aware of. The bond is so well under way that any genital contact would bring on intercourse and could scar the formation of a solid bond. Engaging in intercourse would introduce an undercurrent of mistrust and high levels of anxiety that would haunt the pair later should they marry. Communication is vastly different. The verbals shut down and eye contact and nonverbals take over.

7. Face to face   Three types of contact take place here: face-to-face hugging, deep kissing, and prolonged eye contact.

The body position has shifted from side by side to that of facing each other. Close body contact in this position combined with deep kissing brings on strong sexual arousal, particularly when repeated or prolonged. Much restraint must now be exercised by the couple since the position and activity quickly excite sexual sensitivities. Even though they are several steps away from genital contact, sexual desire has been activated and becomes a factor with which each couple must deal. When kissing takes over, verbals shut down. It now becomes obvious why compatibility and the quality of the relationship must be decided before step 6. If the couple has taken time to talk through all the important issues of life and the foundation has been well laid, deep communication can take place now with very few words. Eye contact becomes long and pronounced. In fact, verbal communication tends to shut down while the couple focuses more on reading each other's face.

The unmarried couple must guard their display of physical affection for one another carefully from this point on.

8. Hand to head   Here one's hand is used to caress or stroke the head of the other while kissing or talking. This intimate gesture of touch is reserved for those who have earned the right. In other words, a high level of trust has developed between the two since few people outside of a barber, hairdresser, or dentist are allowed access to the head.

Few people engage in head-touching rituals unless they are in love or are family members. This act, then, denotes emotional closeness. The sight of a lover running hands through his beloved's hair is a poignant scene indeed. It signals a deep bond of friendship, love, caring, and trust. The bond is well formed.

9. Hand to body   At this level, the hands explore the partner's body. Breast fondling becomes an important focal point for the male. Much "petting" outside the clothing occurs, with some inside the clothing. Eventually, heavy petting wildly takes over and the couple will experience increasing difficulty in breaking the pattern of intimacy that has developed between them without proceeding to completion of the sexual act. It is now that the female usually recognizes she must call a halt or it will be too late. Hand to body is dangerously progressive.

10. Mouth to breast   This step of intimacy requires the baring of the female breast and is usually conducted in utmost privacy. Mouth-to-breast contact once again changes the focus of the intimacy. The couple is not only concerned with pleasure and arousal but with desire to complete the sexual act. Most couples will find it extremely difficult to stop at this point.

11. Hand to genital   The exploration of the partner's body now proceeds to the genitals. Heavy petting and sexual arousal are well under way. Many couples stimulate each other to climax through what is commonly called "petting to climax" or "mutual masturbation."

Dating partners frequently proceed this far but no further, attempting to retain genital intimacy for marriage. But not "going all the way" is faulty reasoning. According to the Oxford English Dictionary, the word *virgin* refers to "a person of either sex remaining in a state of chastity." By that definition, the line of purity has already been crossed.

Furthermore, it could cause a complex. If an obsession or preoccupation with such activity sets in at this level, a couple might be learning bad habits that will make it difficult for them to enjoy intercourse at its best.

12. Genital to genital   The pair-bonding process is complete with penetration and sexual intercourse. The intimacy resulting from the bond that has formed can result in pregnancy and a new launching of the family life cycle, which begins with birth and bonding between parent and child.

A pair bond is thus formed by progressing through these twelve steps, culminating in sexual intercourse. But it should be so much more than just looking to sexual pleasure as the end goal. For a married couple, proceeding through these steps should become part of daily living in order to protect a treasured bond.[8]

The Results of Rushing or Skipping Steps

Desmond Morris notes that when the twelve-step bonding process is altered, several harmful things can happen to the potential bond formation:

1. When steps are skipped, missed, or rushed, the bond is weakened and tends to break or to become deformed. This happens because the couple did not take time to talk through all the important issues of life—values, goals, and beliefs—prior to becoming physically involved. Once the sexual motors get turned on, couples forget other aspects of relationship building. The process of building a relationship that will last a lifetime must be slowed during the first six steps, or a weak marriage may result.

2. When a couple breaks up, the tendency is to accelerate the steps with the next partner. For instance, Dick and Jane are used to engaging in light and sometimes heavy petting (step 9). Although they do not proceed to intercourse, they become accustomed to this level of sexual arousal. Within a few weeks Dick changes to a new partner and immediately attempts to move her to step 9 since he is used to this level of excitement. Jane moves into a new relationship and feels unloved because her new partner is taking his time to reach step 9. She encourages and actually pushes light petting because without it she feels he doesn't care for her. Neither Dick nor Jane takes time in their next relationship to get to know each other as they should. Steps are rushed and sometimes skipped entirely. Should they marry later on, they probably will find themselves in very troubled relationships.

3. A person who previously has had sexual intercourse will tend to rush a new partner to sexual intercourse rapidly. This tracks the previous point. A person used to the level of sexual arousal necessary to achieve intercourse will find it difficult to slow the process or to stop at step 9. This presents a real problem for the formerly married. It may also explain the higher divorce statistics for those entering marriage for the second and third time.

Dr. Donald Joy confirms this thought. He believes defective pair bonding is the real culprit in the rate of divorce in our culture:

> . . . anthropologists faithfully report that our high premium on so-called social experience is contributing to patterns of promiscuity and its defective bonding. Our divorce statistics are likely more related to the amount of unprotected pair

bonding—and to social pressure to be sexually active before marriage—than to any other one cause.[9]

The steps toward intimacy are predictable and progressive. We need to become adept at reading the signals of developing love and teach the signals to our young people, thereby preventing them from making some of the same mistakes already made by us.

Double Bonding: The Tragedy That Stalks Your Life

. . . for a harlot may be hired for a loaf of bread,
　　but an adulteress stalks a man's very life.
Can a man carry fire in his bosom
　　and his clothes not be burned?
Or can one walk upon hot coals
　　and his feet not be scorched?
So is he who goes in to his neighbor's wife;
　　none who touches her will go unpunished. . . .
He who commits adultery has no sense;
　　he who does it destroys himself.
Wounds and dishonor will he get,
　　and his disgrace will not be wiped away.[10]

Double bonding, or what might be termed *adultery*, is highly probable in any male-female friendship where sufficient bonding time is allowed. If respect and admiration are important commodities in the relationship—*beware!*

We tend to classify all "affairs" under one heading. Since bonding can occur with or without genital intimacy, actually three major categories exist:

(1) The emotional affair:　　The couple is attracted to each other but has not engaged in sexual intercourse.

(2) The sexual affair:　　This couple enjoys casual sex without emotional closeness. When one or both are bored in their present marriages, this provides an exciting adventure or challenge.

(3) The sexual and emotional affair:　　The previous two are more likely to end with time. This third category produces a

double bond that sets up all parties for an aftermath of grief and heartbreak.

Pair-bonding instincts are activated whenever opportunity presents itself for (1) prolonged periods of eye contact; (2) sufficient privacy during which two persons engage in any gestures of touching; and (3) the giving of empathy, comfort, and compassion. When privacy exists, the emotions of empathy or even pity are activated, and sexual arousal may result. Over a period of time, unless emotions are carefully guarded, two persons who had no intention of "falling in love" find themselves becoming attached to each other.

At particular risk are those in the helping professions, such as doctors, psychologists, ministers, and counselors. People in such fields find themselves besieged by those who are hurting and in deep pain. A natural instinct to assist and alleviate pain is aroused. A bond of trust and confidentiality develops. And anyone—yes, even you—could become vulnerable to sexual indiscretion when dealing with the soul-stirring emotions of another human being. It's a perfect setup.

Two-couple friendships provide both time and opportunity for a double bond to develop. Frequently, adulterous bonds begin in the workplace, where associates spend many hours a day together working on and sharing common interests. Seeking another's advice during times of stress creates another opportunity.

When nurtured, innocent-appearing friendships set off the pair-bonding instinct. Even though a mate is totally unaware that an outsider is invading the original protected bond, a pattern is developing that will haunt the adulterer all the days of his/her life.

Stretching the Bond

Certain conditions are conducive to the formation of an adulterous bond:

1. Separation   When a couple is well bonded, brief separations will not disturb the bond. However, repeated absences, when frequent or prolonged, stretch the capacity of the best of bonds.

A friend of mine sought advice regarding her husband's accepting a more suitable job in a town three hours north of where they lived. She would maintain the family home and retain her high-salaried position. He would come home on Friday night and leave early Monday morning. Weekend marriage. I strongly advised against it.

Separation weakens a bond through loneliness. The lonely individual is emotionally vulnerable to contact with others. Any prolonged eye contact, conversing, or occasional light touching with an acquaintance could set off a chain reaction of circumstances that could lead to adultery.

2. Stress   Stress, in its many forms, can weaken a bond. The stress may be caused by a job, finances, fatigue, illness, a rebellious teenager, or any number of other stress-related problems. Extreme fatigue resulting from stress may lessen sexual desire. When sexual interest wanes or dies, it weakens the sexual bond. If a new love appears on the scene, awakening a dormant sex life for either partner, an adulterous relationship could easily replace a monogamous one.

3. Grief   Grief which follows divorce, death, or abandonment of a spouse must be worked through before beginning a new relationship. Two often hurting partners rush from one relationship to the next. Frequently, Harry and I observe this phenomenon at work in singles groups where individuals gather to recover and support one another after deep loss.

Bob and Janet asked for an appointment to discuss their budding relationship. Janet was twenty-nine and twice divorced. Bob was a thirty-one-year-old father of three who held in his arms Janet's two-year-old, a product of her second marriage. Bob's divorce had been contested in the courts for the past three years because of custody rights. Their initial question to me was, "We've been attending your Compleat Courtship seminar and have been thinking about getting married. We'd like your opinion about our relationship." Further questioning revealed that they had been going together for three months and were planning a Thanksgiving wedding!—this was June. Between them they already had three marriages and four children, and in eight months they wanted to rush into another marriage!

Deep grief tends to hurl individuals more rapidly into new relationships. The hurting partners often feed off each other's pain and feel deep bonds of attachment as they share their common sufferings. This produces an atmosphere of high vulnerability and impaired perception regarding needs. A recovery period of at least two years following divorce, death, or separation is recommended in order to stabilize one's emotions. Another two years should be spent moving slowly and securely through the steps to bonding with a new partner.

Persons who commit adultery are not necessarily promiscuous. One who has established a strong bond in marriage can be drawn away to an opposing bond, but such relationships are not like "one-night stands." The same affection and fidelity enjoyed in the previous relationship is simply extended to the new partner. Such affairs are deeply emotional in nature.

Note: This does not mean the marriage is dead.

The original bond has been severely strained, but hope still exists for the marriage if pain and grief over the loss of the relationship is manifested. The marriage is dead only when little or no grief is experienced. A healthy bond can be restored to those who give attention to strengthening the original bond rather than resorting to separation or divorce.

Daily Bonding

Question: If you and your mate interacted while dating the way you are interacting now, would you like each other and know each other well enough to marry? All too often the answer is, "Uh . . . I think so" or "I hope so" or "Maybe" or "I don't know" or "I seriously doubt it." If a strong bond is to be maintained, it must be renewed daily.

A few years ago a couple would have stayed together regardless of how they felt, for the sake of the children or because of their faith. Not so today. We are demanding more of marriage than ever before. With increasing longevity and greater expectations, it becomes imperative that we do our homework early and nuture the pair bond in order to experience the greatest rewards from marriage.

Maintaining a high level of interest requires constant reapplication of each of the pair-bonding steps. Emotional closeness cannot be attained while remaining emotionally distant. Without constant nurturing, communication and trust will disappear and the bond will disintegrate.

How do you keep a bond strong? Is there any way to prevent or restore a bond once it has been broken or damaged? The pathway to intimacy and a bond strong enough to last a lifetime is embodied in the following four principles:

1. Communicate verbally   Is there anything sadder than two people who are married and yet can't communicate? Many couples get caught in a web of ineffective communication habits which have gone on for so many years they think it is hopeless or impossible to change.

Unsatisfactory communication skills is one of the easiest characteristics to identify in a crumbling relationship. When a couple communicates unsatisfactorily, they will function poorly as a team. Verbalization takes the form of "speeches" rather than an easy flow of conversation. Such couples may talk more but say less. Some will use silence or withhold the fulfilling of each other's needs. Tremendous power struggles may dominate the relationship along with blaming, judging, and put-downs during times of stress.

Thousands of couples are communicating with each other through these shallow methods. They simply have not learned any other way of communicating. They continue in the rut they have created for themselves, as miserable, meaningless, and isolated as it may seem.

Well-bonded couples have learned to keep the channels of communication open. They tend to listen with respect and accept all feelings, even when they don't agree. Each is free to interrupt the other on occasion without hurt feelings. Sentences will not always be completed, yet the other appears to understand the message being sent. Each experiences joy in hearing the other's experiences—empathizing appropriately during times of sorrow and crisis as well as celebrating during times of joy.

Because these partners communicate well and feel free to express feelings, they work well together as a team in accomplishing family tasks in a shorter period of time with less energy expended. When conflicts arise, they can deal with them constructively, solving them with less hurt and friction. Each problem is tackled with optimism and confidence that it will be worked out to the highest satisfaction of both.

Each assumes responsibility for his or her own words and actions. An atmosphere of respect is present for self and each other. Such persons do not speak for one another, nor do they expect their partners to read their minds. They do not invade the privacy of the mate's feelings.

When the lines of communication shut down between two people, it is like a terminal illness, and it is rarely reversible unless the partners work together to halt the dread disease.

Any couple who can master three basic skills of communication—the verbalization of feelings, attentive listening, and reactive feedback—can save or restore a weak or damaged bond. If both partners can learn just this much, the marriage can survive. Mastering those skills is what this book is all about.

2. Look at each other   Some couples never look at each other directly. They see one another only over newspapers, through television screens, or out of the corners of their eyes. Sometimes this path is chosen to escape hurtful memories of the past. A direct look into the other person's eyes would resurrect hurt, anger, and bitter memories too difficult to face. Still other couples rarely look at one another due to time pressure.

Eye contact also fades when people have something to hide from one another. It is difficult to look someone in the eye and hold the gaze if you are operating from a base of deception and dishonesty. A lack of eye contact and dishonesty seem to go hand in hand. Openness and trust in a relationship begin with penetrating eye contract. Eyes are the avenue to the soul, and much nonverbal communication takes place through lingering affectionate glances.

While seated in a restaurant, I can frequently distinguish the married from the unmarried couples. Unmarrieds gaze warmly into one another's eyes. The meal is often eaten slowly, interrupted by looks, smiles, and dialogue. Hands intertwine. Among married couples, the communication may be limited to such directives as, "Be careful. You're gonna spill." Where are their eyes? Studying their food, the walls, others in the room—anywhere but on each other.

It is possible to recapture the magic you felt when you first met, but it will take time, eye contact, touch, and persistence. Begin by sitting across from your partner at the table. Look directly into his or her eyes and tell the truth. It might sound like this: "Rose, I've failed you. Something is gone from our relationship and I am to blame. I've neglected you. I do care deeply about you and I intend to mend my ways. Be patient with me. I promise you something better for the future. You are *important* to me."

Whereas all couples must spend time daily interfacing with direct eye contact, this is particularly true for a couple in a troubled relationship. A damaged bond can be repaired when the couple takes even a small step toward honesty and eye contact.

3. Touch each other   The adult need for touching is more basic than the need for sex. The need begins at birth and is the infant's first reassurance of nurturing. The cuddling and stroking the newborn receives is critical to his future development. Infants who lack this kind of affectionate care grow up to be emotionally disturbed adults. Touching is essential for physical well-being.

Adults are not very different from children when it comes to the need for physical closeness. We all have deep needs for touching and the intimacy it creates.

Another word for touch is *caress*. Webster defines *caress* as "an act of endearment; a tender or loving embrace, touch. To touch, stroke, pat, tenderly, lovingly, or softly." Nurturing is involved in each word of the definition. If you trace the origin of the word *caress* to the Latin word *carus*, from which it was derived, you will find it was a term for "dear," which implies caring and nurturing.

Some people insist they do not want to be touched; they don't need it or enjoy it. Such a reaction can usually be traced to early childhood experiences or a marriage relationship in which emotional barriers have been erected to isolate oneself from real or imagined hurt. However, even the most troubled couple could within a short period of time experience a dramatic change in their union simply by touching one another in affectionate ways.

Tremendous rewards await any couple who begin weaving the joy of touch into the everyday fabric of their lives. For instance, a couple can join hands during prayer; give a loving pat; hold hands when going for a walk or while riding in the car; cuddle at night with no demands for sex; sit close at church or while watching television; greet each other with a hug and kiss after being separated; give a loving pat as they pass in the kitchen.

Someone has said that three hugs a day keep depression away. According to new medical evidence, touching can also stabilize the heart rate of the intensive-care patient; improve movement for cerebral palsy victims; heal the sick by the "laying on of hands," as evidenced both in Bible and present times; raise children's grade-point averages; activate hemoglobin and brain wave activity.

The Communication Inventory (CI) investigated the amount of nonsexual touching couples were experiencing. Eighty-four percent said they had the kind of touching that did not signal intercourse some, most, or all of the time. Twice as many women as men, however, indicated they found nonsexual touching a factor in caring and healing. Women have a tremendous need to be held, aside from sex. It gives them a feeling of emotional satisfaction to be held outside the bedroom. Any woman who associates each touch with a sexual encounter will begin to resent it.

Shere Hite conducted a survey on female sexuality and found that even women who did not achieve orgasm during intercourse still enjoyed sex very much.[11] The reason? The feelings of intimacy they derived from the experience—the physical touching and closeness—were so rewarding.

Such habits, regularly followed, will build feelings of warmth, psychological satisfaction, and emotional security. It is essential that troubled couples who wish to rebuild a relationship begin with simple expressions of caressing. Couples who say they have fallen out of love with their mates could rebuild a relationship just by reinitiating loving caresses. Touching can do more to heal the wounds of bickering, hostility, and negative attitudes than any treatment modality.

A Fabulous Four-Minute Formula

Verbal communication, eye contact, and touching are what keep a marital bond interesting and vital over the long haul. But how do you put all this into practice amidst hectic schedules, rearing children, work, church activities . . . and exhaustion? Here's a fabulous formula for putting it all into practice in just eight minutes a day: *Make the first four minutes of contact every morning and the first four minutes of contact when you reunite at the end of the day a pleasant interlude.*

Observing morning and evening rituals between a couple can provide a revealing portrait of the concern they have for one another. To a large degree, the success or failure of the marriage can be predicted on the basis of these eight minutes.

Leonard and Natalie Zunin have confirmed this in a book titled *Contact: The First Four Minutes*, in which they emphasize the importance of the first four minutes of contact in handling crucial business deals as well as interpersonal relationships.

To capture how you interact, put a video camera on the pattern of interaction you and your partner follow first thing in the morning. What did you see? The silent treatment? Complaining about an aching back? Compulsive grooming? Demands about errands to be run before the end of the day? Persistent pessimism?

Caressing and holding is almost always welcome in healthy relationships and should become a regular part of every couple's morning routine. Establish verbal contact as well. Talk about something pleasant, anything that will lead to reinforcing positive feelings. Hold each other close before bounding out of bed; have a leisurely hot drink before dashing off to work; take a brisk walk together; reflect on a

Bible verse and pray while holding hands. Try anything that will make your early-morning routine more meaningful. And don't be afraid to vary your approach from time to time.

Just as the first four minutes of contact in the morning determine the quality of the relationship for the day, so will the second four minutes of contact, as you reunite at the end of the day, shape and determine the interaction during the evening hours. What do you see and hear as you put the video camera on a typical greeting at the end of the day? How a couple spends their evening hours is an accurate gauge of their overall marriage relationship.

Couples who analyze their evening contacts objectively are often embarrassed by what they recall: "Where's the mail?" "The kids were awful." "I'm so tired I could die." "There's more trouble at school." "Where are you, for Pete's sake?" Many messages can be projected through body language—a downcast mouth, the squint of an eye, the scent of body odor, crumpled or disheveled clothing. All of these provide significant information about attitude and mood.[12]

Six Easy Ways to Strengthen a Bond

A warm and friendly greeting after a period of separation can have a positive influence on husband and wife. Here are some pointers for making the second most important four minutes of your day more rewarding:

1. Prepare yourself mentally   Prior to your reunion, prepare yourself mentally to meet your spouse. Think good thoughts. Some people actually *plan* to dump bad feelings on their partners. Instead of planning in such a negative direction, rehearse in your mind at least one positive incident from your day that you can share with your partner upon greeting him or her. Questions, problems, and phone messages can be discussed later. Pray on the way home that the Lord will prepare you to be a blessing to your partner. Sometimes a quick phone call in advance helps to prepare the way.

2. Check your appearance   The first glimpse of each other affects how you will relate throughout the evening. A neatly groomed wife who dabs on a bit of perfume and accents her femininity will naturally elicit a more positive response from her husband. A man, too, can make a difference. A slob who enters the house with crumpled clothes, greasy, grimy, and reeking of body odor, will probably get a much different greeting from the man who washes up before he leaves work, combs his hair, and applies a dash of after-shave lotion. Your grooming says a lot about how you feel about yourself and your partner. Try your best to be appealing to your spouse.

3. Shower your partner with smiles   Plan your time so you can greet your partner smiling. Let your partner know he or she is a priority in your life, not someone to be fit in after other responsibilities have been taken care of. A smile can say "I love you" with more meaning than an expensive gift. A smile is free and readily available. Even if you don't feel like smiling, do it anyway. Act the part, if need be, for the first four minutes. If you act nice, good feelings may follow and the hidden negativity may fade. If you feel lousy and enter the house acting lousy, you'll probably kill any possibility of getting the empathy you want and need from your partner. However, if you enter the house with a positive attitude, you can set the mood for resolving your feelings more satisfactorily.

4. Greet each other with a hug and kiss   I used to have real competition in getting to Harry with hugs and kisses. Buffy, our dog and "the blond" in Harry's life, used to lie in wait at the front door, anticipating his arrival home. Once Harry was inside, Buffy would dance on her hind legs while barking a most enthusiastic greeting. We were in competition for the same man and he loved it. We all might enjoy a reunion more if we put as much into it as Buffy did. If kissing isn't your style, have some other physical contact: holding hands, patting, fondling. Do something that reestablishes touch.

5. Say something nice   Rather than greeting your partner with the "didyas"—"didya go to the bank?" etc.—or a curt hello, greet your partner with some verbal pleasantries. A warm "Welcome home, honey," or a compliment will do. You can also tell some amusing or interesting incident that occurred during the day. Once a week plan a surprise greeting, some small thing that says, "You are special to me and I care about you."

6. Create a pleasant atmosphere   Give each other time to relax before tackling any problems. Anyone who enters a home with kids running wild, the TV blasting, and everything in chaos might want to run away. Whoever gets home first is responsible for setting the mood, but both are responsible for maintaining a pleasant and peaceful atmosphere. Each couple needs to talk through their expectations and find a workable plan for bringing peace out of chaos. Those who work outside the home may need a decompression period that involves a few minutes of quiet. Others are okay after they've read the paper. Some want fifteen minutes of quiet music and little or no talk. Still others want to romp and play with the kids. Whatever it is you want, talk about it and then attempt to create this for your partner. This will reap big dividends.

Those who are serious about strengthening their marital bond, or who wish to salvage a deteriorating relationship, must begin with revitalizing these crucial eight minutes. These contact minutes, to a large degree, symbolize how a man and woman have integrated their lives.

Some people assume that routine comings and goings are no big deal. They don't realize that each day we make swift and durable impressions on our mates—impressions that influence how we relate to each other on that day and all the days to come. Couples who insist on using phrases, words, and messages that alienate one another will eventually drift apart.

With new insights and by carefully structuring these eight minutes per day, a couple can experience a sense of renewal between them and realize how good it is to face the world together.

The formation of the pair bond in the early stages of a relationship requires a careful and extensive investment of time and energy. Young lovers willingly behave like lovers.

Married lovers must also behave like lovers and move through the bonding steps, renewing and affirming their love for each other. This way the bond is well tended and will ripen with age. A friendship and magnetic force will draw and hold the couple affectionately together in a permanent adventure. This truly is the pathway to intimacy.

3 Heart Listening: A Way to Show You Care

Listening is the most neglected and least understood of the communication arts. Perceptive listening doesn't require a degree, but it does require learning.

Some people just don't listen, and by the time they discover their carelessness they frequently find themselves at the brink of disaster.

Such was the case at 8:00 P.M. on October 30, 1938, when some 6 million radio listeners across the United States heard an important announcement that caused a panic in the nation. It was a radio promotional that was simple and straightforward, yet it was destined to have far-reaching consequences.

"The Columbia Broadcasting System and its affiliated stations," the announcer began, "present Orson Welles and the Mercury Theater of the Air in *The War of the Worlds*, by H. G. Wells."

It was that plain, yet most of it didn't even register. And why should it? The strains of romantic dance music that followed were much more appealing.

But a few words stayed in mind—and unknowingly they set the stage for panic.

"War of the Worlds! . . . WAR OF THE WORLDS!"

The threatening words had been part of a routine announcement, but to the million or so radio listeners who had caught only part of the message, it meant the beginning of doom and the end of the world. "Hearing" that the world was about to end, they succumbed to their fears and, grabbing whatever valuables they could, rushed out of their homes, looking for places to hide.

When fearful and desperate, people have been known to do strange things. In Newark, New Jersey, panic set in when twenty families ran screaming into the streets after hearing the program's announcement, wet towels covering their heads to escape what they thought was a poison gas attack. Others were seen dragging their furniture to safety. People kept the police phone lines blocked, volunteering their services to fight the martian invasion. In Mount Vernon, New York, a man who had been considered a hopeless invalid got up and stumbled out of his house the moment he heard the word *invasion*; he crawled into his car and disappeared.

Scores of people in cities all over the nation picked up their phones, tearfully whispering last farewells to loved ones. Others simply sat down in shock, immobilized by fright, or gave in to good old-fashioned hysteria.

But safely within the studio, Orson Welles and the other actors had no idea of the national panic their program was creating. They thought it was going well, sound effects and all, until they happened to look through the glass window into the control room, where scores of wildly gesturing uniformed police were demanding that the program be cut immediately.

Minutes later, Welles and his colleagues were told they had caused a panic of national proportions. It had been a skillfully executed show with a good cast. Furthermore, it aired at the right time—to create panic, that is. For months, America's nerves had been jangled by European war rumors and the probability of its own involvement. The agreement drawn up by Adolf Hitler and Neville Chamberlain promising "peace in our time" was less than four weeks old. Invasion was on everyone's mind. For maximum effect, Orson Welles and CBS could not have chosen a better moment.

The fact remains, however, that radio listeners apparently missed or did not listen to the announcements informing audiences they were tuned to the dramatization of a play, the name of the play, and the author. There was no association between the program and the newspaper listing, which read "8:00–9:00 P.M., play by H. G. Wells, *War of the Worlds*."

Listeners ignored or did not even hear three additional announcements made during the broadcast emphasizing its fictional nature.[1]

Studies later proved that those who did not panic were the ones who heard the message and then put their minds at ease through careful listening, but the fact remains that about one-sixth of the radio listeners did not use their listening ability in a critical fashion to discover what was really happening. Listening is a problem most of us don't realize we have.

Is listening a problem in marriage? The Communication Inventory attempted to explore this question by having participants respond to the following statement: "My partner listens attentively to what I have to say." Forty-seven percent said their partners listened attentively "some of the time," "rarely," or "never." Fifty-five percent admitted their partners accused them of not listening all, most, or some of the time. More complained that their partners were easily distracted and acted uninterested while they were talking. Others complained their partners avoided looking at them while conversing. Wives complained their husbands wouldn't listen to them and men said their wives never heard what they were told. Yes, listening is a problem within marriage.

Listening Versus Hearing

Many of us assume listening is something we do with our ears. Ears are vitally important to the process of hearing, but true listening goes beyond only hearing what is said. Many people hear but do not listen.

Hearing refers to the process by which sound waves hit the ear with lightning speed and are transmitted to the brain—an unlearned process occurring without conscious effort on our part. Listening describes *a skill which one learns*. The process of listening is tuning in or tuning out voices, noise, music. A conscious choice is made about what will receive our attention.

A "Dennis the Menace" comic strip describes the process perfectly. Dennis greets his neighbor, Mr. Wilson, while Mr. Wilson is reading his paper. No response. Dennis tries again, speaking louder. No response again. In desperation Dennis tries one last time, then turns to leave when his last attempt has failed. In a normal voice he calls good-bye over his shoulder.

"Good-bye, Dennis," Mr. Wilson replies. Dennis remarks on his way out the door, "There's nothing wrong with his hearing, but his listening's not so good."

Researchers estimate that we spend 70 percent of our waking hours communicating with others—speaking, listening, reading, or writing. Thirty-three percent of that time is devoted to talking and 42 percent to listening. Since a commanding amount of time is spent in listening, it assumes primary importance in our lives.

Listening Bloopers

Poor listening stems from bad habits. Some of the most irritating of these habits are as follows:

Interrupting is the number-one detested listening habit. Interrupters spend their time not listening to what is being said but in forming a reply. Interested only in their own ideas, they pay little attention to the words of others and wait for a split second when they can break in with, "Oh, that's nothing. You should hear what happened to me."

It may be a human tendency to jump right in when something is said that triggers a thought. But you must let the other person finish a sentence no matter how boring he or she is. When you interrupt, you are stepping on someone else's ideas, and this is just as rude and sometimes as painful as stepping on their toes.

Lack of eye contact came in second on the "most irritating" list. Listeners who fail to look at the person speaking to them convey disinterest, distrust, and a lack of caring.

Ordinarily, Harry is a good listener, but recently I stopped him in the hallway to share something important to me. While I was talking he was looking over my shoulder, squinting his eye, and obviously measuring to see if something in his line of vision was crooked. I stopped midsentence. I could not and would not continue with no eye contact.

In relationships that are deteriorating, couples rarely look directly into each other's faces when they talk. The magic of face-to-face conversation in which eyes meet, hold the gaze, and communicate more than words can explain is gone. In a very troubled relationship, a couple may not look into one another's eyes for weeks or months at a time. All they have in common is infrequent lovemaking episodes which tend to leave both unfulfilled since emotional needs are not being met.

Lack of eye contact is used as punishment. Couples refuse to look at each other in order to convey displeasure. Consciously refusing to maintain eye contact with a partner is cruel. Eye contact also fades whenever dishonesty is a factor.

Those wishing to rebuild deteriorating relationships must begin to establish eye contact and nonsexual touching.

The bored listener has heard it all before. When Mr. J rehashes complaints about his job, Mrs. J says to herself, *Here we go again*, and puts her brain in neutral. Yet on occasion, when Mr. J says something new and looks for support and encouragement from his wife, he isn't likely to get it.

A *selective listener* picks out bits and pieces of conversation that interest him and rejects the rest. For instance, a husband may be watching the six o'clock news while his wife is talking. Most of what she says goes in one ear and out the other, but when she mentions spending money he becomes all ears.

Other people do not want to hear anything disagreeable, upsetting, or different—Michael's behavior at school or more expenses on the car.

We do not gain anything by rejecting what we do not wish to hear. In many situations, we need all the facts in order to make a decision.

A *defensive listener* twists everything said into a personal attack on self. One wife casually remarked to her husband that the new styles left her with nothing to wear. Although she never mentioned purchasing a new wardrobe, he flew into a rage because he felt her remarks were directed toward his lack of ability to earn a living. A hurt wife gave her husband the silent treatment all evening because she felt his disgust with the children's table manners was a personal attack on her ability to train them properly.

The insensitive listener is one who cannot catch the feeling or emotion behind the words. A young wife asks her husband to take her out to dinner. She does not need to be taken out to dinner as much as she needs reassurance that he still loves her and is willing to make the effort to please her. If he tells her bluntly that they can't afford it or he is too tired, he hasn't listened to the meaning behind her request.

Other annoying listening habits include the following:

- one who makes you feel you are wasting his time
- pacing back and forth as if impatient or in a hurry to get away
- no facial expressions indicating understanding or hearing
- prestating your point or prefinishing your sentences
- rephrasing what you say so that words are put in your mouth
- asking a question to which you've just given the answer
- contradicting what you say before you even state your case
- everything said reminds hearer of a story or something just heard
- speaker phones
- standing too close

Bad habits abound because we have not been trained. Listening is the most neglected and least understood of the communication arts. Perceptive listening doesn't require a degree but it does require training. Let's learn to do it right.

Listening Know-How

Listening sounds simple, but becoming a perceptive listener is infinitely more difficult than becoming an eloquent speaker. Listening is serious business because it involves more than hearing words. It involves discernment, observing nonverbals, caring, eye contact, watching for underlying motives, asking the right questions, giving appropriate responses, and sometimes being silent. It is hard work, but the payoffs for developing closer relationships are worth the price.

I have researched and narrowed down perceptive listening

to seven basic skills. If you can master these skills, you can become a more sensitive listener.

Total Body Listening: Look Like a Listener

If you are going to be a good listener, you must look and act the part. If you do not look as if you are listening, you might as well not be. Total body listening can be described as an activity in which you utilize every part of your body to show your partner you are listening. It makes the speaker feel special, valued, and worthwhile.

Listen with your eyes.   Look at the person who is speaking to you. Supposedly, the powerful preacher Charles Spurgeon once said, "To me it is an annoyance if even a blind man does not look me in the face." How would you like to be speaking to someone who all the while looked over your shoulder and rarely at you? This is a real turnoff and immediately breaks down the communication process.

Make sure your partner senses you are listening. Without staring, boring holes, zeroing in, or making your partner uncomfortable, make certain your eyes are not darting here and there or moving indiscriminately about the room when something important is being shared.

People feel distrust and suspicion for those who do not look at them when communicating. Distrust is one of the biggest blocks to effective communication. When someone looks you directly in the eye, it conveys confidence and builds a trust in the relationship.

Recently I had two ideas to illustrate a point for our Compleat Marriage seminar. Late one night while Harry was deeply engrossed in a television drama, I asked him to decide which of two ideas best illustrated the point I was trying to make. He hit the mute button on the remote control so he could hear me but without looking in my direction said, "They are both good. You could use either one." In spite of the fact that he responded, with his eyes focusing on something else, I felt as if I weren't there.

Granted, my timing was off. Never ask a man to solve a marriage problem during the World Series!

Eye contact is important in all close relationships but

especially so in marriage. In controlled experiments, psychologists have found that people who are deeply in love with each other engage in much more eye contact than do other couples. Eyes are capable of conveying many messages: love or hate, surprise or disinterest, happiness or sadness.

Listen with your head. Unless you nod your head in agreement, there is little motivation for the speaker to continue. A nod at the appropriate time says, "I understand." "I agree." "I'm with you."

Resting a forefinger on the side of your face, head in hand, indicates thoughtful listening. In contrast, perhaps one of the worst listening habits is to slouch backward in a chair, chin in palm, as if almost asleep or in a trance. A disinterested expression on the face completes the picture and indicates, "I'm here, but I don't want to be. Let's get this over with."

Resting your chin on your fist as in the famous *Thinker* fashion is perhaps one of the best head positions. Lean toward the speaker as though hanging on every word, but be sincere.

Listen with your hands. The hands are capable of many gestures which can communicate approval or disapproval. Thumbs-up says agreement; thumbs-down, disagreement. Pointing your finger at your mate is accusatory, but turning your hand upward and curling the index finger toward you repeatedly indicates, "Come here. I want you closer."

Avoid doodling or drawing pictures while you are listening. Fidgeting with paper clips or pencils and clipping or cleaning fingernails are silent but often hurtful and frustrating nuisances which say, "You aren't as important to me as this is."

Instead, use your hands to say, "I care." Why is it that when couples are going together they can hardly keep their hands off each other, while after marriage they hardly touch except to communicate sexual readiness? So much more warmth could be communicated to a partner by taking hold of, stroking, or even pressing a partner's hand to your lips. Slip an arm around your mate's shoulders while pulling her close. A love pat or a tender squeeze of the hand could soothe so many hurts.

The human touch is vital to emotional health. Touching shows we are paying attention. Touch heals, lifts up, affirms others, and conveys a message that can't be expressed in words.

Listen with your body.   We convey either openness or defensiveness through body postures. The gesture for defensiveness is arms folded across the chest. One who leans back in a chair with legs crossed, ankle on knee, hands clasped behind the head often conveys superiority or smugness. In contrast, arms outstretched, palms up indicates openness and sincerity. Leaning forward toward the speaker is a sign of interest and involvement.

Listen with your mouth.   Mouth listening includes smiling, laughter, a low whistle, a light kiss, and other ways the mouth might be used to show caring. Verbally adding an occasional, "Hmmm," "No kidding," "I see," and otherwise casual but genuine responses lets your partner know you are listening.

Listen with your mind.   In learning to listen, the ability to listen for feelings is frequently emphasized. Intentional listening searches for thoughts, intentions, and action statements as well.

Following a lecture, a researcher tested participants to determine what proportion of the material presented was retained. Immediately following the lecture, the all-professional group could recall only about 50 percent of what they heard. What might be expected if the group were to be retested a week, a month, or a year later?

A physician would become exceedingly alarmed if a patient retained only 50 percent of the food he ate. Emergency treatment would be started immediately. Yet few would be concerned if this same person said he remembered only half the information given him.

You may need to develop deliberate listening skills for banking information. At least a limited "listenability" is needed to process information, analyze it, recall it at a later time, and draw conclusions from it. The listener must be able to pick up the basic idea being conveyed and interpret the data. Effectively understanding the concept or idea in order to give it intellectual attention is a basic listening skill.

Some logical and highly analytical persons can listen to a fault in this manner. Listening only for data and becoming too analytical can keep a listener from hearing what is said. In marriage, we are continually giving and receiving information. As much as possible, profit from the facts presented; listen effectively for ideas. Guard against becoming so involved in analyzing concepts of what has been said that you miss the importance of the message given.

Match your listening responses to your partner's behavior. While not mimicking your partner's behavior, match your body language to his or hers. This means that if your partner is sad, you match your listening responses—head, eyes, hands, and body—to respond to sadness. It does not mean you must sob because your partner is sobbing, but show responses appropriate to unhappiness.

If your partner is happy and excited about something, adapt your total body listening to a spirit of joy. If your partner is really intent on sharing something with you, get in the spirit of it through your body responses. Assume many of the same body postures and facial expressions.

Total body listening can be used in another manner, also. If a person is too excited, you can assist in calming him or her by reflecting control. If you got excited too, it would be like pouring gasoline on a bonfire. If you speak a little slower and lower your voice while modeling control, it will have a calming effect.

Mirroring quickly establishes a rapport. The sooner and quicker you establish such a rapport and trust level, the more effective the communication process will be.

To be at your listening best, think through where and when you can listen with the fewest distractions. For important listening occasions, select a place that is private, comfortable, and one which allows maximum eye contact along with opportunity for observing your partner's nonverbals.

Lag Time: Tuning In, Tuning Out

Most of us speak at the rate of 100 to 150 words per minute. Some speak slower at only 80 to 90 words per minute, and others gust up to 170 words per minute. We can listen at the rate of 450 to 600 words per minute. This means we can think five times faster than we can talk.

If you are listening to someone who is speaking at one hundred words per minute while you can listen at close to six hundred, what is your mind doing the rest of the time?

The time differential between the two speeds is called "lag time."

Have you ever asked your husband to do something for you and then later noticed he hasn't done it? When you ask him why he didn't do it, he says, "I never heard you." You say, "Well, I told you." He says, "No, you didn't. When did you tell me that?"

This frequently happens due to lag time. Information tends to go in one ear and out the other without penetrating the gray matter. Attention was focused on something else and thoughts may have been running rampant on another channel so that the listener caught only a portion of what was being said.

Other people use lag time to formulate their next response, failing to recognize that by doing so they are probably missing information, conveying disinterest, and missing cues which might indicate deeper problems. We want to be thought of as intelligent, helpful, and witty, so we often use lag time to think up amusing anecdotes, helpful thoughts, or appropriate responses. Such replies may be desirable, but to allow our minds to wander in an undisciplined manner in order to come across as brilliant conversationalists is selfish, to say the least.

Dale Carnegie, one of the most gifted of all men in effective human relations, once told of an event in his own life: At a dinner party, he found himself seated next to a botanist who kept him literally on the edge of his seat with astonishing facts about the humble potato, even solving some gardening problems for his listener. When it was time to say good night, the botanist turned to his host and paid Mr. Carnegie several flattering compliments. Mr. Carnegie was "most stimulating" and a "most interesting conversationalist."

The truth of the matter was that Mr. Carnegie had hardly said anything at all. He had, however, used his lag time creatively. He acted interested because he *was* interested. This is the highest compliment we can pay anyone: to listen attentively to what is being said.

Good listening and a productive use of lag time requires responding to the entire message being conveyed. It means evaluating what is being said and processing the information. It also means observing nonverbals and acting interested.

It is entirely possible for an adept listener to know more about the other person than he knows about himself!

The Invitation to Say More: Opening the Door

If you remain silent in a marriage relationship for very long, your partner will get the idea that you don't care. Your partner wants some type of verbal support. The kind of response he or she receives determines whether or not he will continue to open up to you.

A good listening technique is found in responding with a "door opener" or the invitation to say more. This response does not communicate a judgmental evaluation of what your partner is trying to say, or any of your own ideas or feelings. It simply invites your mate to share his thoughts.

Some of the simplest door openers might include the following: "No kidding," "How interesting," "I'm happy to hear that," "Good!" "Great!" "I see," "I understand."

These are more explicit door openers: "This sounds exciting! Tell me more"; "I can see how important this is to you"; "Tell me more about this"; "I'd be interested in hearing what you have to say about this"; "I'd like to hear your point of view."

Such responses reveal that you are interested in your partner; he or she has the right to express feelings on things; you might learn something from him; you'd like to hear his point of view; his ideas are important to you.

They also keep the conversation with him. He will not get the feeling that you want to take over and begin telling your own experiences, preaching, giving advice, or threatening. The responses you get from the door openers might surprise you. They encourage a person to talk, move in, come closer, and share feelings.

Anyone would respond favorably to such attitudes. You feel good when others respect you, make you feel worthy, and indicate that what you have to say is interesting. Your mate is no different. We need to offer our mates more opportunities to express themselves.

Creative Questioning: Tapping Private Space

Creative questioning prompts the other person to talk and lets him or her know you are interested and you are hearing what is being said. You can also discover what the other person is thinking and guide the thought process in a productive direction.

Note: Creative questioning is really a listening rather than a speaking skill, since you will be unable to phrase an appropriate question unless you have been listening.

Questions are invaluable aids in collecting information. You can discover much about your partner by asking questions. Personal sharing on an intimate level often has been stimulated by a well-phrased question. Questioning helps you grow in your knowledge about each other and has the ability to break down barriers of alienation. Creative questioning also extends conversation, thereby giving you and your mate more to talk about.

Questions can motivate a person to more serious thought about a matter as well as assist an individual in applying new concepts in his or her life. Thoughtful inquiries also enable you as a listener to reflect on what you just heard. The versatility of questions allows you to clarify what was meant: "You just said you were tired. Does this mean you are not planning to go to the church board meeting tonight?"

Creative questioning is a skill based on the ability to ask insightful questions about free information. Free information is that which is given without the prodding of questions. Creative questioning gives the go-ahead for the other person to tell more.

In creative questioning, however, you will follow the other person's agenda, not your own hidden agenda. Your questions will lead your partner where he or she wants to go, not where you want to take your partner.

Creative questioning involves open as opposed to closed-ended questions. A closed question is any question which requires a one-word or yes-or-no reply: "Did you have a good day?" An open-ended question would be phrased in the following manner: "Tell me about the most interesting thing that happened to you today." This invites the speaker to share more than customary perfunctory remarks.

Such inquiries must be used skillfully, however, or they may have negative consequences. Probing interrogation can be interpreted as invading private space. Some questions are too private or intimate to be asked and depend on the existing relationship and manner in which they are asked.

Questions can be manipulative or "loaded": "You call that being loving when you are never home in the evenings?" (a put-down hidden in the form of a question). A good response to any loaded question might be, "I'm confused about whether you are asking me a question or telling me something" (a perception check).

Blocking questions ("Is that all?") and interrogating questions based on information you want rather than what the other person wants to tell you are poor uses.

As much as possible avoid the question Why? It sounds accusatory and tends to make others defensive. A why question may get you the information you need but it doesn't help the other person. Whys get you realizations regarding feelings. A better way to ask a why question is this: "Tell me about your feelings regarding this matter." Some people are noticeably inquisitive and may even refer to themselves as why persons, but this doesn't change the effect.

Creative questioning can be a powerful tool when used in the right way at the right time by a skillful listener.

Body Language: Do Actions Speak Louder Than Words?

The following story was excerpted from an account by a reporter walking a beat in a simulated police-training situation. A loaded .38 rested on his hip to capture the mood of the moment. Without warning, a man appeared from a clump of bushes between two houses.

He was a big, rangy hippie, wearing a sloppy Zapata mustache. In his right hand he was hefting a baseball bat. At the sight of me, he slowed a little, but kept coming. His face had a mean and nasty aspect, a tightheld scowl. He turned towards me, his hand choked up on the bat, his eyes direct at me; his stride was determined, menacing.

I cleared my uniform jacket away from my gun butt, just in case. That bat could clobber me, all right, but except for the glare on his face, he hadn't jeopardized me, yet. The question was, had he just left three dead bodies in one of the houses? Had he burgled them? Assaulted a housewife? What?

He was within striking distance, three feet away. The tendons in his right forearm rippled. My hand was on the pistol. As he came abreast, the first clear break in his manner and behavior flashed on his face; he smiled and walked on by.

Whew! I had come that close to plugging a guy who was guilty of nothing more than heading out for the ballfield.[2]

A judgment based on facial expressions, gestures, and body cues—important as they are—led to faulty conclusions that were almost deadly!

All body responses and emotional expressions are part of nonverbal communication—a silent persuasion that tells the real story. The term also includes manner of speech as well as voice intonations and rate of speech—which all support what is being said.

Few people grasp the importance of nonverbals. In normal communication, the words used or content accounts for only 7 percent of what is conveyed; tone of voice and gestures amount to 38 percent; facial expressions alone account for an astonishing 55 percent.

Because a total of 93 percent of what is communicated is done so without words, understanding nonverbal communication is probably more important than any other listening skill. If you were really angry at your partner, could you hide it? Could you be filled with genuine anger and reveal nothing on your face through body posture or gestures or tone of voice? It would be difficult if not impossible.

Some people do become adept at masking nonverbal cues. Any facial expression, gesture, or posture that might give them away is carefully hidden from view. This leaves the listener at a severe disadvantage since he has only the 7 percent verbal from which to make an analysis.

We communicate nonverbally through three different modes:

1. Body language   All body positions either support or deny a verbal message. A direct message is sent even without the spoken word. Sagging shoulders might communicate discouragement; slouching in a chair, disinterest; head in hands, despair; a shrug of the shoulders, "I don't know"; a rigid sitting position, tension; crossed arms, defiance, and so on.

When not in agreement with what is being said, a person may put more distance between himself and the speaker; affection and intimacy, on the other hand, may draw two people closer.

Facial expressions are a part of body language and the strongest silent message sent. Eyes are the most expressive part of facial expressions. Their shiftiness, narrowing, widening, a slow roll, dullness, and rate of blinking all tell the mood of their owner. A quick wink at your beloved can communicate more than a whole spoken sentence. "I have no interest in you" or "You are important to me" are divulged through the eyes alone.

Other facial expressions also convey important messages. Imagine what a simple lift of the eyebrows, a wrinkling of the forehead, an uplifted chin, a dropped chin can intimate. When smiling, warmth and happiness are signified; when frowning, sadness and displeasure are evident.

Gestures are also included as part of body language. The outstretched arm with palm up demonstrates openness and acceptance; the outstretched arm, palm down, indicates closure and distance. The handshake, embrace, clenched fist, slammed door, thrown objects, clasped hands, upturned thumb, and pat on the back all send clear messages when coupled with other nonverbals and the spoken word.

Dress. Someone has said that by what we wear we hang a sign for all the world to see and judge. "Loud" clothes beg for attention; sloppy dress indicates carelessness and low self-worth; immodest or revealing dress, a desperate plea for attention. Our choice of clothes sends a silent but powerful message about what's inside.

Body language rarely lies because it springs from the subconscious. A person can hide feelings but not body language.

2. Voice cues   Words convey information, but how those words are spoken—volume, speed, inflection, and emphasis—carries more weight (38 percent of the impact). The teasing tone, touch of humor, judgmental chastisement convey friendliness, happiness, or anger. Cues tell the other person whether to come closer or back off.

Much of what might be termed *miscommunication* occurs because of reaction to tone of voice or style of talking. Style is measured in terms of signals sent—the speed at which one talks, loudness or softness, intonations used as well as choice of words. What actually was said as well as when also must be taken into consideration.

Such patterns are always at work, but we fail to see this as we tend to measure results in terms of intentions: "She seemed interested"; "She cared about my concerns"; "She attacked me." Our style of communicating, which is clear and normal to us, may be perceived by others as wrong or something to be distrusted.

The meaning of any sentence can be changed, depending on which word is emphasized. Read the following sentences aloud, emphasizing the boldface words:

I never said Jim stole the money. (Someone else said it.)

I **never** said Jim stole the money. (My intention was to keep it a secret.)

I never **said** Jim stole the money. (I only implied it.)

I never said **Jim** stole the money. (His name was never used in my account.)

I never said Jim **stole** the money. (I said only that the money was gone. Everyone just assumed it was stolen.)

I never said Jim stole the **money**. (I merely voiced a conviction and everyone assumed the money was missing.)

Interesting, isn't it? Six words, six sentences, six different meanings.

Speech mannerisms. Attitudes, meanings, and emotions are

communicated through a variety of mannerisms. Speech mannerisms are used so unconsciously that the sender is most likely not aware of them, and the listener may let them slide. One such mannerism is "Yes, but." Anytime a comment or opinion is given, this person contradicts with "Yes, but." Another is, "I know," which conveys, "You dummy! You can't teach me anything I don't already know."

3. Emotional cues   A tear running down a cheek, a giggle, sobbing, open laughter, and heavy sighs are all emotional expressions of inner feelings. Each heavily influences how the spoken message is interpreted. By tuning in to emotional clues, a listener can sense warmth, coolness, despair, friendliness, or hostility.

Silent Persuasion: It's Easy to Misinterpret

Nonverbal communication is revealed in many forms, but certain aspects are common to all forms. Generally speaking, nonverbal communication is used to express or highlight emotions. Norman Wakefield, counselor and author, points out:

> Feelings seem to be ventilated more easily through nonverbal channels. One possible reason for this is that the emotions can work through the nonverbal routes subconsciously whereas the verbal expression is dominated by the conscious mind. What we are reluctant or fearful to admit consciously, we will often release subconsciously. This somehow seems safer, although it is potentially more dangerous.[3]

Second, the nonverbal message is easier to confuse due to its more ambiguous nature. A listener is wise to give a cautious tentative interpretation of what he has gathered. Perceptions should be checked out with the speaker for accuracy and confirmation.

Third, nonverbal communication is more limited in scope. Whereas the nonverbal message carries more weight and is more intense and powerful than the verbal message, it has a more limited range for expressing concepts and ideas.

Note: Verbal is not more important than nonverbal, and vice versa. They have different functions, however. The primary function of the nonverbal is to strengthen, augment, and intensify the verbal. Nonverbals put life into the spoken word, lending vitality to what otherwise would be monotonous and boring.

A listener can more quickly interpret the true message when combining the nonverbals with the verbals. But nonverbals are much more difficult to interpret than verbals. The following suggestions may help:

(1) Develop a sensitivity to nonverbals.   Awareness of nonverbals is the first step in becoming a more sensitive interpreter. Consciously practice deciphering body, voice, and emotional cues. For practice, turn on the television and observe a program with the volume off. Can you guess intentions without the spoken word?

As you develop your sensitivity and awareness, practice checking out your perceptions with your mate rather than leaping to conclusions and giving a negative evaluation: "You have been quiet and distant all evening. Is something troubling you?"

(2) Learn to recognize a "mixed message."   When all three—the spoken word, the tone of voice, and body language—give the same message, they are said to be "congruent." When a person's words say one thing, but his body language or tone of voice contradict his words, it is a "mixed message." Since tone of voice and body language make up 93 percent of the message, they are more believable than the words used. Words are the least believable of what is conveyed. The words may be believable but denied by the tone of voice.

"I am not angry with you!" (*accompanied by a fist being slammed on the table*)

"I love you too." (*said in a mechanical, lifeless tone*)

"Of course I want to talk with you." (*while continuing to watch television*)

Would you believe the words—or the tone of voice?

Mixed messages confuse the listener and make interpretation more difficult. Whenever an unclear message is received, the listener must check out the observations to avoid misinterpretation and a potential misunderstanding.

Whereas mixed messages are generally troublesome, when the timing is right they can add spice and wit to conversations. A husband can growl with a special sparkle in his eye and a come-hither look, "Who wants you, baby?" For fun, or when we deliberately want someone to guess our intention, a banter of mixed messages and hidden meanings becomes a game of matching wits. Just be certain your partner is in the right frame of mind.

Paraphrasing: Unmuddling the Muddled

Paraphrasing is the skill of responding to the content and meaning of another person's verbal statement. Through paraphrasing, the listener clarifies the statement for accuracy and conveys to the other person that he is being heard. You can verify that the assumptions you are making about what you are hearing are what is intended by the other person. Your responses show interest in what is being said.

Paraphrasing deals primarily with the content being conveyed—the facts, information, ideas, opinions, or circumstances being described by the speaker. Responses might sound like this:

"I hear you to say that. . . ."

"From what I'm hearing, you are saying. . . ."

"You mean that. . . ."

An example of paraphrasing might go as follows:

WIFE: "I attended the most interesting in-service workshop at the office today. The speaker introduced a method of screening applicants through personality testing that could be invaluable to me. It could drastically change the present hiring system for the company."

HUSBAND: (using paraphrasing response) "If I perceive you correctly, this new testing method could change the present rate of turnover in your office. Right?"

Unlike active listening, paraphrasing deals only with the information shared, not with feelings. The listener works at understanding the information and sends it back, sometimes in question form, for verification. You show interest in what is being shared but avoid sending back duplicate phrases in parrotlike fashion.

Clarifying what has been said is important in all relationships but especially in marriage. Many misunderstandings which begin innocently could be avoided if the listener would only check on whether his perception was clear.

Harry and I could have saved ourselves some grief along the way if someone had taught us this skill years ago. For example, one day he came into my office and asked me (I thought) if I was going to use the car. Confused, I responded, "How do you think I am going to get to the store if I don't use the car?" In reality he was asking, "Whose car are we going to use?" (referring to a trip we were to take the following day). If only I had used a paraphrasing response, misunderstanding could have been averted!

Active Listening: Excellent Pattern for Intimacy

"Deliberate listening" is the ability to process information, analyze it, recall it at a later time, and draw conclusions from it. "Active listening" hears the *feelings* of the speaker first and processes information secondarily. Effective communicators must learn this important skill.

We tend to think of listening as a passive activity. However, when we add the word *active*, it implies participation and caring by the listener. Both deliberate and active listening are necessary in effective communication, but listening for feelings is far more important in marriage.

In active listening, the listener has the responsibility of attempting to grasp emotions often veiled behind the spoken word. But the active listener will go one step further and attempt to assist the speaker in expressing innermost emotions. It sounds simple enough in principle but can be extremely tricky when we hear criticism, a negative emotion, or something personally threatening or opposed to our values and beliefs. When someone confronts us, the natural inclination is to tune him out or straighten him out.

Active listening is best used when your partner experiences a problem: anger, frustration, resentment, loneliness, discouragement, hurt. Your first reaction upon hearing such feelings may be negative. You may want to argue, defend yourself, withdraw, or fight back. But in active listening, you simply lay aside your personal feelings in order to assist your partner in airing his or hers.

It is through such venting of feelings that a solution will be found. The fact that your mate can ventilate pent-up feelings to you and receive understanding rather than censure will be a giant step toward intimacy.

In active listening, you lay aside any preconceived ideas about how your partner should be feeling. Active listening requires total acceptance of your mate the way he is feeling right now. His emotions are neither right nor wrong. They simply are what they are: transitory feelings that come and go. The negative feelings you may hear expressed are not permanently engraved in your partner's heart or mind. Remember also that your partner is responding to the intensity of the moment. If at any moment your partner senses in you a lack of acceptance or a judgmental attitude, he or she will probably get angry or withdraw.

When your preconceived ideas are put aside, you are then free to listen, not so much to the information your partner shares with you but to the feelings behind the words. You attempt to crawl inside your partner, see the problem through his eyes, experience the same feelings, walk in his shoes. Another word for this process might be *empathy*. Empathy says, "I feel what you feel and I care about what is happening to you right now." Empathy implies caring, and this is what active listening is all about.

In preparing for active listening, listen with your eyes. If you see the muscles at his temples pulsating, you might guess great stress or tension. What do his eyes tell you about what he is experiencing? Listen to the tone of voice. Do you hear despair? Anger? Discouragement?

Remember that you are sending nonverbal signals too. Certain body signals such as nodding, a touch on the hand, and leaning toward your partner show acceptance and caring. Use these to your advantage but be genuine.

Putting It Into Practice

(1) Restate the feeling(s) heard.   Let's say a wife is feeling resentful because her husband is not spending enough time with her. She puts this into proper I-statement form (to be fully explained in the next chapter). "I am feeling resentful because you are gone almost every night of the week. When you are home you are so tired you watch TV or fall asleep. This is making me feel lonely and unloved. I need more of you than I am getting" (an open and honest statement of feelings).

Her husband listens for the feelings. He restates them, and the reason for her feelings, in his own words. "I hear you saying you feel neglected because I am spending too much time at work and not enough with you." It is important that he restate his wife's statement until she feels he has heard her.

(2) Wait for agreement.   He must agree with her feelings. He may *think* he has spent adequate time with her and may wish to prove his point by citing examples regarding his position. "What do you mean, I'm not home enough? I was home three nights last week." If he does this, he proves he is not listening to her *feelings*.

The fact is, his wife feels neglected. No counterargument will change this. In fact, it will probably only make her more defensive of her position. He may know for a fact that she is being unreasonable, but at this point nothing short of listening for feelings and understanding those feelings will do.

The husband may have his own opinions and feelings. His right and the opportunity to express them will come. But not now.

Active listening also requires that the husband listen to everything his wife has to say without offering any solutions. Far too often, solutions are offered before the problem is understood.

Carl R. Rogers, eminent psychiatrist, wrote on this subject:

> Can I let myself enter fully into the world of his feelings and personal meanings, and see these as he does? Can I step into his private world so completely that I lose all desire to evaluate

or judge it? Can I enter it so sensitively that I can move about in it freely, without trampling on meanings which are precious to him? Can I sense it so accurately that I can catch not only the meanings which are only implicit, which he sees only dimly or as confusion? Can I extend this understanding without limit?

... I am impressed with the fact that even a minimal amount of empathetic understanding—a bumbling and faulty attempt to catch the confused complexity of the client's meaning—is helpful, though there is no doubt that it is most helpful when I can see and formulate clearly the meanings of his experiencing which for him have been unclear and tangled.[4]

Even the "bumbling and faulty" efforts of husbands and wives are greatly appreciated. You need not be a pro to show you care and listen empathetically.

(3) Give adequate feedback.   The easiest proper response to ensure that you are picking up the feelings rather than the facts is "You are feeling . . ." and then state the feeling, the emotion you just heard expressed. A restatement of the feelings will get you into an active listening episode. It might sound like this:

Situation 1: Wife becomes irritated because she feels son is being treated unfairly at school. She says, "I am so angry over this. They can't do this to Jeremy. I have a good notion to march right over there and pull him out."

Husband's response (whether or not he agrees): "You are really upset over this latest incident. Tell me more." (a door opener)

Situation 2: Husband is despondent over personnel problems at work. He doesn't verbalize easily, but his astute wife observes his despondency and leads in this way: "Honey, you look troubled over something. Tell me about it." (the door opener)

Husband: "It's nothing I can't handle, but it just goes on and on. Joe is causing me no end of grief. I have no idea who promoted such a turkey to supervisor. It's useless to talk to him about anything!"

Wife: "You are really feeling pressure, aren't you? I'd be interested in hearing the whole situation from your point of view."

Situation 3: Wife, after a long hard day: "I am so tired I could die. I do nothing but race from the moment I get out of bed in the morning 'til I collapse at night . . . the kids, the meals, keeping this house up [*with a heavy sigh she sinks into a chair*]. Life in the fast lane is too much for me."

Husband: "You are really feeling exhausted tonight. Is there anything else connected to this that is getting to you?" (*a door opener*)

Notice that in each of the situations, the active listener responded appropriately by identifying the correct feeling and then provided the opportunity for the speaker to go on, verbalize more feelings, and get it out of his or her system.

Here are other ways to get into active listening:

"It sounds as if you are really feeling. . . ."

"I understand. You feel. . . ."

"If I am hearing you correctly, you feel. . . ."

"Let me see if I fully understand how you feel. You are feeling. . . ."

Gear your response level to the mood of your partner. Reveal empathy without overshooting or undershooting. It must come across in a believable way that you care.

Few active listening episodes will end with just one response. Generally speaking, when a big problem is being verbalized, the episode will continue for a series of exchanges. Stay with listening for feelings and continue to act as an escape valve for the ventilating of feelings.

Let's go back and continue Situation 3, in which the wife feels she is living life in the fast lane. Her husband responds appropriately and then gently probes to see if this is the real problem or if there might be anything behind what she said.

JOAN: (*pausing to ponder the question*) "Yes, I think I could take all the pressure I'm under if I felt you really cared about me."

JACK: "I see. You feel I don't care about you anymore and you are really frustrated about it."

JOAN: "Well, we used to have time for each other . . . to talk . . . to go out to eat . . . just you and me. We haven't been out without the kids in months. By the time I get them fed and to bed, I'm so tired I don't even care if I see you—let alone talk to you or make love to you."

JACK: "If I'm picking up what you are saying, the real reason you're upset is you feel we are growing apart rather than closer together."

JOAN: "Right! You take time to play racquetball twice a week, but you don't have time for me. There's always time and money to do what you want to do."

JACK: (*bristling but not becoming defensive*) "You feel I'm not being fair to you and you resent it."

JOAN: "You bet! I don't really mind my busy life. I rather thrive on it, but I've got to feel you care about me, that we are a team, not two separate people going in different directions. Well, I can dream, can't I? I'm dead tired. Turn out the lights and let's get some sleep."

Joan ended the conversation abruptly. Not once did Jack defend himself, in spite of the fact that he felt Joan was making some unfair jibes about racquetball and his not paying enough attention to her. Nor did he attempt to solve the problem at this time. The hurt evidenced by Joan touched him. How easy it would have been to placate her by saying, "Okay, okay, we'll begin going out together once a week without the kids. Okay?"

That might have solved the immediate problem, but what would have happened to all the feelings Joan had stored up inside her about what she perceived was happening to their relationship? Instead of attempting to solve her problem immediately, Jack allowed her to ventilate—a true act of caring that would draw them closer together.

She shared; he cared. A great pattern for intimacy!

Something may happen to you when you practice active listening. Your own attitudes or opinions may change as you understand accurately how another person feels. Allow this to be an exciting experience and revelation in your life. Opening yourself to the experiences of others invites the possibility of reevaluating your own experiences. Introspection and self-evaluation can be very uncomfortable to a defensive person because he cannot afford to expose himself to ideas and views that differ from his own. A flexible person is not afraid of being changed; hence, he experiences inner peace and freedom even in a state of flux.

Six Powerful Listening Rules

How is your "listenability"? Have you been a poor listener? Merely deciding to try to improve will not work. You must discipline yourself and make a firm commitment to improve this skill. Here are six power-packed ways you can practice listening with feeling on a daily basis:

(1) Maintain good eye contact.   Focus your full attention on your partner. (Turn off the television and put down the newspaper.)

(2) Sit attentively.   For a few minutes, act as if nothing else in the world matters except hearing out your partner. Block all other distractions from your mind. Lean forward in your chair as if you are hanging on every word.

(3) Act interested in what you are about to hear.   Raise your eyebrows, nod your head in agreement, smile, or laugh when appropriate.

(4) Sprinkle your attentive listening with appropriate phrases to show interest and understanding.   "I agree." "Is that so!" "Great!" "I hear where you are coming from!" Your partner wants to know you understand the ideas being presented.

(5) Ask well-phrased questions.   Give encouragement by asking questions that illustrate your interest.

(6) Listen a little longer.   Just when you think you are through listening, listen thirty seconds longer!

His and Her Listening Styles: Are They Different?

According to studies conducted on the listening habits of the sexes, women and men have different ways of showing they are listening. Women tend to denote keen listening through "uh-huh," "mmhmm," and "interesting." Women will include affirmative head nodding and other positive listening habits more frequently than men.

Men include fewer of these behaviors in their listening. This leaves women with the impression that their husbands aren't listening and men with the impression that their wives are overlistening.

Furthermore, what men and women mean by their listening behaviors may differ vastly. When women nod their heads and say "uh-huh," they do so to indicate they are listening and understand what is being said. Men use listening noises more to show agreement. It could be that women are listening less but are more convincing actors. Or it could be that men are hearing as much as women but are agreeing less!

This complicates the listening process. If a wife listens attentively to her husband, echoing many "ohs," "yeahs," and "uh-huhs," indicating good listening and understanding (from her point of view), and he discovers later that she did not agree with what he was saying, he might get upset and even accuse her of being deceitful. The same is true for a woman. If she shares something with her man and he gives no response, verbally or nonverbally, she thinks he is not paying attention.[5]

Occasionally I get the idea that Harry is not listening to me. I share something with him that is very important to me. No response. So I say, "You're not listening to me." He repeats, word for word, what I just said. It is so irritating! Men could, however, improve their listenability by getting into the act of listening with an occasional "I see" or "uh-huh" and a nod of the head.

A woman needs this kind of listening response from her husband in order to feel heard. She seeks understanding more than a solution. A time will come to search for a solution, but while she is upset she wants to be listened to. If her husband listens with one eye on the television, or gives a string of solutions, it won't suffice. Most of all, a woman needs to have her feelings validated and accepted. A woman who feels she cannot be heard also begins to feel unloved. Usually she will talk louder and longer in an effort to be heard and feel loved.

Notice that men's and women's listening behaviors are consistent with their focus in communication. Using listening behaviors to show interest and caring rather than agreement serves the emotional aspects of the relationship, a primary focus for women. Using listening behaviors to show agreement with what was said focuses on content or the nuts and bolts of a conversation, the primary focus for men. So in listening, as well as in many other aspects of communication, men and women remain consistent in style.

Many of us think listening is something we do with our ears. Nothing could be further from the truth. Ears are involved in the listening process, but true listening goes beyond only hearing what is said. True listening demonstrates caring.

Are you willing to put yourself out to hear and feel your partner's problems? Forty-six percent on the CI said they did. That leaves 54 percent who need more willingness, more acceptance, and more understanding. Are you doing all you can do?

The Listening Heart

A couple reached the very brink of divorce. Both were Christians and well intentioned, but something had swept into their relationship and threatened the fibers of their marital bond. A heretofore unknown weakness in the husband's character suddenly surfaced. One night he was arrested because of it.

Although only the arresting officer, those involved in the court system, and the wife knew of the problem, deep feelings of humiliation consumed the wife during the days before the hearing. She vacillated between shame and intense pity for the one who had fathered her four children. Divorce became a serious option as she contemplated a future with a man she now doubted she had ever known. What basis was there for a relationship where honesty and trust were nonexistent?

In desperation, the woman sought the advice of a trusted minister who was specially trained in working with severely troubled families. His only request was that she postpone any final decision regarding divorce until after the court hearing. In deference to the minister's wishes, she complied.

The husband remained in the house, although they secluded themselves in separate bedrooms at night. The atmosphere was tense. At night you would have found her sobbing quietly into the coolness of her pillow as she pondered the frightful situation in which she found the children and herself. Days passed in a confused fog.

The court hearing was humiliating. Words were used she had never heard before. How could she possibly understand what drove him to such unnatural acts? As suddenly as it had begun, it was all over. The judge dismissed the charges if the defendant agreed to get in-depth, long-term counseling. Except for the degradation, embarrassment, and bitter memories, it was over.

He was free. She could now file for divorce.

She had agreed, however, to see the trusted minister with her husband one time before she filed. They arrived in separate cars, minutes apart. She entered the minister's office with a polite but curt greeting, her eyes carefully avoiding her husband, who was already seated. She seated herself as far from him as possible.

Cautiously, the minister asked the outcome of the court hearing.

"It's over. The charges were dismissed. He needs counseling. I stuck with him through the hearing as you asked me to do. Now all I want is a divorce. I want nothing more to do with this man. He's sick!"

The words tumbled out of her with staccatolike rapidity.

Without waiting to be called upon for a response, the husband spat back a reply: "And if that's what she wants, she can have it! I'm sick and tired of the whole mess. And I'm sick and tired of her. All her accusations . . . the questions . . . through this whole thing . . . she's never cared about me . . . all she's cared about is herself! Divorce is the only answer. The sooner the better!"

The case appeared settled before discussion had even begun!

Wisely the counselor asked for a moratorium on all judgments, accusations, and anger during the upcoming hour. He requested that during this one session they both put all charges and assumptions on hold in an effort to deal with the feelings involved.

The wife described feelings of humiliation regarding this strange weakness of her husband, his being arrested, and the court hearing. She felt she could cope with the situation had it been another woman, whom she could fight, but not this. She went on to describe intense feelings of rejection and loneliness resulting from his strange behavior.

The counselor encouraged her to probe the recesses of her mind for everything she had been experiencing since the discovery of her husband's secret vice. He encouraged her to explain her feelings so graphically that the two of them could see it through her eyes, feel the situation with her, taste of her loneliness and hurt. She plunged on, graphically describing the personal disappointment she felt in her own lack of ability to cope with the situation . . . ordinarily she was strong . . . now she felt inordinately weak . . . for the first time in her life she was unable to change or cope with a situation . . . her fear for the children's future. A dark forest enveloped her . . . she was running . . . deeper and deeper into the foreboding forest . . . darkness was closing in on her . . . terror surrounded her . . no help in sight . . . no way out.

Judging by the husband's reactions, he had heard none of this before. The intense anger which had consumed him only shortly before had dissolved into a look of bewilderment and confused hurt, even compassion for his wife and mother of his children, who felt so betrayed by someone who had promised to protect her.

A trace of hope appeared on his anxious face. Did even the remotest possibility of a reconciliation exist? His manner softened ever so slightly as he listened to the continued revelation of feelings that consumed his wife.

Half an hour had passed. Many tears had been shed. She was near exhaustion as she relived the torment of the last few weeks. When she paused, the counselor leaned forward in his chair and asked if she hated her husband. Wasn't she filled with rage against one who had caused her so much anguish?

Her answer came quickly: "Hate? Oh, no! All I feel for him is compassion. I love him even now!"

Now it was time for the husband's eyes to fill with tears. And it was his turn to talk. He went back into his childhood, describing the feelings of alienation he felt due to his weakness. He felt lower than the lowest man on earth, totally without worth, weird, filthy, not worthy of a fine wife and beautiful children. He expressed deep love and concern for the children and his fear of infecting them with his weakness. He described feelings of living in his own private hell.

Somewhere in the midst of the man's description, his wife silently walked across the room and sat next to him, putting her arm around his shoulders. No words were spoken but in effect this gesture said, "Carry on. I am with you." More fear, shame, guilt, and hurt poured out of the grief-stricken man.

Toward the end of this emotional scene, he told of his greatest desire: a relationship with someone who could know about his weakness and still care for him, someone who would love him in spite of this "thing." He longed for someone to hold him just as a mother would even if she knew the real him.

A new dimension to the drama unfolded at this point. The woman reached over and put both arms around her husband, drawing his head to her shoulder and embracing him compassionately. He sobbed out the bitter despair of thirty-four years while she held him and their tears mingled.[6]

One hour earlier this couple had been bent on divorce. Now they held each other as if nothing on earth could ever separate them. These two people almost never got to know each other. Other problems will surface that will test the bonds of their love, but on this occasion they learned the importance of sharing what is inside rather than trying to hide feelings from the world.

Furthermore, each of them learned to listen without preconceived ideas or judgments. Until now, neither of them had really known the other because each was so busy building a protective wall as a shield against further hurt. Each learned before it was too late to risk exposing self. In doing so, they found someone to whom they could "tell all"—someone with whom they could be fully known and share all their inner thoughts, weaknesses, and foibles. Rather than driving a loved one away, the episode drew them together in unfathomable bonds of closeness and intimacy. Each risked transparency and found intimacy!

Just as those who listened carefully on the evening of October 30, 1938, were the ones who had no reason to panic, today those who listen carefully, to show they care, are many strides ahead of the pack.

Listening is the key, my friend!

4 Hearttalk: How to Talk to the One You Love

The most important function of talking is not the giving of information but the establishing of a relationship. A couple who can't talk to each other have no basis for a relationship. By opening up and sharing, you can turn a stranger into a friend.

"While we were going together we spent much time talking," Sharon shared. "We were best friends. I could tell Ed anything and he shared everything with me. Now we hardly ever talk and when we do, we argue. We can't discuss the smallest matter without tempers flaring. Is there something wrong with us?"

Sharon and Ed married with the platitude "If you really love each other you will work everything out" ringing in their ears. Not necessarily! The more a couple loves each other, the higher the expectations are for success and the greater the potential for hurt and misunderstandings.

Sharon and Ed knew how to solve their problems only by talking them out, but if there are misunderstandings, hidden angers, and indirect messages, talking won't solve the problem. Continued discussion merely gives exposure to more confusing talk, which drives both partners up a wall. Without realizing it, Sharon and Ed were engaged in a game of mutual aggravation.

The advice "talk about it" given to couples with communication problems assumes that each can state what he or she means and the other can understand what is said. Focusing on the words alone to see what sparked a crisis won't cut it. The real culprit is more likely in the body language, tone of voice, unstated implications, assumptions, meanings attached to the words, or resentment from past experience.

The time a couple spends talking assumes great importance, for talk can either bring two people together or it can distance them. How a couple talks to each other can either build or destroy a relationship.

Through talking, we can express feelings, convey emotions, clarify thinking, reinforce ideas, and make contact with a partner. It is a pleasant way of passing time, getting to know each other, releasing tension, expressing opinions, and deepening intimacy. The basic and most important function of speaking, then, is not the giving of information but the establishing of a relationship. The quality of this relationship depends a great deal on the ability of each to express himself verbally.

Killer Talk: Messages of Pain

Much of our everyday talk consists of alienating messages that can be aptly described as "killer talk." We get so used to using some of these phrases that we become unaware of how offensive they can be. When a partner reacts negatively, we accuse him of being oversensitive or overreacting. Here are some killer messages that are guaranteed to make your partner want to leave home:

The "solution sender" weights down his speech with orders, directions, and commands: "Get over here." "Hurry up." Warnings and threats fit here also: "If you ever do that again, I'll. . . ." Another habit is moralizing: "You know enough not to. . . ." Most of us resent being told we *must, should,* or *better* do something.

Many people resort to put-downs in spite of the fact that we know what it feels like to be discounted. Put-downs judge, criticize, and blame: "Not a bad idea, considering *you* thought of it." They name call, ridicule, and shame: "You're a slob." They interpret, diagnose, and psychoanalyze: "You say that only because. . . ." They attempt to teach: "Honey, we shouldn't act like that in public."

Dr. James Dobson tells of a game husbands and wives play. He calls it Assassinate the Spouse. In this destructive game the player (usually a husband, he notes) attempts to punish his wife by ridiculing and embarrassing her in front of their friends. He can hurt her when they are alone, but in front of friends he can really cut her down. If he wants to be exceptionally cruel, he'll let the guests know how stupid and ugly she is—the two areas where she is the most vulnerable. Bonus points are awarded if he can reduce her to tears.

Then there is the "corrector." For example, while the wife tells a story to friends, her husband helps her keep the facts straight:

"We had dinner at Peaches last Wednesday night—"

"Not Wednesday night, honey. Tuesday."

"Well, anyway we had dinner and their specialty is Italian food and I had the best manicotti I've ever had."

"They don't specialize in anything. Besides, I thought it was awful."

"After supper we went shopping and I bought this gorgeous dress on sale for only sixty dollars. It was a steal."

"The dress cost eighty dollars plus tax!"

A corrector has the compulsion to concentrate on proper reporting of facts. Such interruptions are often attempts to draw attention to self. They show a gross lack of sensitivity in not allowing someone else to tell a story the way she remembers it.

The "judge" tries to second-guess what will come next. A wife might say, "They are showing a really good movie at the church Wednesday night." Her husband doesn't wait to see what point she is going to make, but cuts her off with, "Yes, but we're not going." He *assumes* he knows what she was going to say. Many miscommunication problems could be avoided by clarifying what you think was meant before leaping to a conclusion.

The "topic switcher" changes the subject before meaningful communication can take place or when he does not wish to discuss a topic.

Some people bicker or quibble, raising trivial objections to dispute an event seen differently by others.

Some are "topic avoiders" who refuse to discuss certain subjects.

"Topic overkillers" talk excessively about a subject.

"Underresponsiveness" speaks for itself—it describes the reactions of those who say too little in response.

A list of killer talk is almost endless. You cannot control killer messages sent by your partner, but you can stop killer messages you are sending. When you do, you will notice you and your mate drawing closer to each other without conscious effort. You will feel closer when you don't have to deal with residual hurt accumulated from killer communication.

Breaking the Silence Barrier

The most deadly killer message of all is the silent treatment. To clam up, withdraw, retreat, refuse to talk about something, or hide behind a curtain of hurt does more to clog communication than any other killer message. It has been said that adultery slays its thousands but silence its ten thousands.

The caption "Talk About a Quiet Marriage: 12 Years Without Speaking" caught my attention. The story from England told of a husband and wife who had maintained a strict code of silence for twelve years! Out of spite, neither would lower themselves to speak, but they did communicate by passing notes. At some point, a divorce was suggested by one of them in this manner. The other responded by returning the note with the words "Go Ahead" written on it. Yes, silence will eventually destroy a marriage.

Silence is used as a weapon or a form of control. Both men and women use the silent treatment but usually in different ways. A man is silent when strong emotions such as anger or fear build inside. A woman usually uses silence to get even for some injustice to her or when she reaches the stage of total despair and desperation. The silent treatment may be given because one refused to listen last time, or the silent one may be suffering from a deep hurt. Some Christians feel it isn't right to say what they think. Others resort to silence for the children's sake. This bottling of emotion takes its toll physically, mentally, and spiritually.

The "silent husband," according to some marriage counselors, lies behind one-half of all troubled marriages they encounter. Many women complain that their husbands won't talk to them and cannot be prodded into it. These husbands communicate primarily on the "small talk" or "factual" level.

Several attitudes account for male silence. Some men, particularly workaholics, consider little but productivity to be of value. Their answer to all of life's problems is action, not talk. Other men are so dogmatic and authoritarian they refuse any further discussion and hand down edicts. Still others detest discussing what they term "trivia."

A man under emotional stress usually clams up, closes the gates, and retreats within himself because he has been trained since birth to keep tight control of his emotions. He will cut himself off from anything that differs from the logical and detached way of life to which he has become accustomed. As he grows older, he grows tougher so his peers won't detect any sign of softness or emotion.

Whenever feelings well up within him, a man's automatic response is to turn them off, especially in the presence of a woman. If he gets angry and lashes out at her, he isn't a gentleman. If he cries, it is perceived as weakness. Consequently, he uses silence as a method of escaping from his feelings, failing to understand how this maddens his wife when her aim is to get it all out in the open.

When a man is charged with not communicating, he often responds this way: "What do you mean I'm not communicating? I'm talking to you right now," or "Okay. I'll talk. What do you want to talk about?" or "Talk. Talk. Talk. That's all we do," or "You want to talk? Let's discuss what's in the newspaper." That last one is funny because everyone knows that current events is not necessarily what a wife wants to talk about.

A man's verbals and nonverbals deny the reality of his words. When confronted with this, he adopts "crazymaking" techniques of insisting there is nothing wrong with him or it's all in his wife's head; she makes mountains out of molehills. Such denials lead nowhere and end in stalemates.

Those who retreat to silence—male or female—generally see it as a safety device. They think if they keep their inner thoughts and feelings hidden, others cannot attack or discredit them. But withdrawal and indifference convey a vital message concerning involvement in the relationship. In effect, the person is saying, "I have little or no responsibility to become involved with you or the relationship." However, every married person does have a responsibility, by virtue of marriage, to become involved. Marriage implies involvement, not separateness or indifference.

To celebrate a birthday, recently we went to a dinner theater production of the musical *Paint Your Wagon*. We were seated at a table for six with two people we knew and two who were total strangers. Though it would have been acceptable for us to ignore the unfamiliar couple and converse only with our friends, for the sake of courtesy we made small talk with them. Point: There was no commitment to them and therefore no obligation to converse.

When one chooses not to communicate in marriage, however, it is considered an offense. The choice not to communicate seriously undermines the validity of the commitment to the relationship. By withdrawing, the silent one acts as if he has no obligation toward maintenance.

You can't do much about your partner's silence, but you can do something about what may be causing the silence (if you are causing it). Begging, pleading, getting angry, or responding in kind is hardly the remedy. By using other tactics, you are more likely to get your spouse to open up. One approach is this: "There are times when you have trouble talking with me. There must be something I am doing that is making it difficult for you. I'd like to discuss this with you so I can make some changes."

If you ask a question and get no response, try, "What do you think of what I just asked you?" or "Your silence says to me that you are very angry/hurt/upset over something. Is this what you are trying to tell me?" or "I'd like to talk with you about your silence and how it affects me. But first I would like to hear what you have to say about your silence."

Most people would prefer a good argument to silence—at least they get feedback. If you want your partner to resent you and possibly leave, talk only when you feel like it, pay little attention when your partner is speaking, and use silence frequently!

Body Language: What Do Your Nonverbals Say?

Fifty-five percent of the total message delivered is made up of nonverbals. Your nonverbal behavior actually carries more weight than the words you say.

The film *A Cry in the Dark* well illustrates the primary function nonverbals play in conveying a message. The movie is based on the extraordinary true story of Lindy Chamberlain, who was convicted of the murder of her infant daughter, whom she insisted was carried off by a wild dog. Meryl Streep, who played Lindy, was fascinated at how the Chamberlains, who were victims of a tragedy, so swiftly came to be seen as deceivers and murderers. In an interview Streep said, ". . . There was something about the way she behaved, the way she set her face, the way she appeared on television that changed the way people felt. . . . The Chamberlains . . . didn't seem to make an appropriate expression of grief. . . . She wasn't seen to grieve—although she did—and therefore she was seen as guilty."[1]

In another article about the film Streep said, "I'm fascinated in how we judge each other on the TV and how much how you look and sound has to do with what you're saying in terms of legitimizing it, making it palatable. . . . Lindy was judged based on how she communicated." Lindy Chamberlain spent more than three years in prison because her nonverbals were more believable than her verbals.[2]

Powerful messages can be delivered without ever opening your mouth: the finger pointed accusingly, a roll of the eyes, or a deep sigh. Other strong messages come through if you fold your arms across your chest, stand with your hands on your hips and feet far apart, or walk away during a conversation.

A lack of eye contact, not answering when spoken to, pulling away when touched, and a host of other nonverbal behaviors speak louder than words. Each possesses killer power.

Winning Conversation: How to Talk Sweet

The voice has been called the melody of conversation: it can be loud, soft, harsh and angry, or mellow and soothing. The tone of voice, which represents 38 percent of any message delivered, can draw your mate toward you or push your partner away. Next to nonverbal communication, it carries the most weight in any spoken message.

Voice pitch, volume, tone, speed, number and length of pauses, stammering, intensity, and emotion conveyed all give a meaning far beyond the words themselves. A word may be a word, but how it is received is dependent on how it is said. Some messages are so loaded with emotional overtones that they deny the reality of what was said.

Jim enters the house after a miserable and frustrating day at work. June inquires, "Did you have a good day, dear?" The emotional overlay that accompanies June's innocent-sounding question can convey sarcasm, irony, gentleness, or concern, which can shape, change, and modify her question. Subtle nuances can contradict words, adding a totally different dimension to the message. Any two people can say the same sentence, yet each sentence is delivered and received differently due to the voice intonations that accompany the message.

Meaning is given to words by the sender as he chooses the words, but also is taken by the listener as she listens and interprets. Not everyone interprets meanings in the same way. The five hundred most-used words in the English language during everyday communication have over fourteen thousand dictionary definitions.[3] "Meaning" here, however, is not referring to the dictionary definition but to the meaning attached to a word by the sender and receiver. Others don't always use words the way we do, and we can end up with all sorts of misunderstandings.

At the dinner table Rich exclaims, "Do you know what happened at work today?" His wife responds, "No." That one-word response can say, "No, and I couldn't care less," or "No, and I'm really interested to know." Take the sentence we all love to hear, "I love you." Give special emphasis to "you" and raise your tone slightly. Now say it again, dropping your voice. There's no conviction behind the second message.

Even the rate of speech can alter and affect meaning. A fast talker can be both persuasive and expressive, but fast talk can also irritate a more slowly paced individual. Words that tumble out with rushed urgency may make some people uncomfortable. Equally irritating to others is a slow speaker who implies apathy and indifference. As a fast and slow talker attempt to converse with each other, misunderstandings could escalate.

Talking has a rhythm and flow. A clever speaker can shift his normal rhythm to hammer a point. Hitler became so adept at this, he frequently used drumrolls keyed to the rousing rhythm of his speeches. This added impetus and excitement to his words. Some talkers speak with a soothing smoothness, others with awkward, unpredictable pauses that create an uncomfortable feeling.

Volume can be used to soothe or irritate. Noise frightens the enemy, therefore increased volume can be a very successful weapon. A loud, angry voice is an effective weapon in most arguments. However, lowered, subdued tones can be used to gain attention. A top television executive deliberately lowered his voice during important meetings and always held center stage as his listeners had to lean forward to hear what he was saying.

Jennie was raised in a quiet family of soft-spoken people. Low voices were the norm unless someone got angry. She married Ken, whose family was the exact opposite—a loud and boisterous group where everyone spoke loudly whether happy or angry. Family background differences caused many misunderstandings. Jennie found Ken's family loud and obnoxious and couldn't wait for peace and solitude after they visited. Ken found Jennie's family withdrawn, cold, and unfriendly.

Many situations can be softened by proper tuning. A loud argument can be more properly paced by taking the volume down a notch or two. A soft voice can reassure and comfort a hurting partner. It says, "I'm here. I care and I understand." Scripture backs up this assertion: "A soft answer turneth away wrath" (Proverbs 15:1 KJV).

Your voice can transmit cold, uncaring messages of indifference or it can transmit love, caring, and warmth. Each of us needs to expend tremendous effort to break negative habits and move toward a pleasing tone of voice that is supportive and productive.

Smooth Talk: Establishing Rapport

Before moving into more effective speech habits, it is appropriate to look at how we might create the kind of atmosphere in which a partner would want to listen to us.

From a wise judge come these words: "I have found it effective at times to meet people on their level and to use their language to convey ideas they would not understand if presented in any other fashion." Meeting a person at his or her level and creating a positive atmosphere is not only good advice in business but in marriage as well.

A couple synchronized with each other will experience rapport exemplified by agreement and harmony in both their verbals and nonverbals. A couple who is out of sync will experience alienation and disharmony. Rapport can best be established through pacing.

You can pace in many ways: through mood, body language, tone of voice, volume, rate of speech, words, phrases, and images. You can pace opinions, ideas, beliefs, and even breathing patterns. The better able you are to pace your partner's behavior, the more harmony you will create between you as you interact.

Pacing moods   An old axiom states that misery loves company. Likewise, cheerful people prefer to associate with similar people. Some people awake early in the morning ready to set the world on fire. Others resent wake-up calls prior to 9:00 A.M. and even then present themselves puffy-eyed and grumpy. I have not yet figured out why such people marry each other, but I do know the early bird will not endear himself to his partner by chirping each morning at 6:00 A.M.

Some think their cheerful ways are superior, and they attempt to influence and change a grumpy morning partner. If your partner responds with a lack of cooperation and/or sheer hatred, it might be wise to mollify your behavior. By doing this, you will say, "Your mood is important to me. I will respect it." Rapport is established.

Pacing body language   Nonverbal behavior far outweighs the impact of words when the two are out of sync. But rather than attaching an interpretation to the behavior, it is more important that you respond to your mate's nonverbals appropriately. Pacing your behavior by adjusting your nonverbals to those of your partner establishes greater harmony.

Picture a pair of lovers sitting across the table from each other, staring deeply into one another's eyes. Can you see them each fiddling with silver, chins in hands, legs crossed at the ankles? Each is oblivious to the rest of the world but so in tune with the other that they appear almost as twins, mirroring each other's body language unconsciously.

The more movements, postures, facial expressions mirrored, the greater the sense of acceptance and belonging between them. Much of this occurs on an unconscious level, but what happens when it doesn't occur? It blasts a message: "I am different from you." This message can mean the difference between cooperation and resistance, acceptance and rejection.

Researchers have noted that women are better than their counterparts at pacing. Females are naturally more adept at picking up nonverbal cues and probably have had more social conditioning to do so. Men can become adept at pacing with practice but tend to feel they've lost their individuality and power when they have to adjust their behavior to someone else's.[4]

Pacing verbals   Learning to pace verbal communication can also influence marital harmony. A businessman dramatically increased his list of subscribers to the answering service he owned by adjusting his rate of speech to those who called for information. If the potential customer spoke slowly, he responded slowly. If the customer spoke rapidly, he responded in kind. This one change resulted in a 30 percent increase in subscribers. Unless partners adjust differences in rate of speech, the fast talker will constantly irritate the slow speaker and vice versa.

Pacing volume   This is another smart and useful technique. The soft-spoken partner may respond in terror to one who speaks loudly. Likewise, you will probably gain respect from a partner who speaks loudly if you respond in kind.

One woman whose husband was a yeller cowered before him for years. While he stormed around the house pounding on tables, slamming doors, and shouting, she remained silent, attempting to model for him the type of behavior she wished him to demonstrate. Some coaching finally convinced her to match the intensity of his verbals and nonverbals without attacking. On one occasion she did, agreeing with everything he said while pounding a table for emphasis. Her astounded husband fell amazingly silent, put his arms out to her, and said, "Honey, calm down and let's talk about this rationally."

The message is clear: Effective pacing allows you to establish a profound level of empathy with your partner.

Sensing the Right Time

While we were picnicking by a lake during a sizzling hot spell, Harry complained of the heat. After several such complaints, I responded, "Well, go jump in the lake." He took my suggestion literally and found some welcome relief from the heat. On another occasion, we were engaged in a rather heated discussion and I once again suggested that he "go jump. . . ." His reaction was significantly different due to timing.

Often we create pain in our relationships through poor timing. Maintenance of close relationships is dependent on awareness of the other's "sensitivity line." When this invisible line is crossed, it creates pain. The line may be crossed more rapidly in some people than others. It also is influenced by mood, temperament, and wellness. The closer the relationship, the more sensitive each person becomes.

Timing involves raising your awareness level, respecting the emotional state of your partner, and monitoring your honesty and openness with real concern for the other's present feelings. Unfortunately, many couples use timing negatively, catching and attacking a partner when he or she is most vulnerable, thereby causing tremendous hurt.

Carefully consider the issue of timing in your relationship

regarding both problem- and nonproblem-oriented discussions. Are you being considerate of your partner's sensitivity line? Respecting that line can greatly influence the closeness a couple feels for each other.

High-Level Talks

So far we have talked about other elements of speaking beyond the actual words. Now let's focus on the message itself. John Powell, in his book *Why Am I Afraid to Tell You Who I Am?* describes five levels on which we can communicate. An understanding of these levels is essential when conversing.

Level 5: small talk   At this level, shallow conversation takes place: "How are you?" "Whatcha been up to?" "How are things going?" Such conversation borders on the meaningless but is better than embarrassed silence in social situations with those we do not know well. However, if communication remained at such a superficial level in marriage, it would lead to extreme boredom along with deep feelings of frustration and resentment.

Level 4: factual conversation   This reads like the evening newscast: Information is shared but no personal comments along with it. You talk about the day's events, but you don't tell how you feel about them. Conversations are constructed so that news, facts, and information are shared while you remain uninvolved. Factual conversation is easy because it requires minimal risk. Almost nothing of self is exposed. Men are more likely than women to communicate on this level. They find it logical, factual, and safe. It requires little but you get less in return. A couple communicating only on this level can never attain intimacy.

Level 3: ideas and opinions   Real conversation is approached here as you describe ideas and opinions. Because you feel free to express yourself and verbalize personal ideas, your partner has a better chance to know you. At this level, you test the waters by exposing some personal thoughts. If these are accepted, you can move to a deeper level. If not, you stay here or back up to level 4, where it is safe again. Real intimacy has not yet taken place, but when level 3 communication is met with acceptance, you are laying a good foundation and are approaching it.

Level 2: feelings and emotions You now feel secure enough to share the feelings that lie underneath the ideas and opinions expressed at level 3. You describe what is going on inside you—how you feel about your partner or a situation. A part of you remains slightly cautious, keeping a watchful eye on your partner's response. Before revealing more or telling all, you test your partner's acceptance level. Unless you receive the acceptance you need, you will probably say only things you know your partner can handle and will agree with—a real communication killer. When a couple can share honestly at this level in a give-and-take manner, with each respecting the other's feelings, their relationship will be greatly enriched and intimacy created. Flashes of insight into your partner's personality will be gained and provide a basis for understanding and intimacy. A good combination for daily interaction is to alternate between the levels of ideas/opinions and feelings/emotions.

Level 1: deep insight The deepest and rarest level is deep insight, where complete emotional and personal self-disclosure takes place. You feel secure enough in the relationship to throw yourself open to view. It is risky because you become very vulnerable. Usually some deep personal and emotional experience is shared, perhaps something you've never shared before. Communication on this level usually makes a deep and lasting impression on both partners and enriches the relationship.[5]

Deep insight is the most difficult of all levels to master. Only one in five on the Communication Inventory were satisfied with their level of communication, with the other 80 percent indicating they wanted deeper and more meaningful levels of conversation. How easy it is to stay on the superficial levels of 5, 4, and 3 due to a backlog of rejection and fear. Before a couple can communicate on the deep-insight level, there must be a level of trust between them. A person who neglects levels 1 and 2 and does only what is safe due to fear will never have what he or she could have with a partner. There never will be an intimate conversation on a deep and personal level. This person's partner will never share him or herself openly, either.

All five levels are useful and necessary in maintaining relationships, but communication on the deep-insight level is a must for couples today. Couples of yesteryear could survive in a "functional marriage" without it. But today's "relational marriage" requires a depth beyond functionality.

What levels are you using in your marriage? Are you able to share on levels 1 and 2? If not, why not? Isn't it time to seek a more meaningful level? The quality of a relationship can be judged by the level of communication it most frequently attains.

Frankly Speaking: Learning to Express Yourself

One of the big challenges in marriage is how to talk with your mate about something you don't like or a behavior that is irritating to you. During the course of any given week, situations will come up where needs and preferences clash. When this happens to you and you find your partner's behavior unacceptable, rather than defensively blaming and judging him or her, assume ownership of the problem. In other words, your partner may be the cause of the problem, but if you are the one who is irritated, you now own the problem.

Once you have determined that you own the problem, you can decide the best way of responding. Here are several alternatives:

(1) Make a request.   In a relationship based on mutual respect and caring, if one person does something unacceptable to the other, a simple request not to do it again might solve the problem. Such a request must be framed so that blaming, judging, and condemnation are not implied. The tone of voice also needs to be monitored. In many relationships, however, a simple request doesn't work.

(2) Suggest an alternative.   When an irritating behavior

occurs, the offended partner might suggest an alternative. Harry has next to no sense of time. When he leaves home to run an errand, it can become an all-day trip. This interrupts meals as well as other schedules. I suggested that he call to let me know if he is going to be late. Suggesting an alternative has worked in this instance (most of the time).

(3) Use I-messages.   Sending an I-message is a method of expressing your feelings directly when upset, irritated, or annoyed by your partner's behavior. I-messages let your partner know you have negative feelings about the behavior, but you do not attack or ridicule. You are more likely to be heard because it is less threatening. It establishes openness and honesty and is an excellent method of venting feelings of irritation.

I-messages identify your actual feelings and report them openly and honestly, yet kindly, to your mate. Rather than attacking, blaming, or judging, say, "I feel irritated when you . . . because. . . ."

Compare the different reactions to these two messages sent by wives after their husbands refused to take them out to dinner.

Wife Number 1: "You're so inconsiderate! You never think of anybody but yourself. All you want to do is watch TV. You make me sick!"

Wife Number 2: "I feel hurt when you won't take me out to dinner because I have a real need to be alone with you to communicate on an adult level, just to feel close to you."

Wife Number 2 tells only how she feels, a fact her husband can hardly argue with. She selects suitable words to let her husband know she too has feelings which, in her opinion, are being ignored. Wife Number 1 blames, judges, and puts down her husband. This gives him ammunition for an argument and will probably cause him to become more stubborn and defensive than before. Furthermore, for a wife who wants to go out to dinner in order to feel closer to her husband, "You are so inconsiderate! You never think of anybody but yourself . . . you make me sick," is a poor selection of words to convey her message. Always ask yourself, *Are my words distancing or drawing?*

An I-message rather than a you-message exemplifies the

difference between assertiveness and aggressiveness. An assertive individual can speak the truth concerning his feelings without blaming the other person. Aggression clobbers your partner with your feelings in a hostile manner. The assertive I-message says, "I feel starved for some time alone with you." The aggressive you-message says, "You never want to be with me." It is much better to say, "I feel frustrated when you don't respond to my questions" rather than "You are mean. You never answer me when I talk to you." The assertive I-message appeals to the person to reflect and consider, whereas the aggressive you-message arouses defenses and retaliation.

An effective I-message has three parts:

1. A statement of how your partner's unacceptable behavior makes you feel. (Use a descriptive feeling word.)
2. A nonblameful description of your partner's behavior. (It is acceptable to use the word *you* in this description.)
3. An explanation regarding the tangible effect of that behavior on you. (Tell what you have to do as a result of the behavior.)

Examples of how to use the I-message properly follow:

* Husband turns on television to watch the news during supper when the couple has agreed not to watch TV during meals. Wife: "I feel upset when you break the agreement we had not to watch TV during mealtimes because it is one of the few times during the day when we can communicate with each other."

* Wife gives husband the silent treatment. Husband: "I feel angry when you clam up on me like this because I don't know what you are thinking and it makes me feel shut out."

* Husband criticizes wife in a sharp and degrading manner. Wife: "I feel deeply hurt when you criticize me in such an unfair manner because it makes me feel I am not respected or loved."

I-messages contain an explanation of how you feel about the annoying behavior. They do not attack or condemn your partner but refer only to the unacceptable behavior, differentiating between your partner and his behavior. I-messages contain no put-downs and do not tell your partner what to do. The CI confirmed that when attacked most people tend to defend themselves. "Clam up" ranked next with "attack back" as third choice. Only 2 percent of all respondents would tell their partners how much they were hurt by the attack, which should be the response of choice.

I-messages can bring some startling results. It surprises people to learn how their mates really feel. Often they say, "I didn't even know that bothered you" or "I didn't think you cared if I . . ." or "How come you never told me before how you really felt?" We are often totally unaware of how our behavior affects others, and this is particularly true in marriage. Many people, out of love and consideration for a partner, will change an annoying behavior once they understand the impact of that behavior on the other person.

I-messages are much more likely to produce positive behavior changes, but that is not actually the main purpose of an I-message. A major goal is to release your feelings of irritation. Your partner may or may not change his behavior, but you are staying in touch with your feelings and communicating them in a direct way rather than suppressing them. Unattended little resentments and irritations can fester into big, bitter fights. The head of steam that builds up can be let off daily by learning to communicate in this open and direct method.

More about I-messages: (1) Use them when you first become irritated. Don't wait until you are boiling over a problem. (2) Avoid sending a solution or telling your partner what to do. Telling someone what to do brings defensive reactions. (3) Your tone of voice must match the intensity of your message. Avoid over or undershooting. (4) If your partner does not respond to your first I-message, send another, rephrased in a new manner, until you are heard.

I-messages are powerful speaking tools, yet the majority of people can't or won't use them. Why? Many people are so out of touch with their own feelings that they wouldn't recognize one if they met it in broad daylight. While growing up, without being aware of it, they received messages telling them which emotions are acceptable and which are not. A host of emotions has been cut off due to messages from the past. These people simply don't recognize emotions as they occur. Since it has been learned that certain feelings aren't okay, they are pushed out of the consciousness. Eventually such people have difficulty recognizing any feeling that doesn't appear on their acceptable list. This lack of spontaneity in expressing feelings becomes a real problem since feelings add an extremely important dimension to any message.

Others have tried I-messages a time or two and gotten a "Tough!" or "So what? You're always upset!" or some other defensive reaction which led to further conflict. They gave up before giving this method a chance. Eight-two percent of the respondents on the CI had difficulty with this, stating that their partners rarely or never responded effectively when feelings were expressed to them.

Let's look at an incident in which a wife is irritated because her husband didn't return for hours from an errand that should have taken a few minutes.

SHE: (*I-message*) "I really get frustrated when you go on an errand that should take only a few minutes and you leave me home fuming and wondering where you are."

HE: (*defensively*) "I wasn't gone that long. It takes longer than you think to. . . . And besides that. . . ."

A couple who is earnestly working on improving their communication will stop right here and evaluate where this pattern will lead them. NOWHERE! In order to break out of this destructive, self-defeating pattern, a new strategy is needed. She must now send a new I-message.

SHE: (*new I-message*) "I've got a new problem right now. When I tell you about my feelings and get a response like the one I just got, I feel I've not been heard or haven't made my feelings clear to you."

Another way of putting it might be, "You may be right. I may be upset frequently, but I would be less than honest with you if I didn't tell you how I feel."

There is still no guarantee that the defensive communicator will stop defending himself, but a partner interested in breaking destructive patterns will cooperate. Some people, however, might ignore all attempts to communicate positively. At this point, you must recognize that you have a more basic problem than the undesirable behavior. Your partner will not respect your feelings, and you need professional help regarding your inability to speak and listen with respect.

If you really want to have your feelings recognized, you must *continually* communicate them directly until you are understood. Don't let your partner force you offtrack. Don't give up just because you didn't get the desired response. You simply do not have that many constructive options at this point. Even if your partner fails you, resolve not to fail your partner.

Double Talk: Why Can't My Partner Say What He Means?

What we say offers clues to what we mean when we talk. The trouble is, we don't always say what we mean! In other words, we often speak in an indistinct, confusing array of surmising and hints referred to as "indirectness." Dr. Deborah Tannen, associate professor of linguistics at Georgetown University in Washington, D.C., and author of *That's Not What I Meant!* relates a personal experience which well illustrates the point.

She and her husband were having one of their frequent conversations about plans—in this case, the issue was whether or not to accept an invitation to visit her sister. Cozy in the setting of their home and willing to do whatever her husband wished, Deborah asked, "Do you want to go to my sister's?" He responded, "Okay." To her, "okay" didn't sound convincing; it indicated condescension. So she continued, "Do you really want to go?" He blew up. "You're driving me crazy! Why don't you make up your mind what you want?"

That explosion sent her into a tailspin as it was so typical of what went on between them. Outraged at his irrationality, she shouted, "Make up my mind? I haven't even said what I want. I'm willing to do whatever you want, and this is what I get?" Trapped in a theater of the absurd, she thought her husband was crazy and that she was crazy for marrying him. He was always getting angry at her for saying things she denied she said, or for not paying attention to things she was sure he had never said.

Trying to solve these communication impasses was almost

abandoned when Tannen heard a lecture on "indirectness." The lecturer explained that people prefer not to say exactly what they mean because they are concerned not only with the ideas they are expressing but also with the effect their words have on those to whom they are speaking. To avoid imposing, they give (or appear to give) the other person a choice in the matter being discussed. Different people have different ways of achieving these potentially conflicting goals.

Suddenly Tannen understood what had been going on in her marriage. She had taken it for granted that she could ask her husband what he wanted and he would tell her. When she asked if he wanted to visit her sister, she was seeking information about his preferences in order to accommodate them. He wanted to be accommodating too but assumed that people don't just blurt out what they want. To him that would be coercive because he found it difficult to deny a direct request. He assumed that talkers hint at what they want and listeners pick up on those hints. One way to hint is to ask questions. He assumed she was letting him know, indirectly, about her desire to go, and since he had agreed to go she should have gratefully accepted! When she asked, "Are you sure you want to go?" he heard that she didn't really want to go and was asking him to let her off the hook. From his point of view, she was being unreasonable and he agreeable—exactly her impression but with their roles reversed! The intensity of his explosion (and of her reaction) came from the cumulative effect of repeated frustrations.[6]

We avoid directness because absolute honesty leaves us wide open to question or attack. Stating what we mean might also hurt others. Indirectness prevents confrontation and protects us from rejection. Irony, sarcasm, and joking are forms of indirectness.

When one expresses needs and wants directly and the other in oblique terms, only hinting at wants and needs, enter misunderstandings. According to Tannen, women are more likely than men to be indirect.

There are several things that can be done to clear up misunderstandings about directness and ensure cooperation when making requests of each other. Marilyn says to Jack, "Honey, I want to talk to you about something." The request is phrased and delivered in a positive manner, yet Jack's response is totally negative. When asked about it, Jack explains that he always feels like a child when Marilyn approaches him in this manner.

A statement of Marilyn's intentions in advance might have defused his defensive reaction and created a climate of openness. "Jack, I need to discuss a problem that involves both of us. My intention is to gain input from you, not to blame you. I am looking for a solution that will be acceptable to both of us." This statement of intention in advance reduces the possibility of attack and allows Jack to relax. Marilyn has created an atmosphere of listenability.

If a person perceives what is being said as an attack, he will become defensive and immediately withdraw to shield himself from the expected blast. *Defensiveness* is probably the greatest single barrier to effective communication. The sooner you recognize the part you play in producing defensiveness or in reacting defensively, the sooner you will experience more satisfying interpersonal relationships. Stating your intentions clearly in advance may help in numerous instances.

Some people say they do not expect or like directness. Such individuals usually are not so much unwilling as unable to be direct. They simply cannot bring themselves to state their intentions directly. To them it appears rude and wrong. When two people who are married to each other have different views of how ideas should be advanced—directly or indirectly—they will have to adjust their expectations and attempt to make one another comfortable. Working at this will pay off in rapport and feeling more as if they are on the same wavelength rather than feeling as if, "I know you believe you understand what you think I said but I am not sure you realize that what you heard is not what I meant."

His and Her Talk Styles: Are They Different?

Is there a difference between the way males and females talk? All you have to do is listen in on any group of males and females to note some of the differences. Men and women will naturally have differing communication patterns from past experience. Boys and girls are raised in different worlds, even when born into the same household. From birth on boys and girls are spoken to, treated, and taught differently. As a result of this, along with brain sex differences and temperament types, they also talk differently.

Talk styles will not always follow the sex-related patterns observed here. Approximately 15 percent of all males and females will tend to display more typical patterns of the opposite sex.[7] This is particularly true of those who are left-handed. It is interesting to note that male/female styles tend to predominate even when styles are reversed. However, an explanation of general male and female tendencies may allow for a better understanding of what is going on between you and your partner.

For centuries, women have been accused of talking more than men. But is it true? Yes, studies at Harvard show that girls learn to talk earlier than boys, articulate better, and acquire a more extensive vocabulary than boys of a comparable age.[8] From their earliest years, girls talk more than boys. One study even showed that infant girls moved their lips more while in the hospital nursery.[9] Diane McGuiness, a prominent researcher at Stanford University, confirmed the same point by studying the amount of vocalization taking place among two-and-one-half- to four-year-olds. It was noted that while little girls performed designated tasks, they talked—to themselves, to others, to the objects they were working on. One hundred percent of their time was spent with audible, recognizable words. A totally different pattern was observed with the little boys. Only 60 percent of their communication was recognizable words. Forty percent was comprised of one-word exclamations like "Wow!" or noises and sounds such as "uh" and "mmmm," or sound effects like "Yaaaah!" and "Zoooom!" Girls get the verbal edge early and seem to retain it throughout their lives.[10]

Boys and young men have more difficulty with reading, writing, and speaking than do girls. Most teachers can attest to this phenomenon. Nine out of ten reading and speech disabilities involve boys.[11]

Even as adults, men never seem to catch up. It is estimated that the average male speaks about 12,500 words per day while the average woman doubles that with more than

25,000![12] This could explain why many men don't want to talk much after getting home at night. They have already expended their 12,500-word limit. The women may have expended 12,500, but they have saved as many for their husbands!

Furthermore, men and women talk about different things. She gets bored as he goes on and on about sports, cars, and business. He tunes her out when she rattles on about her friends or about others he doesn't even know. To her it is natural to talk about people and relationships; it proves involvement, interest, and caring. Sharing this with someone she loves proves closeness. When this kind of sharing is shut off or ignored, a vital element of self is closed to her husband.

Men consider it normal to talk about sports, politics, cars, jobs, the stock market, and how things work. Women frequently perceive this as boring or even as a lecture: "I'm the teacher; you're the student. Now learn!"

Couples can also be talking on different wavelengths. From the time we were married, I knew Harry's brain was created differently. I couldn't prove the difference, but I could *feel* it. On any given subject, I'd be traveling one road and Harry would be trucking down another. We'd come up with totally different conclusions. I used to think it was because I was right and Harry was wrong. Harry felt the same way, only in reverse. I was only partially right, however. His brain comes up with totally different conclusions, yes, but that doesn't make me right and him wrong—different, maybe, but not wrong.

Medical studies have shown that something happens to the fetus between the sixteenth and twenty-sixth week of pregnancy which forever differentiates the sexes. Researchers have actually observed a baby boy's brain getting a chemical bath of testosterone and other sex-related hormones during this time period. As these chemicals saturate the baby boy's brain, the right side of the brain recedes slightly. Also affected at this time are some of the connecting fibers which send messages back and forth to the two hemispheres. Simply put, it means a boy begins life more left-brained oriented.

Because little girls don't get this chemical bath, they have quicker and easier access to both sides of the brain. What occurs during pregnancy sets the stage for men and women to "specialize" in two different ways of thinking. The left-brain dominance promotes the tendency of men to specialize in more logical, factual, analytical, and aggressive thought. Women tend to use the right side of the brain, which is the center for feelings, language, and communication skills. It is the more relational of the two sides.[13]

As a result of this, women tend to operate on Channel E for Emotion while men tend to operate on Channel L for Logic. When Lisa shared a problem with Hal, she was looking for sympathy and support. Hal didn't understand what she was searching for, so he responded with logical advice, not realizing that was not what she wanted.

Men tend to be "solution oriented" (except where the marriage is concerned). The male ego is usually threatened at the prospect of airing marriage problems. Therefore, when a woman becomes emotionally upset, the male mind automatically seeks a solution. If she cries, in order to stop the tears, he might say, "Don't cry, honey. It isn't that bad." All this does is discount her feelings when she needs a simple validation such as, "Tell me about it, honey." This would provide her with the emotional support and understanding she is seeking.

A little directness on Lisa's part initiated healing. When she wanted Hal to listen empathetically, she asked him to hold her without giving advice. With this simple technique, long-avoided subjects were brought into the open, and within six months their marriage was revitalized.

While communicating on differing channels, the actual talk styles of a man and woman differ. A woman tends to dramatize the story through tone of voice and gestures in an effort to recreate the experience.[14] She relives it as she tells it. A man is more likely to give the *Reader's Digest* version of an event. In brief summary form, devoid of emotion or particulars, he reports the facts. If she presses for details, he feels he is being grilled. He probably can't remember more than he told her anyway.

As men and women take part in conversations, they tend to concentrate and remember what they know they will need to recall later on. Women usually aren't interested in scientific explanations. They pay little attention and are likely to recall less. Men usually aren't that much into the details of relationships and the lives of friends, and their attention lags here. Neither males nor females have poor memories. What comes into question is the type of subject matter each remembers or forgets.

Women's conversations with women keep them in training to converse well with other women, but men enter these conversations with little or no training.

Women generally have a more significant circle of personal friends than do men. They will discuss at length with their friends what men would describe as "frivolous stuff" or gossip. But it is their ability to keep talking that nourishes the friendship. Many men simply don't have friends as women do. This may be in part because they don't talk to each other unless they have something significant to discuss, and significant happenings don't occur daily. Consequently, women usually find themselves with more personal friends than men do.

Women are more people-oriented. They rely on social cues, can pick up on body language and emotional tones in speech, remember names and faces better, and are more empathetic.[15]

Men are more curious as to how things work and are more exploratory. They are object-oriented people who like to examine and take things apart and excel in a wide range of skills that require mechanical manipulation. Women tend to live in a world of people and feelings while men attach more importance to ideas and intellectual concepts.

Women have a need to talk things over, especially their relationships, according to Ted Huston, Ph.D., a psychologist at the University of Texas at Austin who studied 130 couples.[16] Men appeared bewildered by this need and made such comments as, "I want to *do* things with her, and all she wants to do is talk." This tendency doesn't show itself until after the wedding because while dating, men are willing to spend time talking in order to build the relationship. After the wedding, the male tendency is to devote more time to work and male friends. Women want to talk through difficulties and resolve differences so they can feel closer to their husbands, while men will do almost anything to avoid a

blowup. Men don't view discussing difficulties as an opportunity to gain intimacy as women do. Men are more content
just being with their wives, and they feel no burden for
constant sharing of thoughts, feelings, and needs. Each
obtains his or her feelings of connectedness differently.

According to Robin Lakoff in *Language and Women's Place*,
women send out signals of uncertainty, indecision, hesita-
tion, and subordination.[17] For instance, when in a restaurant,
a man might say, "The food is terrible," a simple declarative
statement. A woman would more likely say, "The food is
terrible, isn't it?" tagging a question on the end in search of
support of her opinion. In ordinary conversation, we drop
our voices at the end of a statement, raise it at the end of a
question, and keep it level if we intend to continue speaking.
These subtle signals cue a partner as to when to respond and
when to wait. Women tend to answer a question with a
question. A husband asks, "When do you want to go for a
walk?" and his wife answers, "In half an hour?" The rising
inflection on *hour* turns an answer into a question. In effect
she is saying, "I'd like to go with you in half an hour if that's
okay."

This is an attempted accommodation and politeness, according to Lakoff. In general, women are more polite in
almost all situations. Their grammar is better and the use of
obscenities more restricted. But men control the conversation
more.

A researcher analyzed hours of conversation between
couples. In spite of the fact that they knew they were being
taped, the men controlled the conversation by withdrawing
as well as through positive effort. The women raised twice as
many topics to discuss, but the men simply refused to
respond to the topics they didn't like. Women resorted to
attention-getting devices when faced with long silences and
occasional grunts. Women asked three times as many questions as men, used more introductory remarks such as, "Do
you know what?" or "This is interesting." When talk lagged,
they interjected "you know" more and more often. Men used
some of the same devices when conversation failed, but they
usually didn't have to as the women responded so enthusiastically whenever their husbands talked![18]

In addition to controlling the conversation, men also are accused of dominating conversations by talking too much. When questioned about this a man will say, "Well, when I stop talking you don't say anything." A woman, endeavoring to be polite, fears interrupting and therefore has a tendency to wait before asking a question or giving a reply. The man, who is less adept at picking up nonverbal cues, misses that she is about to speak and goes right on talking.

Women are more tuned in to the metamessage—what is implied but not stated, a combination of reading attitudes and nonverbals. Men focus more on the actual words.[19] Vickie asks, "What's the matter?" when a frown crosses Mack's face. Since Mack was only thinking about a football game, he resents her line of questioning, which he thinks invades his privacy.

Lee Ann always asks about Howie's day, yet Howie never inquires about hers. In exasperation she demands, "Why don't you ever ask about my day? I always ask about yours!" He replies, "Why should I have to ask about your day? If you have something to tell me, just tell me. I shouldn't have to extend an invitation." She would view his question as evidence of caring about her and her day, and when he doesn't ask, she feels he doesn't care.

When Len announces, "I'm going for a walk," Mim feels hurt because she wasn't invited. Len says she's welcome to go, but this doesn't change Mim's feelings. Mim probably would have said, "I'd like to go for a walk. Will you go with me?" including Len immediately. On the other hand, Len would not feel hurt if Mim failed to ask him to go, and he would feel free to ask to be included if he wished to go.

Please note: There are men who are very emotional and women who respond logically; men who are more verbal and quiet women; women who achieve acceptance and approval by reaching goals and men who start arguments to find closeness. It has not been implied here that men always respond one way and women another. There is a wide range of crisscrossing among the sexes that is normal and healthy. Hopefully this discussion of sex-related *tendencies* helps you understand your partner in a new light.

Male and female just may be marching to different drummers. Misunderstandings resulting from a lack of knowledge about male-female talk styles can lead to frustration and misery. Rather than assuming something is wrong with your partner when you come up with different conclusions, why not accept these differences as part of God's marvelous plan for male and female. A change in attitude can bring rich rewards.

Making the Most of Talk Time

"We just don't talk anymore," couples frequently lament. After years of marriage, many couples are out of the habit. Caught in the aftermath of neglect, they somehow lose the knack.

Some couples are too busy. The fast pace of today's life-style, with family members all running in different directions, is definitely a contributing factor. Other obstacles include each doing his or her own thing such as hobbies, classes, aerobics, and church business—solitary pursuits that neglect conversational skills. Still other couples have the television on so many hours a day that time to chat is severely limited. In time, family members become accustomed to not speaking, not being heard, speaking only during commercials, and fielding frequent interruptions.

Lack of time to talk can be both an excuse and symptom of deeper problems. "When couples complain they have no time to talk, they are often—unwittingly, perhaps—choosing not to," notes Richard H. Mikesell, Ph.D., a psychologist in private practice in Washington, D.C.[20]

Phil and Elsie are good examples. After six years of marriage, both were miserable but neither could figure out why. "It isn't pleasant to talk with Phil," Elsie complained. "All we do is criticize each other. When this happens, we each clam up and spend the rest of the evening hostile." Phil and Elsie sought the help of a counselor who assisted them with taking an in-depth look at their relationship. Their counselor showed them that taking time to talk meant sharing positive experiences and ideas, not just criticisms, worries, or arguments. The counselor got a commitment from them to spend fifteen minutes per day talking about positive things. "In one week's time," Elsie commented, "we noticed a tremendous change in how we felt about us and our relationship."

Though couples are slow to recognize it and loathe to admit it, after a few years of marriage boredom sets in. A predictable pattern that can bring sudden death to conversation engulfs the relationship. Whatever the reason, the message is clear: A couple who talks little today sets the stage for more difficulty in talking tomorrow.

There is a great deal couples can do to improve their talk time in the home, and the good news is that it is never too late to begin:

(1) *Work at talking.*   *Make* time to talk and create things to talk about. Encourage each other to tell stories about each other's day-to-day experiences, about your families, about each other's past. Bring up topics for discussion you know are of particular interest to your partner. Read a book about these topics, clip magazine articles, share a clever cartoon. Take a class so you can discuss your partner's special interests intelligently and enthusiastically. And feel free to introduce topics you wish to discuss. Talking should be fun and will be if certain guidelines are followed: no interruptions, put-downs, criticisms, giving advice too quickly, or asking too many questions.

(2) *Maintain a daily talk time.*   Set aside time each day to talk about noncontroversial marriage matters. This daily talk time is not for intensive sharing of feelings or deep problem solving. Instead, it involves talking about everyday life—the kids, jobs, neighbors, the boss, what-happened-to-me-today, and what-I-did type of thing. This swapping of information leads to involvement in one another's life and strengthens the marital bond. Some couples set aside the first ten to fifteen minutes upon being reunited after the day's activities for this type of conversation. Some find that mealtime is good. Others linger at the table after the meal. When it occurs isn't important; that it occurs daily is.

(3) *Observe the marriage meeting.*   Ideally, once or twice a week a couple should have a set, previously agreed-upon time when family business is discussed. Problems are solved at this time, decisions regarding family plans are discussed,

and schedules for the upcoming week are coordinated. Disagreements that occur during the week may be saved for the marriage meeting and thrashed out appropriately. The atmosphere should be relaxed and no interruptions allowed— no eating, driving, or phone calls. A time limit can be set on this weekly meeting if necessary.

(4) *Use pillow talk.*   When your heads actually hit the pillow, instead of recounting the horrors of the day, talk about some pleasant memories, such as, "The most pleasant experience I shared with you during the past month was . . ." "My favorite hobby is . . ." "One thing I really like about you is. . . ." This is not the time to solve problems, recount negatives of the day, spout angry feelings, or conduct a gripe session. This is a sacred time for pleasant sharing. You might play soft music, even a recording of "your song." While talking, hold and hug each other closely. This full-body touching can give each of you an enormous sense of peace and well-being.

(5) *Try the walk talk.*   Are you a tennis, golf, or racquetball buff? Have you ever thought of switching to walking for fitness? Walking could be done with your partner. It is possible to walk at a fast pace and still communicate. If you are not in the habit of exercising regularly, you should begin with a stroll around the block, gradually increasing the distance and pace if you are in good health. Eventually, you should be able to complete a mile in fifteen to twenty minutes and handle three miles. If you and your partner could build the walk talk into your daily life, the benefits from your dialogue and fitness could add a richness to your emotional closeness.

(6) *Communicate using car talk.*   Another way to utilize time together is to use commuting time to full advantage. I suggest to couples who have completed our Compleat Marriage seminar that they carry their *Compleat Marriage Workbooks* with them in their cars. When on vacation, taking a trip, or when not in heavy traffic, they can use one of the many "Let's Talk It Over" communication exercises. Many also use the *Compleat Marriage* audiocassettes while driving. Their hours together studying and discussing have rejuve-

nated their relationships, improved their time together, and rekindled closeness.

(7) *Play games together.*   Playing games such as Trivial Pursuit, Uno, Sorry, and Monopoly create a pleasant, relaxed atmosphere in which a couple can banter without undue pressure to communicate. Games provide an opportunity and a reason to talk and beat boredom by creating new situations and life experiences that bring you together. You might also select a project to work on together. One couple painted a Nativity set before Christmas. Sharing this creative experience got them away from the television, exercised their creative talents, added a new dimension to their lives, and built a memory to treasure.

(8) *Make the most of mealtimes.*   Table time can be one of the most pleasant or most hated times of the day, depending on the atmosphere. Each family develops its own atmosphere: silence, television viewing, griping, pleasant chitchat, or general commotion. Realistically, we may not be able to gather twice daily for titillating discussions or intimate sharing. But we can wake up to the opportunities that lie before us and establish a tradition of pleasant sharing. Think of it: Twice a day, seven days a week, you could talk for twenty minutes or more. Around the table you will be facing one another, which encourages eye contact. Caution: If the TV is on, attention will be focused on the conversation killer, and dinner will become a nonevent.

(9) *Deliver a verbal bouquet.*   A verbal bouquet is any affirmation which shows acceptance, appreciation, or respect for your partner. The most desired verbal bouquet might say, "You are the most important person in the world to me. I love you and care about you. I may fail you, but even when I do I want you to know I care. I am trying to meet your needs. I want to smile at you, caress you, talk with you, and tell you all the wonderful things about yourself. And if you do the same for me, I will be joyous!"

Unfortunately, we all fall short of the ideal. We speak unkindly, take each other for granted, or withdraw. However, negative interactions are easier to take within the context of a four-to-one ratio. In other words, if you deliver four times as many verbal bouquets as negative or killer talk, there will be a strong foundation to support you through troubled times. Make sure a day never goes by that you don't appreciate some good quality in your partner. Expressing affection and appreciation every day is one of the most effective techniques for smoothing the rough edges of life.

The Last Word

Even when our talk methods fail to bring desired results, we keep talking. Woody Allen knows why. In his film *Annie Hall* he reveals the secret. Heard in a voice-over at the close of the film is this: "This guy goes to a psychiatrist and says, 'Doc, my brother's crazy. He thinks he's a chicken.' And the doctor says, 'Well, why don't you turn him in?' And the guy says, 'I would, but I need the eggs.'" This pretty much sums up why we keep trying to talk: We need the "eggs"— connectedness with others.[21]

Many people are reluctant to talk to their partners. It isn't the right time; they don't know what to say; they might say the wrong thing; they are too angry. The real failure in refusing to talk is the loss of a relationship. A couple who can't talk to each other have no basis for a relationship. By opening up and sharing, you can turn a stranger into a friend. Your life can be enriched immeasurably by learning hearttalk—the language of love.

5 Anger Workout: Coping With Conflict

It's risky to fight, but fighting between two people who really care about each other does not have to be destructive. Learning how to fight fair might be the most important communication skill you will ever learn.

High in the Big Bear region of the San Bernardino mountains, a couple was out for a Sunday-afternoon drive. Steep granite cliffs pressed on one side with treacherous chasms on the other. Their conversation drifted to their horse-boarding business and recent struggles with collection of bills. Each had assumed a portion of responsibility for operating their business. His tasks included repair of buildings and fences along with the care of the animals, while she handled accounting and collections.

The wife had fallen behind in collections and was greatly agitated as she felt that some of the people refused to take her seriously because she was a woman. There was some question about their ability to keep the business afloat. She openly verbalized her concern and asked her husband to step in and assume some of the phone calls. He staunchly refused.

With a tight grip on the steering wheel, she became angrier by the moment as she negotiated the tight mountain curves. Why was he so unwilling to help? How could he be so uncaring? Did he want to lose the business? Their voices rose to fever pitch as they hurled obscenities and hateful accusations against one another.

Suddenly the woman could not handle the intensity of the situation or her husband's attitude. With her emotions now well out of control, she decided to leap from the moving vehicle. No sooner had she made the leap than she thought better of it and wildly gripped the steering wheel, causing the car to veer toward her and roll over the lower portion of her body with crushing force.

Medical examination revealed a fractured spine and pelvis, a compound fracture to one leg, and multiple cuts and bruises. Eight hours of surgery spared her life, but she would be forever paralyzed from the waist down. In the subsequent six months of hospital confinement, her days consisted of traction and physical therapy. Her husband was now challenged with collections, repair of the buildings, and caring for the animals *and* an invalid. All of this occurred because of anger out of control.

Perhaps this newspaper story, "Wife Runs Over Self in Angry Fit," is an isolated case. Most couples don't deal with anger to this degree . . . or do they? Let's look at anger within marriage.

Anger: What It Is and Isn't

When we say a person is angry, we think of terms such as "boiling mad," flying into a rage," or "getting hot under the collar." Anger comes in different degrees of intensity from mild to intense. It covers a range of severity from simple feelings of annoyance or irritation to the vehemency of rage, hate, fury, bitterness, and resentment.

Today's usage of the word gives a negative connotation of extreme intensity, which can be misleading. David R. Mace, author of *Love and Anger in Marriage*, defines anger in a broader and more correct way: "Anger is any feeling of displeasure directed against a person (or object) accompanied by a desire to remove the cause."[1] Such a definition is more accurate as it leaves room for the range of feelings included when referring to "anger."

Anger is a basic defense mechanism designed to protect self or the personality. Just as the body prepares a defense against an invasion of germs, so does self need protection. When self is attacked, a warning system activates anger to respond to the threat.

Admittedly, the major portion of our anger arises from less noble and much more selfish reasons: *concern over not getting our own way.* Anytime our wants and wishes are denied, we become angry. When we make plans and someone does not agree, perhaps even refusing to cooperate, our blocked desires give way to anger. Let's look in on a couple on their way to dinner:

He: Let's go to the Chinese Pagoda. I feel like having some good Chinese food tonight.

She: I get sick every time we eat there. I'd rather go to the Country Inn for a plain dinner.

He: That's too far to drive. It'll be an hour before we're there and I'm starved. Let's go to the Chinese Pagoda. Just don't eat too much.

She: If it's too far for you to drive, I'll drive.

Resulting frustrations from blocked desires develop into full-blown anger. This puts tremendous strain on the marriage relationship.

Anger in Close Relationships

David Mace aptly points out that anger is not a primary but a secondary emotion. Anger is prompted by an attack of some kind. Whether the attack is intentional or unintentional is immaterial. Let's say a husband verbally attacks his wife. The emotion behind the attack is usually frustration over something he disapproves of in their relationship. At first a polite request is made since only minor irritation is experienced during the early stages. If this request is ignored, he will probably interpret it as a challenge or rejection.

His wife views the situation from a different perspective. She may interpret his request as illogical, unreasonable, or ill-timed, which prompts her sense of danger, resulting in the emotion of fear. Intuitive awareness suggests a difficult situation looms before them. A wrong response at this time could propel them into a crisis situation she wishes to avoid. Mingled with her fear may be frustration. She might be annoyed that he brought up the issue at this particular time.

If the fear response is stronger than frustration, the wife may withdraw to silence. If feelings of frustration dominate, she will probably launch an effective counterattack that will in turn elevate her husband's level of frustration. He too may experience some fear as he evaluates where this episode of anger is heading.

Anger, then, is prompted by another emotion that is the core issue of what is going on between the two. *The motivating emotions behind most anger are frustration and fear.* These two emotions cause us injury and pain in the form of hurt feelings, which serve as a launching pad for anger. Generally speaking, feelings of frustration launch the cycle, with fear and hurt following close behind.

The Inner Workings of Our Feelings

Intellectually, we understand that it is normal and natural to possess feelings. The ability to experience emotions is as much a part of being human as the capacity to reason and think. The intellectual wizard who can deal only with life in abstract concepts, but is unable to relate feelings, appears incomplete and is pitied by us. We know this and yet we become uncomfortable when someone expresses strong feelings. Furthermore, many of us fail to recognize, let alone accept, our own feelings. Feelings are viewed as a disruptive force, one that fills our lives with obstacles and problems in close relationships.

Due to our fear, ignorance, and discomfort with our feelings, we spend an enormous amount of time and energy denying or ignoring them. This problem usually begins in childhood. When you were growing up, were you taught, "You shouldn't feel that way!" or "Zip it up!" or "Simmer down," or the like? If so, you most likely learned to control or repress your feelings. The business world reinforces this concept. Surely you have heard someone say, "Keep personal feelings out of this. You can't run a business by emotions."

The more detached we are from our feelings, the easier they are to discuss. I can more easily tell you what angered me a year ago than I can tell you what you are doing now that angers me. It follows that I can tell you what I didn't like that happened a month ago, but I can't talk about yesterday's problem, about which I am still angry—especially if you are present and involved.

We get angry in the present but aren't free to discuss

present anger. We are basically uncomfortable dealing with our own intense feelings. Our God-given emotions—even strong emotions—are viewed as problems because we recognize we have less control over what we feel than over our behavior.

Feelings, however, cannot be turned off and on at will. Once angry feelings have been activated and adrenaline is racing through the system, a choice to return to the preanger state won't help, as it will take time to deactivate the threatened system. I can't stop the anger merely by deciding not to be angry. Nor can I accomplish this when someone tells me I shouldn't be angry.

Feelings are spontaneous reactions to situations over which we may have little direct control. In order to control the feeling, we try to structure the environment so that it will not produce the feeling we wish to avoid.

In marriage, a vast amount of effort is expended to control what feelings will be aroused. It works like this: I am going to try to get you to treat me the way I want you to treat me rather than the way I don't want to be treated. You will do likewise, attempting to get me to act in a way that meets your needs. Each of us then attempts to control the relationship and the other's behavior in order to control our own feelings.

We also try to make it appear that others have more control over our feelings than we do. Emotionally we'll say, "You make me so angry!" rather than "I am very angry." We blame the other person for arousing our feelings.

Perhaps in admitting to the anger that rises up in me against you, I recognize that you have more control over me and my behavior than I would like. If you are the cause of my anger, I will probably want you to stop doing whatever aroused my wrath. More than a feeling, then, my anger becomes a tool or a weapon to force a behavior change in you.

Much of our anger arises out of power struggles, a desire to maintain control in a relationship. If I am bent on winning and controlling a relationship, then my yielding to you in any matter would be to relinquish control. Therefore, I will use my anger to control you. If you dare to cross me, I must either increase my anger or withdraw from the relationship. If I am frequently challenged by you, then I must maintain a state of anger at all times lest I lose control of the relationship.

In any close relationship, feelings will be aroused. We can't get around it except through total indifference. Our feelings cannot be turned off and on. Persons who enter the state of matrimony cannot avoid each other. Marriage calls for constant interaction. All feelings aroused by your partner connect you to him or her, whether they are positive feelings of joy and pride or negative feelings such as disappointment and anger.

The thought of giving up total control of our feelings to others may frighten us. Yet becoming emotionally attached to someone we care about is one of the greatest rewards in life. In order to find that emotionally satisfying relationship, we may have to risk giving up some control over our own emotions and control over others. To love is to risk.

Usual Responses to Anger

There are three well-known methods of handling anger: (1) suppress it; (2) express it; (3) repress it.

Suppressed anger   In suppressed anger, you recognize you are angry but you don't know what to do about it. You conscientiously try to control it instead of letting it out. By keeping a lid on such feelings, you keep bad feelings from spilling out or poisoning others. Anger boils and seethes inside, but it is hidden from the world and possibly even from an unsuspecting mate.

Jim grew up in a home where anger was suppressed. His family and his church rigidly taught that anger was a sin. The unwritten rule was enforced in spoken and unspoken ways. If he dared to express anger he was severely punished. He remembers throwing his books on the floor after an exasperating day at school. That cost him a stern lecture on self-control and an evening in his room alone without supper. Other displays of temper were handled by a trip to the basement, where he got a beating with a belt. Feelings of resentment and anger boiled within but he dared not express them. As an adult, he experienced no open battles or arguments. Friends would rate his marriage as very happy because of the appearance of harmony and lack of obvious friction. But he and his wife were painfully aware of emotional distance between them. It surfaced as high blood pressure and impotency in Jim.

There are some occasions when suppression of anger is the wisest course of action. No matter how angry you might become with your boss, suppressing the urge to punch his lights out is probably wiser than proceeding.

Expressed anger   In expressed anger, the person tells you exactly how he or she feels, regardless of how much it might hurt. Such people may resort to sharp words, violent shouting, or threats. When the episode of venting is over, they feel better. But what about the person who just got dumped on? What kind of emotional scars will mar the relationship if such behavior becomes a pattern? The CI revealed that 21 percent of the respondents admitted to never or rarely apologizing after expressing anger inappropriately, which could leave some long-lasting scars on the "dumpee."

Hal was raised by parents who were well-meaning but indulgent. He could almost always succeed in getting his way after throwing a fit of temper. In fact, he often thought his parents were actually afraid of him. As a teenager, he threatened to run away when his parents crossed him. It didn't take much to set his temper off. He hassled every person he encountered if things didn't proceed according to his specifications. "Hostile, bitter, and nasty" aptly described Hal's everyday behavior. He was like a ticking time bomb, ready to explode at any moment. Pity Hal's wife, who took the brunt of his rage. Hal excused his behavior by blaming it on his parents.

Expressed anger is usually an excuse for those who *can* control their anger but who won't.

Repressed anger   In repressed anger, you refuse to acknowledge that you are angry. Many Christians get caught in this trap, sincerely believing it is sinful to become angry. In order to live in harmony with their beliefs, they deny all responses to anger.

Jonna grew up in a family that had misconceptions about anger. Anger was often present yet never expressed outwardly. She clearly remembered the red flush, followed by a hasty exit, that signaled wrath within her father. She recalled severe reprimands whenever she displayed any degree of temper. For slamming a door, she had to open and close it quietly one hundred times. "It's a sin to be angry," was taught at home, church, and the conservative church school she attended. These lessons, learned early in life, were carried into marriage. Jonna knew she wasn't happy but didn't know she was angry. She suffered from repressed anger.

Pretending you are not angry solves nothing but prepares the way for an eruption later. Of all the responses to anger, repression causes the most problems.

Processed Anger

Suppressing, inappropriately expressing, or repressing anger are all destructive and immature methods of handling anger, yet many people know no other method. Thirty-five percent of those in the CI felt they were able to ventilate their anger constructively all or most of the time, but this still leaves 65 percent who need help.

The refusal to deal with the presence of anger constructively can create some major health problems: ulcers, headaches, anxiety attacks, and depression, to name a few. When anger is denied or mishandled it will come out indirectly. And remember, when you cut off one feeling, you cut off all feelings. If you turn off anger you will also turn off love, happiness, joy, and sexual feelings.

Being aware of your anger responses is not sinful but healthy. All of our emotions were planted in us by our Creator. Anger is a Creator-given emotion. Scripture instructs us not to suppress, express, or repress anger, but rather to process it. Paul describes processed anger when he says, "When angry, do not sin" (Ephesians 4:26 AMPLIFIED). According to this verse you will be aware you are angry, but you will be in control of your temper and not allow it to get out of hand.

Justifiable anger is approved by God when kept under control and directed toward eradication of sin. Healthy anger fires us up to fight for truth rather than allowing us to remain indifferent. When others are hurt or victimized unfairly, taken advantage of, or are suffering needlessly, we become angry over the conditions that permitted it. Aroused angry feelings can motivate us to change or correct injustices.

How does processed anger work? You recognize that anger is building inside and bring it out into the open where you can deal with it. Processing your feelings before they get out of control is a mature and safe response when tension mounts.

Processing anger is tricky because usually by the time we are willing to admit we are angry, we have sent some obvious nonverbal anger signals that we are irritated. The closer we move to the boiling point, the less rational we will be. Common sense and rational thinking exit when anger takes over.

Dan and Bette are caught in a useless and unproductive web of bickering. Bette suggests that Dan might like to tackle the lawn. Dan reacts, "I can figure out when to mow the lawn. You sound just like my mother. Get off my back." After stinging remarks like these, Bette fights tears while wildly groping for a comeback. The original issue gets lost as feelings mount and irrelevant issues are introduced. The fight is on!

You can avoid such useless and unproductive fighting by following a few simple rules:

(1) Reduce angry feelings.   While either of you is in a state of hot anger, attempting to resolve the problem is next to impossible. The intensity of the feelings must be reduced before either of you can see the issue sanely.

Anger is energy. When you become angry you can swear, spit, cry, throw things, slug someone, kick the dog, or seek any number of other inappropriate and unsuccessful methods of acting out your anger. Instead of turning your anger into an attack, turn the energy into something that will benefit you. Find a safe, physical method that will allow you to vent your energy. You can swim, jog, bicycle, do aerobic dance, chop wood, make or knead bread, pound nails, pull up stubborn weeds, rake leaves, shovel snow, wash windows, hit some tennis balls, or one hundred other things that will relieve the physical stress of anger in minutes. You can write out your feelings and then tear up the paper, or simply take a walk. On his fiftieth wedding anniversary, an elderly man was asked the secret of his lengthy marriage. "We agreed early on," the old man drawled, "that if we disagreed she'd tell me off and I'd take a walk. The secret of our marriage lies with the fact that I've largely led an outdoor life."

Commit yourself to some method of venting your feelings in a constructive manner. When you are upset emotionally, it is difficult to be rational or objective. Reduce the anger and you can deal with the issue.

(2) Assume responsibility for your own anger.   Before you share your feelings, you must come to the realization that you make yourself angry through a process that is under the direction of the will. This comes as a new thought to those who are used to blaming their meanness, impatience, and hostility on others. They say things such as, "You make me so angry when you . . ." or "You embarrass me when you. . . ."

Such statements infer that the other person is in control of your emotions and you have nothing to say about your resulting feelings. Most of us are content to take the easiest route, that of blaming others when the fault lies with us!

No one but you is responsible for your anger. Your partner's actions may precipitate your feelings, but you are responsible for your response. Don't allow your partner to dictate how you will act. You are not at the mercy of anyone. You can and must accept ownership of and responsibility for all anger responses, regardless of what precipitated them.

(3) Verbally share your anger in an acceptable manner.   Avoid using you-messages such as "You make me sick when you. . . ." Instead, state your anger in I-message form: "I really get angry when you give the children permission without checking with me first because it contributes to the children's lack of respect for my authority. I don't want my feelings to get out of control and would like to arrive at a compromise on this issue so that neither of us feels like a winner or a loser."

Stating your feelings openly defuses any angry or defensive response in your partner, and both of you will move closer to being able to negotiate a settlement.

(4) Ask your partner to assist you. Your request for help is not likely to be turned down by one who has been on the receiving end of your anger for years. Your request will most likely be a welcome relief. When the request is accepted, a serious plan can be devised regarding what you want from your spouse when you become angry.

The previous steps will help you regain the freedom to be in control of your life. Having dealt with the physical aspects of anger, you will now be better able to deal with the intellectual and analytical components of any conflict.

Your Partner Is Angry? How to Respond

We all fail each other from time to time. When your partner blows it, here are some suggestions to help you maintain your sanity:

Accept your partner's anger as a valid expression of emotion. His outburst may be offensive and unreasonable, but he has the right to be angry. His anger may not be pleasant, but it doesn't signal the end of the relationship. The best marriages allow room for some turbulence.

Make your partner responsible for his own anger. Your partner may blame you for his anger. Refuse to accept that kind of faulty thinking. You are not responsible, nor are you the cause of his anger despite what he says. He is choosing to display anger, and in all probability it is an attempt to get you to conform to his wishes. Refuse to be manipulated through anger.

Stay reasonable. Even though your partner breaks the rules by cursing, yelling, or acting disrespectful, you can choose to stay reasonable. Quietly confront him with the reality of the situation. With controlled assertiveness state your thoughts, feelings, and convictions in I-message form: "I really hurt when you threaten divorce because it breaks the ground rules we laid down and makes me feel very insecure in your affections." Continue to state your comments in a logical but caring manner.

Set limits on unreasonable anger.   If your partner continues an unreasonable display, becoming increasingly abusive physically or emotionally, it may be necessary to exit the scene. Calmly state that you will be happy to discuss the matter further when he gets his anger under control. Then retreat to another room until he has calmed down.

Refrain from apologizing.   Some people are terrified of another scene and rush to avert it through an apology. However, a verbally abusive partner doesn't deserve an apology. You may be partially responsible for the problem, but to reward offensive behavior with apologies would teach him that such behavior succeeds. An apology may be appropriate at a later time when your partner is under control. Save it for then.

Reward your partner quickly for reasonable rather than unreasonable displays of anger.   Whenever your partner shows progress or makes headway in controlling anger, reinforce the positive behavior by showing a willingness to listen and negotiate.

Give yourself a hug.   Refuse to allow your mate's verbal abuse to devastate your self-worth. His put-downs do not make you inferior unless you choose to believe him. Be good to yourself. Take yourself to dinner or engage in a rewarding activity, hobby, or class.

If you are unable to follow these suggestions, consider consulting a counselor for support and guidance.

Why Couples Argue

"We really love each other, but we argue so much," sighed a battle-weary wife of fourteen years. "Can you explain to me why we engage in such destructive behavior? We have tried and tried to stop but seem unable to."

Do you see yourself in any of these reasons couples argue?

When a partner fails to meet our expectations.   Each of us has a mental picture of how the perfect spouse should behave—a picture that has been forming since childhood. Without conscious effort, comparisons between what is expected and what actually happens take place. Whenever you find yourself annoyed or disappointed with your spouse it is because of the discrepancy between how your spouse has behaved and the picture in your head of how spouses *should* behave.

When reality clashes with our expectations, we experience a variety of sensations: upset, pain, irritation, knots in the stomach—and eventually anger. Anger is the technique relied upon to change the person to match more closely the perfect spouse in our mind's eye. When anger doesn't work, we may resort to depression in hopes of convincing our real spouses to change.

Many couples live together for twenty years or longer with this type of veiled hostility over a failure to meet expectations. These couples will continue to argue and not know why. Arguing doesn't work, but they continue to argue—over the same things!

When there is a sharp difference in values.   Values are the beliefs by which we run our lives. Values dictate our behavior even though we are hardly conscious of it. We all have values that are important to us, but we attach different weights of importance to them. So if one partner values saving and the other spending, if one values works of art, flowers, and museums while the other prefers sporting events, if one values submission and the other equality and independence, some major conflicts will probably surface. Each can agree that saving, museums, and submission are important values but disagree about the extent to which they are important or when they are important.

When a couple differs on values, it can be considered a serious disagreement, regardless of how much they love each other. Such couples will clash every time an issue concerning values surfaces. They will make up and love and pray and still fight and not even know what they are fighting over—or ever tackle the all-important *why*.

Different interpretation of emotional wants.   We all tend to need three things from others: love, appreciation, and respect. Although we attempt to have all three needs filled, one predominates: love.

The trouble is that love is not tangible and thus is difficult to visualize. If I ask a man how he knows his wife loves him, he takes a long time to answer. All their married life his wife has been loving him, but he can't verbalize how since people tend to understand love unconsciously, not consciously.

To further complicate matters, some people (visually oriented people) need to *see* love in action to feel loved. Others (auditory people) need to *hear* love before they feel loved. Still others (kinesthetic people) need to *feel* love in action before they feel loved. It is highly probable that the vast majority of arguments could be eliminated if couples could understand each other's need for actually seeing, hearing, or feeling demonstrations of love, appreciation, and respect.

An obviously angry couple seated themselves in a counselor's office. After being asked about the problem, the wife burst into tears and through her sobs said, "He doesn't love me anymore."

"How do you know?" quizzed the counselor.

"I dress up pretty for him and he never notices or compliments me," she replied.

The counselor turned to the husband and asked if he loved his wife and how he demonstrated that love to her. "Of course I love her. I'm always touching her, hugging her, patting her. That's how it is with a man," he said with a grin.

"That's not love," the wife fired back bitterly. "That's nothing more than an invitation for sex and it embarrasses the life out of me in public!"

Both loved but not in ways that met the needs of the other. Their conflict boiled down to the fact that each perceived and demonstrated love differently. Many marriages could be saved simply by understanding the different ways people perceive demonstrations of love.

The message sent was not the message received.   Another cause of everyday arguments is that the one who received the message (the listener) behaved *as if* he understood the meaning of the message and acted upon his assumption. Without checking, he assumed he understood what was intended by mind reading and reacted according to his inaccurate interpretation.

Suppose your partner says in what you interpret as a gruff voice, "Hey, come in here, will you?" You will probably think, *What did I do wrong now?* You may become defensive because you assume the tone of voice means your partner is angry with you. The tone of voice could mean he is angry, but it could also mean that he is angry with someone or something else that has not yet been identified.

Many hassles begin innocently this way. "I heard what you said and I know what you meant." The other person counters, "No, that's not what I meant." "Oh yes, it is. I know you," the first one says. "Whenever you use that tone it means you are angry with me." "It does not." And on and on it goes.

You can save yourself arguments over nothing if you double-check before coming to a negative conclusion.

What Couples Argue Over

Sociologists Robert O. Blood, Jr., and Donald M. Wolfe surveyed more than seven hundred couples and found that almost all of them fought about the same issues: money, children, recreation, personalities, in-laws, roles, religion, politics, and sex—in that order. Still other couples find that religion, friends, or alcohol and drug usage present the biggest challenge.[2]

The CI turned up similar findings, with slight variations in perceived sources of potential stress.

Males	*Females*
1. Communication	1. Communication
2. Finances	2. Finances
3. Sex	3. Children
4. Children	4. Sex
5. In-laws	5. In-laws

Both sexes ranked the sources of strain in their relationships with almost identical importance, with only children and sex reversed.

Role conflicts—who does what, why, when, and where— are affecting an increasing number of couples where both partners have entered the work force. Even in this age of equality, the typical woman who works outside the home retains the major responsibility for household tasks and child care, thus doubling her load. Even men who encourage their wives to work often fail to accept responsibility inside the home. The end result leads to conflict and disagreements.

According to studies, the frequency of conflict and the issues do not remain constant over the years. Honeymooners tend to disagree most over personality differences—irritating behaviors to which they find adjustment difficult. In this stage they also argue over how to spend their leisure time. "Middle marrieds" argue more over money, but such conflicts lessen in time. The least amount of conflict is found among aging couples.

Fight Styles Are Revealing

Although couples will adopt fight styles unique to them, they will tend to fit into a broad category. Social scientists have identified five different conflict styles.[3]

1. Competitors "Sound the battle cry" quickly becomes the theme of those engaged in competition. Their objective is to win regardless of the cost. Conflict is viewed as open war. There is high concern for self and low concern for others among competitors.

2. Avoiders "I don't want to talk about it," is an often-repeated phrase among avoiders. This group not only will avert their own desires but they have little concern for their partner's desires either. When conflict surfaces, they withdraw and refrain from saying anything. This fight style becomes a deadly threat to intimacy and eventually can kill a marriage.

3. Compromisers The art of compromise, "I will if you will," involves concern for self and concern for others. Those who master this art assert themselves kindly but moderate their demands so both parties achieve a certain degree of mutual satisfaction.

4. Collaborators Collaborators adopt the philosophy that "if you can't lick 'em, join 'em." Collaborators, using the opposite of avoidance, are highly motivated to negotiate creative solutions most likely to satisfy the needs of both. They usually possess high self-esteem, which exhibits itself in significant concern for self and others. Not winning but mutual satisfaction is the goal.

5. Accommodators   "Peace at any cost" is the goal of accommodators. They are so highly motivated toward peace that they neglect their own needs to satisfy their partners. This style is the opposite of competition. Accommodators may engage in conflict, but in the end they always give in for the sake of peace.

Each of us tends to adopt one main style, but we can also alternate between two. For example, a compromiser who is usually open to negotiation may adopt a highly competitive stance on an issue that is extremely important to him. Studies show that a combination of collaboration, compromise, and accommodation seems to facilitate the best overall, long-lasting results.

The Bartons, married for twenty-seven years, have adopted a workable system as to when best to accommodate and when to fight. "Every minor disagreement isn't treated as a major catastrophe," Joe clarifies. "If the issue is of prime importance for me, I'll fight for what I want. If the issue is about something my wife wants to buy—patio furniture, for instance—as long as we can afford it, I'll tell her to go ahead, even if it isn't high on my priority list. If it's a video camera I want, she may give in. We each give and take. It's not one-sided. We've found over the years that fighting over every little thing isn't as important as the stability of our relationship."

It is a mark of maturity to invest time in fighting over only important issues. If a principle you value highly has been violated, fight for it. Let the small issues go. Proverbs 19:11 RSV speaks eloquently to this point: "Good sense makes a man slow to anger, and it is his glory to overlook an offense." Certainly constant bickering over trivial matters may signal deeper problems.

We each have only so much emotional energy. Use your portion for matters that ultimately build bonds.

His and Her Fight Styles:
Are They Different?

Men are more likely to avoid an argument than women, according to evidence reported by Robert Levenson, Ph.D., associate professor of psychology at Indiana University—and for a physiological, not psychological, reason. According to Levenson, who has studied the reactions of couples as they discussed problems in their marriages, men react with a greater increase in heart rate than women to the stress of the argument.

Men are also inclined to withdraw (avoidance) when the conflict is prolonged. Levenson does not imply that men never blow up (competition). They respond to attack much as women do, with a desire to protect self through an increase in adrenaline. But they tend to release anger in spurts rather than in slow-moving negotiations. Such adaptive behavior helps keep stress at a distance.

It is possible that when a wife thinks her husband is withdrawing from an encounter, he is simply reacting to a built-in, health-protecting device. Heated arguing—at least for men—could be hazardous to their health!

The CI showed that females were twice as likely to indicate, "I feel angry most of the time," than males. It also showed that most men say they express anger only several times per month, while women admit to expressing anger several times per week. This indicates that males may have more of a tendency than females to hold in anger. What was disturbing was the large number who said they expressed anger only several times per year or never. These individuals probably consider expressing anger wrong or do not even recognize anger when experiencing it.

Most men and women are aware that when they disagree, they approach solutions according to vastly different methods, directly based on personal value systems. Each sex appears to have built-in codes that direct behavior during conflict and negotiation.

According to Dr. H. G. Whittington, the male tends to believe that solutions should be sought in a manner similar to a game plan that controls sporting events. His game plan dictates that the dispute will take place within certain bound-aries, will last for a specific amount of time, and will eventually end. The game is governed by rules which all players respect and remains fair since an outside force—an umpire or referee—limits foul play.

The objective of the game, when viewed from the male perspective, is to display skill and achieve victory. Other opportunities probably exist for a rematch, if desired. Sports etiquette demands that aggressive behavior and personal opinions be confined to the game and not be carried off the field into relationships. Consequently, postgame socialization is encouraged among opposing teams.

Women too have a game plan, but the game, as well as all of life, is put through an emotional filter. The same rules govern work, play, home, children, and relationships. Aggression and skill may be displayed, but it must be modulated to suit the occasion—especially if males are present. Blocks of time are usually foreign to women, who tend to see all of life as a whole.

Women engaged in conflict would have difficulty socializing, even in a group, with someone with whom they had just battled. Their emotions remain closer to the surface at all times, and they have easier access to them. They might also have difficulty accepting the concept that there is another chance to play the game—a rematch.

Keeping these observations in mind, then, it becomes easier to understand how a couple, even a couple who really care about each other, can experience considerable frustration over stalemates in settling their differences.[4]

Meet the Larsons. They had a blowup after supper, a frequent occurrence. Brad got louder and louder as the argument progressed. His size and loudness threatened Sue, although he had never hit her. His behavior further confused her since he kept shifting from an emotional to a logical viewpoint, pointing out her illogical thinking, overemotionalism, and little-girl behavior. He endeavored to display his superior prowess and game skills and to prove her a stupid, silly child. Objective: Win the war and end the game.

Throughout the encounter, Sue experienced flashbacks to her childhood, when her father had stood menacingly over her, demanding obedience through rigid control. A sense of helplessness engulfed her. When Brad continued to browbeat her with the power of his logical left hemisphere, she intuitively attacked his weak points. She knew he would soon tire of the game and retreat. She criticized a stupid decision he made. As she spoke, another flashback occurred: She saw her mother belittling her father. As clear as the picture was, she was unable to stop herself. The instinct to protect herself from Brad's relentless denigration was too strong.

Brad became outraged because Sue had committed a foul, yet no one called it or punished her. His territory at stake, more intensely than ever he accused her of being nothing more than a crybaby. This prompted her to dump a negative which totally emasculated him.

Retreating to the bedroom, Brad now announced, "It is impossible to discuss anything with you. I'm going to bed." He showered (exactly as any man would do following a sporting event) and got into bed. With a clear conscience, he assessed the situation: "I played by the rules and won fair and square. She will get over her hurt feelings because we can have a rematch any time she wants it." Without further ado, he fell asleep.

The truth is that Brad had not played fairly, or even consulted the rule book regarding guidelines for this game that involves team players of a different mind-set and strategy: women! By faulting and discrediting her method of presentation (emotional rather than logical), he concluded he had won. A logical, rational approach, however, is no more right than is the intuitive emotional approach. Yet a woman can be greatly intimidated by such an argument.

As long as males and females enter into relationships, there will be disagreements between them. Emotions will run high. Resolutions will sometimes prove elusive. Anger, hurt, and guilt will be interwoven with daily life. *Note:* No outside force will magically appear to monitor their behavior or call "foul." In the end it will be the two of them, standing alone, vulnerable, needing each other but hating each other. While trying to hammer out a solution, they are left on their own to utilize the skills they have learned, all the while vigorously attempting to maintain affection for one another. Unless both have learned appropriate skills so that victory can be attained without "winning" or "losing," the conflict will go on. The good news is that hate can be avoided.

Is It Okay to Fight?

You may be one of the many who believe it is wrong to argue, disagree, engage in conflict, or fight. Such a notion has all but collapsed under a barrage of information to the contrary. Couples who say they have never had a fight are deluding themselves or are entirely out of touch with their emotions. Those who refuse to acknowledge the need to fight will suffer from displaced anger such as hostility, emotional instability, depression, a long list of health problems, and/or a lack of intimacy.

Many psychologists consider occasional conflict a sign of a healthy, fulfilling relationship. It shows warmth and caring. George R. Bach and Peter Wyden, in their classic *The Intimate Enemy: How to Fight Fair in Love and Marriage*, comment: "We have discovered that couples who fight together are couples who stay together—provided they know how to fight properly."[5]

Yes, it's risky to fight. But learning how to fight fair might be the most important communication skill you will ever learn. Fighting between two people who really care about one another does not have to be destructive. It can be a highly constructive experience. It means that you care about each other so much you will negotiate and deal with a problem until you find a mutually satisfying solution. Couples who withdraw do not care about one another enough to risk upsetting the status quo.

Fighting is okay—even for Christians. The measure of whether fighting is acceptable for a Christian boils down to the methods and style used during combat and the end result.

The Share-Care Plan:
Your Passport to Conflict Resolution

In a marriage, many minor incidents arise on a daily basis. Constructive methods are needed to solve the day-to-day issues that arise from close living. Negotiation and brain-storming are all well and good for The Big Stuff—major issues—but what is really needed is a plan for handling smaller, day-to-day irritations.

This is what the Communication Inventory revealed the majority of couples wanted—to be able to discuss problems as they occurred. A few wanted to discuss problems before bedtime. Only a scant percentage wanted to discuss problems during a set time each week.

The share-care plan can easily be put into play by either partner when irritation or anger surfaces and a quick resolution is needed. There are four steps in the share-care plan:

(1) A statement of the problem in I-message form. A direct statement of your feelings about the problem is needed without put-downs and without telling the other person what to do. An I-message flows as follows: I feel _____ when you _____ because _____.

(2) A restatement of the problem and the feelings expressed by your partner—a care message. This restatement shows you heard the problem correctly and understand the feelings involved.

(3) A statement of acceptance. This allows your partner to know that you accept his feelings as valid even though you may not agree with his feelings or point of view. To accept does not necessarily mean to agree. Yet this concept is difficult to comprehend. My own survey showed that only 31 percent felt each was able to see the issue from the other's point of view.

(4) Resolution. When the irritated partner has no more feelings to express and the problem and feelings have been restated and accepted, you are ready to move to an apology and resolution. When apologizing, you must say more than "I'm sorry." Sorry for what? You have correctly apologized and asked for forgiveness when you: (a) say "I'm sorry"; (b) state what you are sorry for; and (c) ask for forgiveness. Asking for forgiveness is an important part of resolving a problem.

Let's look in on June and Rick:

HE: (*I-message*) I was really upset when you suggested

inviting your relatives for my birthday but never mentioned inviting my family. This made me feel like my family was not wanted.

SHE: *(care message)* If I hear you correctly, you are upset because you feel I prefer having my family over for your birthday rather than yours.

HE: *(I-message)* Exactly. I like your family, but I resent it when you leave my family off a guest list, especially when it's my birthday. I think my wishes should be considered and my family should be invited too.

SHE: *(care message)* You sound as if you have some resentful feelings about this matter that you've been storing up for a while.

HE: *(I-message)* You bet. Furthermore, I feel. . . .

We have no solution yet, but June has a clearer picture of Rick's feelings. When Rick has no more feelings to express, June can accept his feelings as valid and they can move to apology and resolution.

SHE: *(statement of acceptance)* I have heard your frustration over this situation and accept your feelings as valid. *(apology and resolution)* I am sorry for upsetting you by not including your family as often as mine. Sometimes I feel your family has never accepted me, and I'm not comfortable around them. In the future, I'll try to be more aware of your feelings and include your family more. Please forgive me.

Shifting Gears

Another problem surfaced for June and Rick during the resolution phase. If Rick is a caring partner, he will pick up on this and "shift gears." Now June will become the sender and Rick the receiver.

HE: *(care message)* I accept your apology. If I heard you correctly, you feel unaccepted around my family. I'm concerned about your feelings and would like to discuss this with you.

SHE: *(I-message)* Right. I know you might not understand, but I feel all thumbs around your mother. I feel as if I can't do anything right.

HE: *(care message)* If I hear what you are trying to say, it is my mom who is the source of the problem and is really upsetting you. Tell me more. *(a door opener)*

SHE: *(I-message)* Okay. Remember when they were here for Christmas? All I asked her to bring was. . . .

Each time a partner shares a problem, it should be done in I-message fashion. The one with the problem should be allowed to "dump" as long as there are any feelings, while the other remains in the caring role. It may be that after the dumping has occurred, enough feelings have been defused to arrive at a mutually satisfying solution. Or it may be that the sender has more to share, in which case they will need to shift gears again.

The skill of shifting gears allows both partners the right and privilege to clearly and completely state their views, feelings, and reasons without interruption. It is an orderly manner for airing any potentially troublesome problem.

It will not always result in an immediate solution, but each will know exactly where the other stands. This may not sound like a giant accomplishment, but the number of couples who cannot solve their problems because they do not know what the problem is, is legion. Such couples have been so busy trying to prove *who is right and who is wrong* they never heard what the other was saying, and consequently have never dealt with the real problem. Since the real problem is never uncovered, they go on for years as adversaries.

Before the Conflict: Setting the Stage

The share-care plan solves the small day-to-day issues. Life would be relatively simple if we had little more to deal with than upset feelings because relatives weren't invited to a birthday party. However, life is infinitely more complicated with The Big Stuff that can stretch the bond to the limit. Major decisions and large conflicts can be expected even in the best of relationships. Each can be processed effectively when a couple is trained and knows what they are doing.

Here are some vital items that should be discussed and negotiated prior to attempting to deal with the conflict:

(1) *Schedule the best time.*   Comedians, politicians, and great lovers are well aware of the importance of timing. It

pays to wait on The Big Stuff. It is senseless and unproductive to attempt to solve problems when both partners are very angry. "Take time to cool down first," advises one woman.

What about going to bed with unresolved conflicts? "Let not the sun go down upon your wrath," we read in Ephesians 4:26 (KJV). Is this psychologically sound advice today? Ideally, differences of opinion that arise in daily living can be resolved quickly and lovingly. Unless they are handled in this manner, they frequently grow to a disproportionate size by morning. One man followed this advice religiously. When asked once if he and his wife ever argued, he responded, "No, but once we stayed up for three months."

A word of caution: Don't attempt a solution to a big problem within two hours of bedtime. Factors such as fatigue and high emotional stress decrease mental efficiency and increase irritability. An important issue can wait until morning. Do not, however, allow the matter to go unattended more than forty-eight hours. Tabling the matter for days on end could be as destructive as withdrawal.

(2) Select the best location.   Neutral territory is the key. The family room, basement, or garage may be right for certain couples. Bedrooms and kitchens may provide psychological hang-ups for others. Some professionals recommend going to a motel or other such place to handle big problems. A motel provides an atmosphere free of interruptions, with unfamiliar surroundings encouraging the couple to pull together. The expense and effort involved in reserving a motel emphasizes the importance of the occasion.

Other suggestions include the bathtub, where you sit facing each other. This may sound ridiculous, but it works well. The water has a calming effect and it forces you to interface. However, two chairs in any room will do the trick.

Make sure there is ample time and privacy to talk it out without disruption. Take the phone off the hook, if necessary, and make sure the children are away or well occupied.

(3) Setting the agenda.   Whoever requests the meeting has the right to set the agenda. For example, if Harry calls a meeting to discuss my expenditures, for which I did not first consult him and of which he does not approve, he determines what will be discussed. This agenda can be changed only

with his permission. If I wish to call my own meeting and bring up related or divergent issues I may, but not on his time.

(4) Set time limits.   Both minimum and maximum time limits should be set. If an issue is large enough to require the scheduling of a meeting, it undoubtedly will require a minimum of fifteen minutes to resolve. A maximum of one hour is reasonable on major issues, although you need to remain flexible. If an issue remains unresolved in the allotted time, the one calling the meeting can request an extension of time, or another time can be set to continue negotiating.

(5) Establish ground rules.   Just as a formal debate would crumble rapidly without *Robert's Rules of Order*, so do many disagreements between couples fall apart for lack of structure and clear guidelines. Establishing a set of your own personal guidelines will greatly improve the atmosphere and promote free negotiation. Skilled negotiators set up ground rules, not during the thick of battle, but beforehand in an atmosphere of uncharged emotion. Both partners relax when discussion is governed by rules which prevent emotional harm and promote security. Some general ground rules might include the following: no name-calling, no threats of divorce or suicide, no remarks about in-laws or relatives, no put-downs concerning appearance or intelligence, no physical violence, no yelling, swearing, or interrupting.

(6) Stay on the subject.   Stick with one problem until you solve it. Only 50 percent of the respondents in the CI said they could stay with one subject all or most of the time when attempting to resolve a conflict. The more problems brought up at one time, the less likelihood there is that any of them will be solved. Make a rule that additional problems cannot be brought up until the first one has been dealt with. If necessary, prepare a sheet of paper titled "Agenda for Next Conference" and jot down other issues. Avoid dragging up old scores and arguments. Agree that if the accusation is more than six months old, it is inadmissible evidence.

During the Conflict: Resolving The Big Stuff

The time has come for The Big Stuff. You tried to avoid it, but in spite of your best intentions, you have a Big One to deal with. You have laid your ground rules previously, but what happens now?

(1) Pray together about the conflict.   Praying together might do more to set the proper tone for dealing with a big issue than anything else. Harry and I have reached some real impasses during our years of marriage—impossible and hopeless situations loomed before us. We have been so angry we couldn't talk; we have been choked with emotion, discouraged beyond words. Sometimes without a word, Harry would reach for my hand and quietly begin praying. The words would be mechanical at first, worn phrases about God's goodness and greatness. He would pause. Then his words would come more slowly and deliberately: "Lord, Nancy and I are facing a big problem today. Help us each to express ourselves clearly and to listen to each other caringly. Take over in this situation and teach us each. . . ." Our hearts would begin to melt. At the close of the prayer, the problem was still there, yet we felt hope rather than anger and discouragement.

(2) Stick to the previously laid ground rules.   One couple laid their ground rules: No walking out in the heat of the argument. No yelling, threats of divorce, or swearing. Both promised to limit Big arguments in front of the children and to listen rather than defend themselves. Their resolve to stick to these rules made some difficult times easier.

(3) Sit facing each other.   Assuming the face-to-face position will make it easier to maintain good eye contact and also conveys that both parties are interested and listening. Some couples hold hands during this time, which shows caring even though they are struggling to solve a difficult problem. Develop a signal system that conveys the need for a timeout—a squeeze or raising of the hand in case the situation becomes intense or one breaks the ground rules.

(4) Focus on a specific objective.   As you begin, pinpoint your objective: "To harmonize our hectic work schedules so that we can spend at least one evening together," or "To determine whether our in-laws should come for Christmas or at another time acceptable to everyone." The burden for stating the problem and objective rests with the one who called the conference.

(5) Implement the share-care plan.   The share-care plan is good for more than just solving the small issues of life. Even though the stakes are greater and the issue bigger, the plan still provides the best framework available for solving complicated problems. I-messages will keep you focusing on the issue and the care messages will clarify the problem and demonstrate caring. The negotiation stage will probably take longer. Steps 6, 7, and 8 are needed to complete the share-care plan for solving The Big Stuff.

(6) List in writing all possible solutions.   When feelings have been described openly and constructively, and the problem has been aired and clearly understood by both partners, you will see the issues at stake and be able to work out rational alternatives. At this time brainstorm every possible solution, regardless of how farfetched it may seem. List suggestions on a sheet of paper, but do not evaluate them yet.

(7) Evaluate the solutions.   Once every possible alternative has been jotted down, the two of you can go over the list and share thoughts on the consequences of each. Narrow the list down to the one, two, or three best possible solutions that might work.

(8) Choose the most acceptable solution.   This choice may take a good measure of negotiation and compromise. Solutions can be reached by one partner yielding or by both compromising. Giving in to another in the midst of conflict takes real maturity, because in effect you are admitting your analysis of the situation was wrong and you are now ready to change your mind. Take care to see that one of you does not always do the yielding. It takes two to make a conflict and two to resolve it. Winning should not be the goal, because where there is a winner there must also be a loser, and no one likes to lose. The most acceptable solution is the one that comes closest to solving the problem *and* meeting the needs of both.

(9) Implement the solution.   Two people often perceive agreements differently. In order to prevent misunderstandings, at this time jot down the specifications of what was decided in an agreement book, along with who is supposed to do what, where, when, and how.

(10) Hang in there!   What participants in an argument need to realize is that many times they quit just short of the goal. Anger and frustration mount, and they withdraw or leave prematurely. Within minutes they would have reached a resolution if they'd hung in there.

Harry and I learned this, but far too late. We reached an impasse on something and went to the bedroom to argue this out in a reasonable manner. In the midst of this rather heated discussion, I became furious. More than anything I wanted to scream about his unfairness and how much I had been hurt. I never wanted to talk with him again about this subject or any other. Instead, I hung in there. Within a couple of minutes, we had both moved off dead center (even when I didn't think it was possible), and we resolved the issue. I'll never forget the warmth we felt for each other following this incident. I learned through this experience not to bail out of an argument too soon.

After the Conflict: Harmony Restored

Be patient with yourself and your partner. Even when you have moved through all the steps properly, change doesn't take place overnight. Old habits take time to break. Don't expect too much too soon. Pray for patience.

Now reestablish touch. During conflict, touch seems to evaporate. Of those in the CI, 72 percent said they have trouble touching their partners when angry, which leaves many touch-hungry people starved for some TLC. A simple touch of the hand, a warm hug, or bodies "spooned" as you sleep could melt many hostilities. Tactile togetherness has the ability to dissolve conflict better than anything else. Harmony can be reestablished with something as simple as foot touching. The closeness of a hug seems to go deeper than words. The bond may have been stretched while you were in conflict, but now you are one again and touching reassures you of it.

Talk about something good in your relationship. Conflict conversations focus on problems and are usually troubled and heavy. Whereas no relationship can be stress-free all the time, partners particularly need reassurance that they are loved and cared for after a conflict. Find something positive on which to comment. Give your partner an unexpected compliment, a pat on the back, and a big smile, and you'll find that you can draw closer again.

Arguments that are left hanging in midair with nothing resolved leave you feeling unsettled, misunderstood, and churning. Your arguments no longer have to be left this way if you take the time to negotiate and continue negotiations until you reach a resolution. Feelings of peace and accomplishment are the cherished fruits of conflict resolution. You and your partner no longer have to run from confrontation but can meet it head-on, work through it, and strengthen your marital bond. Your conflicts will no longer threaten your relationship or your intimacy.

When a couple can learn to share feelings, understand each other's viewpoint, search for a solution, and clear the air, not one but both win. *And that's a reward worth its weight in gold.*

6 Best Friends: Secrets of Attaining Intimacy

In a recent survey of four hundred divorced men, all of them felt their marriages fell apart because they stopped being friends with their wives.

Patrice, a wife of seventeen years, speaks as she pulls nervously at the tissue she is using to dab at her tears.

"Our first date was very romantic and unforgettable. We went to dinner but never tasted the food. We were so enraptured with each other, we talked for hours and lost all track of time. I felt I had known him all my life. I was awake almost all night thinking about him.

"We continued to date over the months. I had had numerous relationships with men, but this one was different. We both knew it from the beginning. When John finally asked me to marry him it was inevitable. In the beginning, our marriage was much like our courtship. We shared everything and considered ourselves best friends; we shared things we would never tell anyone else. On some occasions, we'd lie in bed holding each other and talking 'til the wee hours of the morning.

"And now? Gradually, over the years, each of us has pulled back—bottling our feelings and closing up. There is little to say to one another and sometimes I have no feeling for this man I once adored. I get the impression he feels much the same way. The couple who used to be 'best friends' can now barely tolerate each other. The beauty of the love we once shared has faded until I'm not sure we could find it or revive it.

"What happened? Nothing dramatic. He got busy with his career, I with our home, the children, and eventually a career of my own. We were so busy with our separate worlds we

153

hardly noticed that we weren't friends anymore. The signals were all there, but we refused to recognize them. When he came home from work there would be a meal with polite surface talk. Then he'd bury himself in the antique car he was rebuilding, his office, or the TV. I became very resentful of his shutting me out of his life. When he did try to include me in his activities, I would refuse out of spite. Meaningful communication just about dried up from that point on.

"The couple who didn't have enough hours in the day to discuss life didn't exist anymore. I remember how our friends used to tease us. We would get so wrapped up in our discussions with each other, they didn't want to interrupt us!

"That seems like a long time ago. Now we stay together because of the children. We have resigned ourselves to living our lives this way. There must be a lot more like us out there, judging by the number of articles appearing in ladies' magazines on how to improve a marriage. I have read a lot of them, but they are all based on the theory that people *want* to improve their marriages. I think John is satisfied the way things are.

"Besides, we have lived this way for so many years now, it would be very difficult to open up and express how I feel. I doubt if I could accomplish this in a way that wouldn't threaten John and severely interrupt the comfort zone we have each established. Our relationship may not be great, but it is predictable and there is a sense of security in our misery.

"The real barrier between us is not the inability to communicate with each other. We still do on a limited basis. But it's the fact that when we do talk there is no personal caring. We are strangers to one another. We have lost the ability to see things from the other's viewpoint."

People marry dreaming of love, but romance is nourished by an intimate friendship. Most marriages are what might be called "functional"—the partners perform the duties of provider, nurturer, parent, sex partner, cook. Somehow the functional relationship is not fulfilling, complete, or satisfying.

What is the one thing that transforms the functional relationship into a superbly satisfying one? Intimacy—a Best Friends status.

Best Friends Status Comes of Age

When asked, "What keeps a marriage going?" both male and female respondents in a *Psychology Today* survey listed as their first response, "My spouse is my best friend." Reasons that followed included: I like my spouse as a person; we agree on aims and goals; my spouse has grown more interesting; we laugh together; I confide in my spouse; we have a stimulating exchange of ideas; we share hobbies and interests.[1] Notice every item involves sharing, togetherness, and closeness.

We marry dreaming of love and companionship. Yet when asked in the Communication Inventory if they wanted to attain an intimate relationship with their partners, 52 percent of the females responded "definitely yes" whereas 37 percent of the males definitely wanted it. Sixteen percent of the total number said that intimacy was impossible due to the many conflicts they had. Yet 63 percent of both sexes said they considered their partners their best friends. A large chunk, 37 percent, were unsure or definitely not best friends with their partners. This shows there is some conflict in either their thinking or their practice.

Some couples are aware they don't really know their partners, and others have to be shown. The often comical and embarrassing episodes on the "Newlywed Game" point out how little some couples know about each other. A Best Friends relationship might have sounded radical thirty years ago when husband-wife roles were defined in terms of domination and submission. But the age of Best Friends—the attainment of closeness between equals—has arrived.

What does it mean to be Best Friends? Words like *equality* and *partnership* now come into play. Psychologists define *friendship* in the following manner:

- A friend looks for the best in the other and doesn't put his or her friend down.
- A friend will care about another person by putting him first and doing things for that person just because it makes the person happy.
- A friend is a person with whom you can share your strengths

and weaknesses, your hopes and fears, your joys and sorrows. An old proverb says, "A friend is one to whom you may pour out all the contents of your heart, chaff and grain together, knowing that the gentlest of hands will take and sift it, keep what is worth keeping, and with the breath of kindness blow the rest away."

- The Book of Proverbs says, "A man that hath friends must shew himself friendly" (Proverbs 18:24 KJV).
- A friend listens carefully, forgives quickly, and respects the dignity and feelings of his or her friend.

Granted, many differences between males and females will always exist. But in spite of different emotional responses to life situations, intimate bonds of trust, loyalty, openness, and closeness can become the norm. In days gone by, a few couples might have achieved this, but it was the exception rather than the rule. *Goal:* Best Friends. *Reward:* The most satisfying way of life.

Easy to state; difficult to attain.

What Is Intimacy?

So June and Howard had been "intimate"? What would you assume June and Howard had done to achieve intimacy? Most people would assume they had had a sexual encounter. But the term *intimacy* goes far beyond physical contact alone.

The word *intimacy* is derived from the Latin word *intimus*, which means "inmost," referring to a state of confidentiality and a deeply personal relationship. Perhaps it is best symbolized by bonds of emotional closeness between a couple who are responsive to the needs of each other. It is the experience of understanding and being understood by someone who loves us.

Marriage provides the best atmosphere in which such an experience can be attained. In one study, subjects were asked to choose from the following list the most important ingredient for successful marriage: sexual satisfaction; companionship; financial security and material possessions; having children; someone to turn to for problem solving. Companionship was rated first choice by the majority of husbands and wives.

My CI turned up similar results: Both males and females

identified "emotional closeness" as the most important part of intimacy. However, four times as many men as women chose "mutually satisfying sex." Twice as many women as men chose "sharing innermost feelings." A host of other studies rank companionship and emotional closeness the highest. Sexual satisfaction consistently trails way behind.

A look at long-term relationships shows that the marital friendship curve starts high immediately following the wedding but quickly cools. For several years after marriage, there is a steady decline as passion cools and the relationship becomes dull, boring, and humdrum. Early marrieds report their relationships include mutual discussion, shared feelings, comparing new ideas, and planning for the future. As children enter the scene, the curve drops sharply as the complexity of the relationship intensifies. Dullness can and frequently does begin early in marriage.

Dullness or a sense of boredom in a relationship is an early warning sign that all is not well. Today people are less willing than ever to tolerate dullness in a marriage. The now generation desires all the luxuries life can afford materially and socially, plus exciting leisure-time activities, stimulating sex, intelligent conversation, and attractive spouses 365 days a year. Yet the average couple's patience and knowledge of how to attain these goals is at a standstill.

Intimacy doesn't come easy due to human error. This is glaringly evident since the CI showed that only 26 percent of both sexes were experiencing enough intimacy to satisfy them. Three-quarters of all respondents would like to experience it in greater proportions.

Intimacy is the end product of the time and effort given by a couple who want to remain in love with each other for a lifetime. When a couple attains true intimacy, their marriage will become the most meaningful and interesting relationship on earth. The most passionate love novel couldn't hold a candle to what this couple shares.

The Four Faces of Intimacy

Intimacy progresses through several stages. When you meet a person for the first time, you go from the stranger to acquaintance stage. From these basic levels, you may progress to friendship or even close friendship. At this point, it is possible to move into intimacy. But intimacy is not achieved overnight. It develops over a period of time as two people relate to each other in an atmosphere of caring and warmth. We can thus define an *intimate relationship* as one in which trust and honesty are evident in an atmosphere where both parties do not fear undue criticism of their thoughts, feelings, and worries.

Other expressions that might describe an intimate relationship would include the following: caring, sharing, getting to know each other, a giving of oneself, satisfying the other person's needs, telling the other person things you've never told anyone else before, openness. When you achieve this kind of nonsexual closeness with a partner, you have reached the highest level of intimacy. Such a relationship springs from four factors:

Trust   Trust provides an atmosphere of freedom. Neither person experiences recrimination, criticism, or restraint. Each has complete confidence that he or she can bring to the surface hidden thoughts and feelings with the assurance that they will be accepted without reproach. Honesty and respect lay the foundation for trust.

Eighty-five percent in the CI said they trusted their partner all or most of the time, with only the remaining 15 percent indicating varying degrees of distrust. *Remember: Without trust there is distrust.* If you have a tendency to distrust, it is worth making the effort to achieve complete trust. Be willing to move slowly. It takes time to build a trusting relationship. If trust has been damaged or destroyed, it will take longer. Trust is destroyed through lying or pretending.

Openness   Openness implies that each feels he or she can be himself or herself without pretending to be something else. Intimates share the unpleasant as well as pleasant aspects of their lives. Author John Powell describes openness:

If friendship and human love are to mature between any two persons, there must be absolute and honest revelation;

this kind of self-revelation can be achieved only through what we have called "gut level" communication. There is no other way, and all the reasons which we adduce to rationalize our cover-ups and dishonesty must be seen as delusions. It would be much better for me to tell you how I really feel about you than to enter into the stickiness and discomfort of a phony relationship.

Dishonesty always has a way of coming back to haunt and trouble us. Even if I should have to tell you that I do not admire or love you emotionally, it would be much better than trying to deceive you and having to pay the ultimate price of all such deception, your greater hurt and mine. And you will have to tell me things, at times, that will be difficult for you to share. But really, you have no choice, and, if I want your friendship, I must be ready to accept you as you are. If either of us comes to the relationship without this determination of mutual honesty and openness, there can be no friendship, no growth; rather there can be only a subject-object kind of thing that is typified by immature bickering, pouting, jealousy, anger, and accusations.[2]

In an intimate relationship, each partner must feel that his or her feelings are important and that they are being given prime consideration. This lays the foundation for respect.

Freedom   Even in an intimate relationship, you do not own each other. Each has the freedom to move in other directions with or without the other. Independence is allowed without accusations or mistrust. Since honesty, openness, and trust mark the relationship, there is no need to be suspicious or demanding. Each person has the room to develop his or her own likes, dislikes, talents, and abilities without pressure from the other to conform to likes or beliefs.

Time   Many couples tell me it was love at first sight for them. I believe in attraction at first sight, when all the essentials in body chemistry ignite in a gigantic explosion labeled "love." Some may instinctively suspect that marriage is inevitable. But there is no such thing as "instant intimacy." It takes a long time for trust, acceptance, honesty, and openness to take root and expand.

As a couple spends time together, they begin to write a history of their own. Each episode in their life together adds to their own personal history. Each experience is unique to them and makes their story distinct, strengthening the bonds of love and confidentiality between them.

No one can achieve intimacy without personal cost. Sometimes that cost must be measured in terms of hurt and pain. But the benefits of coming close outweigh the pain.

How Intimacy Is Attained

Intimacy is only complete when achieved in the emotional, physical, social, and spiritual realms of life—realms which touch and support the "whole person." Intimacy between two people can be compared to the legs of a chair. Any time one of four legs which supports the chair is weak, there will be a loss of closeness.

Emotional intimacy   Emotional intimacy begins as the newly wedded couple shares how they experience their world with each other—their insights, feelings, beliefs, goals, interests, time. Yet how quickly this couple who vowed to unite their separate lives into one speed down different freeways to opposite locations.

When one man was asked how the communication was in his home, he replied, "What communication? We don't communicate. She has little to talk about besides the house, her friends, and the kids. I'm not interested in that." But this is exactly what builds intimacy. Intimacy comes not so much from the sharing of a devastating emotional crisis as it does from sharing the little things that are important to one another.

In *Blue Collar Marriage,* sociologist Mirra Komarovsky reported that among working-class marriages, one out of three fell short of the ideals most of us hold for emotional intimacy.[3] Instead of soul-searching sessions that involve deep self-revelation, Komarovsky found that nonintimate marriages became that way because to a large extent both partners had little interest in their mate's life. In other words, the ability to speak to a partner about feelings grows out of having a relationship free enough to talk about the trivia of life that pleases or hurts, knowing there is someone who will listen with a caring ear. It seems intimacy is built upon the ability to talk about everyday happenings—what he did and she said, the children's successes and failures, worries over a parent's health, what the boss said, and what happened after you ran out of gas. This swapping of information leads to an involvement in the life of the other as well as a sense of being heard and understood.

In addition, intimacy includes the ability to sense what your partner feels and needs and the inclination to put yourself out to accommodate those needs when the situation calls for it. Does the giving of yourself in this manner mean losing yourself? No, but it implies a reciprocal readiness to respond to the other's desires.

Such emotional closeness can grow only in a place of safety, a comfort zone. If either partner is afraid of being criticized, hurt, put down, or misunderstood, sharing on this level will be next to impossible. Achieving emotional closeness, then, is largely dependent on acceptance.

Nagging and criticism are devastating to intimacy. Each partner longs for emotional closeness, but an atmosphere of faultfinding and censure succeed only in emotional wallbuilding that separates us.

Whereas criticism can be a deathblow to love and intimacy, consistent appreciation is a powerful intimacy builder. In marriage, we are always reacting to each other—positively, negatively, or passively. We have the ability to heal or hurt one another, to restore or deplete, to help or hinder. We can make our mates feel important, alive, and worthy, or we can make them feel inadequate and useless. Let us move in a positive direction.

Physical intimacy   Because we haven't understood what true intimacy is or how it can be found, our culture glamorizes false intimacy: raw sex without close meaningful relationships. The search for intimacy propels people to hop from bed to bed in vain attempts to find a caring experience! For the opportunity of being held in someone else's arms during a lovemaking encounter outside of the bonds of marriage, self-worth is sacrificed. When it's over, the participants feel worse than before, yet so alone they must try again.

Furthermore, people fear intimacy. It is easier to shed their clothes and share their bodies than it is to share themselves. Bodies are used as a substitute for emotional intimacy. When emotional intimacy is short-circuited for the sake of physical intimacy, real intimacy is seldom attained.

In relationships where emotional intimacy has been neglected, sex eventually becomes routine, dull, or nonexistent. A superficial relationship contains little closeness and sex is used mainly to release tension, prove adequacy, or create the illusion of intimacy.

Becoming educated sexually is important, but intimacy cannot be achieved through skillful sexual techniques. Passion and desire that last a lifetime result from shared values, goals, and beliefs. The satisfaction level as well as the frequency level of your sex life are primarily determined by the degree of closeness you have achieved. When emotional intimacy is achieved at its highest level, sexual responsiveness escalates.

The physical dimension of a relationship is not enough to keep a relationship exciting, no matter how beautiful the bodies. Intense sexuality will endure a lifetime only when two people continue to share and explore their intimate feelings.

Emotional intimacy is a rare commodity. When experienced, it results in pure joy, childlike happiness, and fun all rolled into one. Trying to achieve the ultimate sexual experience without first attaining emotional closeness is putting the cart before the horse: the feelings follow the establishment of a close, warm, affectionate relationship over a period of time.

Social intimacy   Social intimacy involves the sharing of each other's interests and hobbies. Some people have such widely divergent interests that they occupy separate continents. A bridge of common interests must be built in order to connect their separateness.

Some people never learn this. Each goes his or her distinct way, developing and nurturing a world devoid of partner interest or involvement.

Frank is a sports addict. A typical week includes jogging every day, racquetball twice a week during the winter, playing on two baseball teams in the spring and summer months, and watching endless games on TV. A trip to Hawaii or some far-off place to catch yet another game is not an unusual event in his life. Frank expects his wife to release him graciously to each event.

Joan enjoys most of this even though she has a different agenda of interests. You will find her attending each game with Frank, being friendly, keeping score and records of errors to amuse herself. She has made a real effort to understand the more difficult aspects of football. Her personal agenda would take her to a concert, play, or maybe even the ballet. Will Frank go with her on occasion in exchange for the massive investment of time and energy she puts into sharing *his* world? Not on your life! "I have no interest in that kind of pantywaist stuff," you might overhear our macho friend mutter. His refusal to share her interests has resulted in growing resentment on her part—a serious threat to intimacy.

Sharing experiences, learning about a partner's interests, spending time together in absorbing tasks promotes caring and knowledge about each other. Couples who desire an intimate relationship must knit their lives together by spending some free time involved in common interests.

Spiritual intimacy   Notice on the triangular diagram on page 164 that as husband and wife draw closer to God, they also draw closer to each other. A couple wishing to experience complete intimacy in marriage must seek spiritual intimacy. Without intimacy in the spiritual dimension, there can never be total emotional or physical intimacy. Spiritual intimacy provides a depth and power beyond what ordinary couples know in their marriages.

Spiritual intimacy can be nurtured by church attendance together. Family worship and attending church functions, both social and spiritual, as well as serving as church officers can build intimacy.

Nothing can draw a couple closer than praying together. A new way of praying that could be a real boost to closeness is "share prayer." Together each night one partner begins share

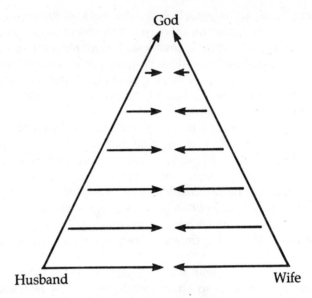

prayer by praying for a specific subject. Then the other prays
for the same subject. Then you pray for the next burden on
your heart and your partner prays for the same thing. You
continue in this manner until you have introduced each
matter you wish to pray about. Tomorrow it will be your
partner's turn to initiate topics.

As you pray for each other's concerns, they become your
own. You will become acquainted with the issues closest to
your mate's heart—an important factor in intimacy. Such
praying will probably be on level 1 (*see* page 103). Soon you
will be so closely identifying with each other's burdens that
you won't remember who had the burden first.

Studies indicate that couples not matched in religious
background attend church less frequently and are more prone
to divorce. Even when a couple shares the same religious
convictions, however, their involvement in religious activities
can become a divisive factor. As he involves himself more
with the building committee and she with women's prayer
groups, they find themselves going separate ways. While it
isn't necessary to share every spiritual experience, it is
important to include some you can enjoy together.

Without the spiritual dimension in our lives, Harry and I

would not be together today. During our early years, we consistently encountered serious difficulties, bigger problems than I imagined any couple could survive. We had had no premarital counseling. Even though we were not teenagers, we were young, naive, and unlearned in the disciplines of married life. We tried to work out all our problems on our own, and they weren't working out very well!

Babies came more quickly than expected: one, two, three unplanned pregnancies (the days before the Pill). Harry was in college training to enter the ministry, and money was tight. We continued to rock along during the early years of his pastoral ministry. We were called to help others get their lives straight, but we couldn't help ourselves. We went to church faithfully, had family worship, read our Bibles, and did all the "good things" Christians are supposed to do, but things got worse.

Had it not been for our faith, we could have thrown our marriage away, figuring that what we had wasn't worth saving and it might be better to separate than torment each other.

At this point, the Lord gave me an experience that forever changed our lives and marriage. I changed, our marriage changed, and eventually Harry changed too. In the end, it was the spiritual bond that held us through our darkest hours.

His and Her Intimacy Needs: Are They Different?

Television's Archie Bunker once quipped to his wife, Edith, "The problem with our communication is I speak in English and you listen in dingbat." Archie's interpretation was slanted from a male point of view but might be echoed by thousands of couples who fail to understand what their partners really want. Males and females appear to have vastly differing intimacy needs, and learning to accept and understand these differences is important.

Enter Phyllis and Arnie. Phyllis is a public defender with the city and Arnie teaches university mathematics. Each leads a busy and involved life. When Phyllis gets home at night, she wants to share it all with Arnie—how she handled the defense, what the suspect said, how the lawyer for the prosecution treated her. All of this is rattled off to Arnie, who would clearly rather be reading the paper or watching the news.

"He listens," Phyllis comments, "but he makes it clear it's a chore. And when I finally get all this off my chest I ask about his day. He usually responds with, 'The same old thing,' and other noninformative remarks. He tells me nothing about his day. I want him to be a part of my world and I want to share his."

Several issues need to be addressed here. First of all, Arnie has a different temperament than Phyllis has and doesn't need to talk out the day's events as she does. In fact, Arnie would rather not talk at all. His work requires talking throughout the day. When he arrives home, he wants peace and quiet until the stress subsides.

One other factor comes into play. Dr. Pierre Mornell, physician and author, notes that the male need for time-out is related to brain function.[4] The left hemisphere of the brain governs speech and analytic thought. The right brain governs the visual, more intuitive part of life. Men specialize in their tendency to use the left hemisphere anyway, but particularly is this hemisphere overworked when a man is employed in a profession such as Arnie's, requiring extreme exertion of the analytical capacities. When Phyllis requires more concentration from him through listening, it is more than he can take.

Phyllis' job is no picnic either, but she has transition time after arriving home before Arnie walks in. According to Dr. Mornell, everyone needs time-out, time to shift from left to right brain to relax. Some time-out activities might include reading the paper, watching TV, working on a hobby, listening to music, jogging, exercise, yard work. Even cooking supper and setting the table provide a change of pace.

Couples need to share what is going on in their worlds to develop intimacy, but most people need time-out after returning from work. Greet each other affectionately and pleasantly, and then take twenty to thirty minutes or more as transition time. Following this, each spouse should grant the other a period of total attention—the kind you gave each other when dating.

Another factor may explain why Arnie doesn't want to talk when he gets home. Dr. James J. Lynch, professor of psychology and author of *The Language of the Heart: The Body's Response to Human Dialogue*, shows that when people talk, their blood pressure rises.[5] Since professors talk all day, Arnie's blood pressure could be high. When a man asks for peace and quiet, he may simply be responding to his body's intense need for quiet time lest he collapse.

A Loyola University study on differing needs showed that men who wanted close relationships were more immune to stress and suffered fewer physical health problems than men who didn't desire intimate ties. Researchers interviewed twelve hundred adults and found that a high-drive intimacy in women provided greater happiness but didn't provide a buffer against stress or affect their physical health. A powerful urge for closeness in men did not provide happiness but did correlate with high stress tolerance and fewer physical ailments. This research implies that intimacy is a strong coping mechanism for males and greatly influences their health.[6]

As mentioned earlier, men and women also have differing communication patterns which originate in childhood and affect later life. Girls tend to play in small groups, frequently with a "best friend." The focus of their friendship centers on discussing life and sharing "secrets." The friendship is dependent on talking and mutual sharing. Whether the information shared is trivial or important is not the issue; it is the experience of sharing that builds closeness between the two. Outside girls usually find it difficult to break into this twosome but if admitted would be treated as equals. Girls prefer conflict-free, best-friend relationships. When conflict is encountered, the relationship is usually broken, with little hope for reconciliation.

Boys, on the other hand, play in large groups. Their time together is spent more in activity than in talking. Outside boys find entry into the group easy, but once in, they must jockey for position within the group. This colors the tone of their conversations. Rather than sharing secrets, boys engage in king-of-the-mountain play and can-you-top-this stories to prove masculinity. To improve their status within the group, they argue about who is best at what and challenge the stories of others, in addition to other ploys.[7]

Both sexes grow up with these divergent, partially learned and partially inherited patterns of communicating, eventually attempting to establish an intimate relationship. A woman is searching for an improved version of her best friend, with whom she can share all. A man who reciprocates by sharing inner feelings, telling secrets from the past and childhood difficulties, will melt her heart.

Reliable data show that men tend to define intimacy in terms of sharing an activity with a woman: eating together, an ocean-side walk, or a visit to a quaint hideaway.[8] To him, little or nothing is lost if there is no sharing of secrets.

Even when a couple shares on an intimate level, it will probably have different meanings to each. She feels a deep emotional closeness as they share feelings and talk things over. He will more likely feel an emptiness or that the relationship isn't working if he has to keep talking things over. If she attempts to strengthen the relationship by talking about a problem, he may effectively sidestep each little talk because he views it as weakening the relationship. Hence the relationship is endangered even when both are doing what they consider their best to save it. Each views the situation through a filtering system which makes sense to them but to which the other responds negatively.

Cathy told Randy about a particularly difficult situation she faced at work. As she got into her story, she relived all the details, trying to make it clear who said what and exactly what transpired. Throughout the story, Randy wisecracked and interrupted her train of thought with side issues. His joking about the situation infuriated her. Cathy wanted understanding of her feelings and perhaps some sharing of an equal magnitude from him. Instead Randy offered advice, attempted to solve her problem, and questioned her interpretation of the situation, in addition to the joking. Not only did Cathy feel that Randy hadn't listened but that he didn't care about her feelings either. Randy did care but responded more as males would in a locker room.

Cathy's bid for closeness resulted in emotional distance. She attempted to reestablish intimacy by talking and sharing secrets with Randy—the only way she knew how. Randy responded in the only way he understood, by offering more advice. The more she strove for intimacy by talking and exposing her inner self, the more advice he gave. Result: Cathy felt incompetent and very alone, and Randy couldn't understand why she couldn't solve her problem when he gave her the answer. Each viewed the relationship as mutually frustrating and completely unsatisfying.

Men need intimacy or they wouldn't seek it, but they find intimacy threatening at their individual level. Once they attain it, they will frequently pull away. Such behavior is baffling to women because once they find intimacy, their heart's desire is to maintain it. Men desire it but not too much at one time. This explains the yo-yo effect of many extramarital affairs. A man will get very close to a woman and then withdraw to the safety of his work and marriage until his need for intimacy resurfaces.

Bickering and quarreling can also become attempts to retreat to safety. If a man feels he is about to be devoured through closeness or demands for it, he may deliberately promote separateness by creating an atmosphere of antagonism.

Attaining an intimate marriage revolves around the ability to understand and accommodate these differing needs. Most of us want our partners to be best friends and lovers, but each may have divergent ideas on how to attain that goal. Simple misunderstandings about how males and females view intimacy can keep an otherwise positive couple stewing in their own juices. Remember: The style may be different, but the goal is the same—to feel closer to someone each cares about.

A couple was driving to dinner to celebrate their twenty-fifth wedding anniversary. All details had been carefully tended to. Her dress was new for the occasion; her hair and nails were specially done. She glanced at the handsome man behind the wheel. Why did she feel so empty on this special evening? What happened to the great love they once shared? In an effort to sort out the dilemma, she almost hugged her side of the car. Finally she verbalized her thoughts aloud:

"You aren't romantic with me anymore. Why don't you love me like you used to?" In his quiet, unshakable manner, he replied, "Who moved?"

Women are frequently quick to blame a lack of closeness on their husbands. In fact, in the CI, women were five times more likely to blame their husbands for a lack of intimacy than men were to blame their wives. A closer look at the relationship might bring a different picture into focus. Before blaming your partner for a lack of intimacy, look closely at yourself.

Drifting Apart

Emotional closeness is rare for some couples. Why are some people so afraid of being known? Respondents to my CI feared emotional closeness for the following reasons, in descending order:

Males	Females
1. fear of rejection by partner	1. fear of rejection by partner
2. painful memories from the past	2. unresolved problems within current relationship
3. unresolved problems within current relationship	3. been hurt too badly to try
4. been hurt too badly to try	4. painful memories from the past

When asked the reasons behind not revealing more of themselves, 10 percent of the males and 14 percent of the females said they were already revealing all of themselves to their partners. Eight percent of the males and 4 percent of the females felt it wasn't necessary. Other reasons ranked in descending order were fear of rejection; fear of having it used against them; too painful to discuss.

When asked about painful memories or unresolved problems from the past, 11 percent of the males and 26 percent of the females had attempted to bury such closet skeletons but were unable to do so. While 7 percent of the men had tried confiding these to their partners, 20 percent of the females had. Women are more likely to risk revealing their pasts than are men.

Many people never feel good enough about themselves or safe enough with their partners to reveal their true selves. They either don't know how or are afraid of the consequences.

It is criticism that breeds fear. Every negative remark pushes a partner away. He or she will retreat behind whatever mask can be created to shield themselves from a partner who is viewed as an attacker.

Many of us remain totally ignorant of how much criticism, condemnation, and insensitivity is conveyed to our partners daily. Some relationships involve constant unacceptance, and it is nearly impossible for a couple to become intimates in such a climate. One husband expressed, "I can't tell my wife how I feel. All she ever does is put me down." As long as this man hears the language of unacceptance, he'll have no opportunity for intimacy and neither will she. Yet she may be just the wife who cries, "My husband never shares his feelings with me!"

We all have a fear of having someone get to know the real us and then be found out. It's risky business. Being rejected is one of man's greatest hurts. If we admit this fear, we might have to admit we are not nearly as confident about ourselves as we like to portray. The mask might slip and reveal our lack of worth.

It is much easier to discuss a problem than reveal a feeling. When discussing a problem, we can always change our minds in order to save face. When we reveal feelings, we expose our inner selves.

I can give you a gift easier than I can expose my inner feelings to you. There is little risk in giving you a gift since I will receive appreciation in return. But if I open myself up to you, reveal my inner feelings, and stand before you emotionally naked, I am at your mercy. Unless you understand and accept my feelings, I could experience a rejection almost as traumatic as a slow death.

So it is safer for me to do things for you, go places with you, and provide for you than it is for me to sit down and bare my soul to you—to tell you truthfully how I feel about you, us, our past, our future, my dreams. But until I am able to do this with you and for you, I have given you nothing. I have kept myself, the most important gift of all, from you.

Madeleine L'Engle, in her book *Walking on Water*, tells of a pious rabbi who was confronted one day by a devoted and youthful follower. In a moment of almost unreasoning passion, the young man blurted, " 'Oh, Master, I love you!'

"The ancient sage looked up from his books and asked his fervent disciple, 'Do you know what hurts me, my son?'

"The young man was puzzled. Composing himself he stuttered, 'I don't understand your question, Rabbi. I am trying to tell you how much you mean to me and you confuse me with irrelevant questions.'

" 'My question is neither confusing nor irrelevant,' rejoined the rabbi, 'for if you do not know what hurts me, how can you truly love me?' "

Likewise, if we are not revealing ourselves to a partner, we are standing in the way of receiving love.

The ultimate would be to attain a relationship in which we could share our deepest fears and greatest joys in perfect safety. Never would there be rejection. But this simply isn't possible. We're all human and sooner or later, after expressing feelings, your partner will fail you, put you down, misinterpret, or inadvertently reject you. Exasperated, you can withdraw, saying, "That's it! I'll never tell her [him] a thing again!" But unless you risk exposing yourself again and again, it is impossible to maintain intimacy.

You must risk something in order to achieve intimacy in a relationship. By sealing yourself off from an open sharing of feelings, you may protect yourself from further hurt, but you also cut yourself off from closeness. Hurts of the past become more bearable when shared with someone you love.

Drawing Closer

Intimacy comes with self-disclosure. Self-disclosure contributes to a more interesting and exciting relationship. The thought of revealing your real self may be as scary as the thought of hang gliding. But even if you are not revealing inner feelings, you can't help disclosing yourself. Your silence and refusal to reveal yourself communicates a strong message to your partner: "I do not trust you or care about you enough to make this effort." Rather than sending this negative message, which is a destroyer of intimacy, why not learn to disclose yourself appropriately and effectively.

Self-disclosure means you will communicate information about yourself to someone, and it must be verbal disclosure. Exposing secret thoughts to a diary cannot be considered self-disclosure. True self-disclosure means you will reveal new information and new thoughts and feelings. It is more than small talk or rehashing things previously discussed. It may include observations about something you have experienced, feelings about your past or present situations, thoughts about yourself or others, needs and desires you have or have had. It also implies implicit honesty.

How Open Are You?

Our "self" is made up of four parts: the Open Self, Blind Self, Hidden Self, and Unknown Self. To help you understand various selves and how open or closed you are in each area, study the diagram.

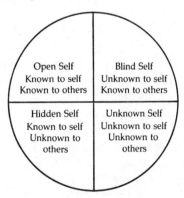

The Open Self contains thoughts and acts known to you and others. The Blind Self represents habits, mannerisms, hang-ups you are unaware of but which are apparent to others. The Hidden Self keeps all your secret thoughts, experiences, and feelings that you never share with others.

The last section, the Unknown Self, houses the unconscious or subconscious, which surfaces only through dreams or reprogramming.

These four human dynamics do not remain static or fixed. Thoughts, feelings, and observations are always on the move. Everything that happens to you is taken in through the Hidden Self and dispersed from there. What is unimportant to you is forgotten and stored in the Unknown compartment. Things you remember but do not feel comfortable in sharing get stored with other Hidden events. Still other events perpetuate behavior patterns and habits of which you are not aware and thus move to the Blind Self. Things you want to share with others get stored with the Open Self. Insights about your Hidden or Blind Self may be gained and shared, thus shifting them to the Open Self.

The shift of information from the Blind or Hidden Self to the Open Self is self-disclosure. Those who excel at self-disclosure are open with themselves and others. The Open Self will be larger than the remaining three (*see* diagram on page 175). The larger the Open section, the more likely you are to experience intimacy. The larger the hidden section, the less likely you will achieve intimacy unless conscious changes are made.

If the Open Self is so desirable, why isn't there a rush on it? Many reasons exist to keep people closed. Unwritten social etiquette dictates that it isn't polite to tell too much too soon. Others remain closed due to fear: fear of being rejected or punished; fear of losing reputation, respect, or friends. Underlying insecurities are also a major contributor to maintaining a closed stance toward others.

You may fear self-knowledge; if your faults and shortcomings become known to self then you'll be expected to change, and that's risky. For these and other reasons, many people consider it safer to remain closed.

The amount of self you reveal to others is not constant but forever changing. Socially you may be open, but on a personal level, with your partner, you may remain reserved and cautious. How much of self you reveal is also dependent on your temperament, mood, and the subject at hand. The

diagrams on page 176 graphically portray the same person in different situations.

Research into the subject of self-disclosure confirms that we tend to be more open with those close to us, particularly marriage partners, family members, and close friends. This is true for healthy persons who have not suffered severe emotional trauma. Unless dealt with and resolved, trauma from the past haunts the present.

Studies show that from age seventeen to fifty, under normal circumstances people increase in their ability to reveal and relate to others. After the age of fifty the tendency is to become more reserved, especially when a person has been emotionally "burned" by a number of trusted people. Becoming adept at the art of self-disclosure is a matter of achieving balance— learning how much to reveal to whom, about what, and when.

If your Blind Self is too large, many detrimental habits and faults can hinder you in achieving successful business and interpersonal relationships. If it is too small, you'll never see yourself as you are. On the other hand, you can analyze yourself, reducing the Blind Self to nothing while becoming a psychological dingdong. If your Hidden Self is too large, you'll be withdrawn and out of touch; if it's too small, nothing shared with you will ever be safe. In other words, balance is needed. In marriage, the ideal is to be more open.[9]

Moving Toward Self-Disclosure

Learning how to reveal yourself progresses through three stages:

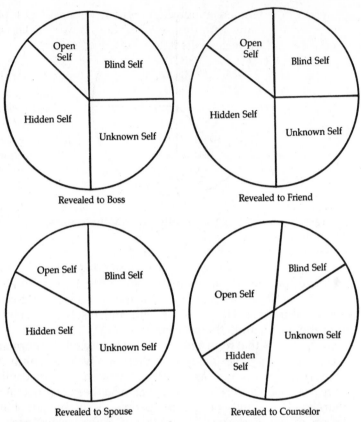

Revealed to Boss

Revealed to Friend

Revealed to Spouse

Revealed to Counselor

Stage 1: the computer stage   At this stage, only facts are dealt with. You share information about your job, car, friends, a hobby, or an interesting experience. Due to carefully constructed emotional barriers, you stick strictly to the facts. No personal feelings or opinions are revealed; emotional topics are off-limits.

Stage 2: the yesterday stage   You move beyond mere facts to include the thoughts, feelings, and needs you have regarding any topic being discussed. Included might be your food preferences, religious beliefs, favorite music, goals for the future, or your saddest experience. Stage 2 sharing builds on the facts from stage 1 but expands by expressing personal convictions, tastes, preferences, and feelings. You tell your partner how you feel about each topic. Experiences or topics revealed deal only with the past or future, however. Discussion about present feelings is too risky at this point.

Stage 3: the present-moment stage   Ultimate self-disclosure involves sharing how you think, what you are feeling, and what your present needs are. You risk revealing how your mate's behavior is affecting you at present: whether you are feeling negative or positive; how you are holding back your feelings; how you are slanting your story to make yourself look good; how angry, nervous, or relaxed you are, and so forth. Only when you can reveal an adequate amount of present-moment feelings are you engaging in complete self-disclosure.

Self-Disclosure Has Its Limits

How much self-disclosure is too much? Can a good thing be overdone? Naturally. You might announce to your spouse, "I am sick of living with you and your faults. I haven't loved you in years." A loose translation might label this self-disclosure. A better label might be "killer talk." A fine line separates honest communication from total devastation.

There is no need to verbalize every negative thought that pops into your head. A current obsession to communicate obscures the fact that, to maintain intimacy, some things should not be expressed. Henry Spitz, a noted psychiatrist, says, "Some of the most devastating things I've ever heard follow the phrase, 'Let me tell you how I honestly feel.' " Total honestly without regard for a partner's feelings is cruel.

Several studies on this topic by psychologists indicate that many of the things couples quarrel over can be traced to the earliest days of marriage, when irrevocable atrocities were verbalized. In one study published in *The Family Coordinator*, couples were asked, "Does your spouse have a tendency to say things that would be better left unsaid?" Those who were getting along fairly well answered no. Those who were having problems answered yes.

My CI showed similar results. When asked this question, 61 percent agreed that their partner at some time had said something that would have been better left unsaid. Over 70 percent of these things involved a former spouse or an extramarital affair. We simply cannot tear each other to pieces and expect love to remain intact. It is wiser to leave some things unsaid for the sake of the relationship.

But how much should be revealed to a partner? This is a key question for the formerly married. Intimate details of a previous marriage are usually better off buried with the past. Revealing too much may impart insecurities, serious questions, or comparisons to an otherwise secure and trusting partner.

Sexual indiscretions committed prior to marriage should be divulged either before the wedding or not at all. This is not to say that every sexual encounter must be confessed. Confession may be honest, but citing confidential details serves no purpose and would probably be detrimental.

Before asking for total disclosure or delivering it yourself, you need to ask yourself some insightful questions: Do I (or does my partner) really need to hear that? What will be the effect on our relationship if I do tell? For what reasons do I need to tell (or hear) that information? Will total disclosure help or hinder in this situation?

Disclosure of adultery and other personal problems must be approached on an individual basis. The wrong move could throw you into a crushing catastrophe. Seek the advice of a professional Christian marital therapist before making any decisions relative to the future, and do it before too many irreparable choices have been made.

Many things are better left unsaid in spite of the push for total openness. Some honesty can boomerang. Withholding hurtful truths is not the same as being untruthful. If an intimate relationship is going to be maintained, cruel and damaging comments and information must be quieted.

Tuning Up and Tuning In

Half the struggle for intimacy lies with self-disclosure. The other half lies with the art of accepting shared feelings. Note this is a two-way street. How frequently I hear, "We have no intimacy in our marriage. My husband [wife] won't talk to me about his [her] feelings." Talking about feelings is only half of intimacy. The other half is having shared feelings openly accepted and understood. True intimacy requires nonjudgmental acceptance. One could spill his guts indefinitely, but without acceptance, intimacy cannot occur.

If you were experiencing an anxiety-producing event, would you feel comfortable in sharing it with your partner? If your partner were going through an emotional crisis, would he or she hold it in or share it with you? Barely half of all husbands and wives in the CI said their partners could accept their ideas and feelings supportively, and 20 percent indicated their partners rarely or never did.

Mastering this ability means you must develop sensitivity in three areas: reflective listening, the clarification of feelings, and the invitation to share more feelings.

Reflective listening   The best way to show understanding and acceptance is to verbally reflect the feelings "heard" from your partner.

HUSBAND: (*I-message*) I really resented it tonight at prayer group when I was giving my interpretation of Hebrews 11 and you kicked me under the table. It made me feel like I can never speak without asking for permission first.

WIFE: (*reflective listening*) When I kicked you, it made you feel rebellious since you viewed it as an attempt at control.

Notice the wife did not attempt to defend her actions, sidestep the issue through an apology, or deny her intentions. She reflected his feelings, clearly acknowledging that she heard, understood, and accepted them as valid.

Clarification of feelings   Sometimes feelings are shared vaguely or indirectly, making it difficult to ascertain what is being conveyed. Under these circumstances it is appropriate to ask for clarification.

HUSBAND: Sometimes I just hate coming home.

WIFE: Do you dislike our home or are you feeling angry?

Questions frequently detract from the feelings, but they can also be used effectively to probe when a situation appears muddy.

The invitation to share more   Some people try to share feelings but are not articulate in expressing themselves. Such persons can respond positively when you assess the feelings accurately and extend an invitation to say more.

WIFE: (*shares vague feelings*) I miss California.

HUSBAND: (*extends invitation to say more*) I'd like to hear more about what it is in California that you miss.

Make sure when first learning to accept feelings that you avoid some common traps:

- Avoid defending yourself: "I did not!"
- Avoid denying feelings: "You shouldn't feel that way."
- Avoid telling your partner he is wrong or bad for feeling "that way": "You shouldn't be so upset over this."
- Avoid analyzing the problem: "The real problem is. . . ."
- Avoid offering to solve the problem: "This is what to do. . . ."

It is impossible to be intimate with someone who does not wish to share intimacy with you. Mutual consent must accompany the desire. If one person desires closeness and the other rejects closeness, there can be no intimacy. An affectionate relationship may exist, but intimacy flows in both directions.

God's plan for marriage is that a couple live together in an intimate atmosphere of respect. Through the closeness of daily interaction, our attitudes and actions are constantly impacting on each other. When we feel accepted, it affirms us and draws us together in bonds of mutually affirming love. Rejection closes us off from each other. We have a profound ability to build one another up or tear one another down.

How Intimacy Changes Over the Years

Intimacy does not remain constant but changes over the course of time. Women in particular seem to get an unrealistic picture of the constantness of intimacy, placing unreasonable demands for self-disclosure on their partners. Intimacy within any relationship is never static but always on the move, shifting and changing.

Over the course of time, any couple may find themselves drifting apart. Demands of work, children, home, parents, church, and friends engulf them. Exhaustion takes over. There is little time or energy for each other. Frustration, hurt, and anger separate the two. Each wonders if their marriage was a mistake and if they'll ever connect again.

Those new at marriage may think the relationship over, but those whose marriages have stood the test of time recognize that if you hang in there, you will get close again. Time is on your side. All of this is part of the ebb and flow of normal relationships. Intimacy is not a constant, unchanging phenomenon but a pattern where closeness comes and goes. In other words, don't scrap the relationship just because you feel intimacy is at an all-time low. When this happens, it is simply a signal to recall closeness. To restore intimacy try the following:

Take a humor break.   "If you and your partner are laughing less than fifteen times per day—including three belly laughs—you are underlaughed," says Hendric Wiesinger, psychologist and researcher on the effects of laughter. Humor contributes to closeness because it indicates similar values, interests, intelligence, and imagination.

If you wish to up your quota of laughs, here are some tips:

- Learn what kind of humor appeals to your partner. Snip cartoons from newspapers, creating a file of smiles. Try putting one next to your partner's place setting at your next meal.
- Share a funny story you've read or heard. By swapping amusing experiences, you'll build bonds of "pleasure closeness."
- Play with words. Rather than accepting everything said at face value, run it through your brain again, looking for a double meaning.
- Tell a joke. If a long-winded joke is out of the question, master one-liners or invent quick-witted comebacks.
- Have a giggle fit. Free your comic side to cut loose; make funny faces and noises. Let your light side show.
- Develop a sense of playfulness. Share private jokes and nicknames. Create private traditions shared by just the two of you. Playful communication creates a sense of confidentiality.

If you and your mate aren't laughing together, it's time to begin. Scripture speaks to this: "A merry heart doeth good like a medicine" (Proverbs 17:22 KJV).

Have a weekly hour of power talk.   Here a couple agrees to spend one hour a week talking without interruption. For thirty minutes, the wife will talk about herself and her needs within the relationship. Off-limits: the failure of her husband to meet her needs. Instead, she must focus on her needs, her fears, and who she is within and outside the relationship. During the wife's thirty minutes, the husband is not allowed to interrupt or make any comments. Because he cannot be forming a response, he is freer to hear things from his wife he might not hear under normal circumstances. Next is his turn to talk for thirty minutes about his needs. He must follow the same plan, talking only about his needs without censuring or blaming his wife for failures. Note: *Do not settle for fifteen minutes of talk.* Experts have noted that people talk rapidly and superficially for the first fifteen minutes and only during the second fifteen minutes do they move to a deeper, more insightful level.

Take on the intimacy marathon.   Nathaniel Branden, Ph.D., counselor and author, recommends a twelve-hour marathon for couples whose intimacy needs a boost. The marathon is not designed for daily use but for that special once-a-year occasion.

Both partners must agree to spend twelve uninterrupted hours together without children, television, books, newspapers, phone calls, or disturbances of any kind except for meals and bathroom visits. Your conversation can include anything that is personal. No talk about car repairs, a child's failing grades, or installation of sprinkler systems is allowed. All talk must be personal and focused on your relationship. If neither of you cares to talk, you may sit in silence.

Some couples immediately discover an unbelievable closeness. Others feel self-conscious and stiff. Some become irritated or actually angry, but invariably they begin to talk. A quarrel may ensue. After their differences have been aired, however, each feels more loving. The resulting closeness often spurs them to make love. The intimacy marathon worked, they conclude!

Frequently couples go their way at this point, even though the twelve hours is not up. Hearttalk is forsaken. A deeper level of communication and intimacy that could develop at this point is missed. Discussion now spontaneously centers on hopes and dreams for the future that may never before have been revealed. An unprecedented level of intimacy comes to those who complete the twelve hours together.

Some other more simple but fun ways to create intimacy are listed below:

Take a class together.   A cooking, art, or landscaping class will develop a common interest and provide a new topic of conversation.

Meet for lunch out once a week.   Meeting at midday breaks the monotony of the week and provides something to look forward to.

Challenge your mate to a pillow fight.   After collapsing in laughter, share some intimate feelings about lovemaking.

Read a book together.   Take turns reading aloud, stopping frequently to discuss your reactions to what you are reading.

Create a new tradition.   This should be something you will remember and celebrate each year. One couple celebrates the date they attended a Compleat Marriage seminar. A special evening is planned and they review their workbooks and commitment to each other.

True intimacy is closeness, fun, and romance all wrapped up together. Experiencing it is an adventure that enhances life. Attempts to live without it result in a vague emptiness. With it, all of life takes on new meaning.

7 Sexually Speaking: Strangers in the Night

Genuine intimacy must first be achieved outside the bedroom before it can be achieved inside. Lifetime passion stems from intimacy, not from expert manipulation of the genitals.

A husband complained to "Dear Abby" that since his wife became an attorney there had been no performance, no common consent, a termination of interest, and no interest in sex. Abby recommended some candid communication (plain talk) between the party of the first part and party of the second part.

A frustrated wife wrote Dr. Joyce Brothers about feeling "used" after lovemaking and her desire to talk and cuddle with her husband. "Do you think it will ever change?" she asked. "It can," Dr. Brothers replied, "but whether it does depends on whether you're able to talk with your husband about your feelings."

A survey of more than twenty-six thousand men and women identified communication as one of the most important aspects of lovemaking. "More than any other factor," the survey underscored, "effectiveness in conveying one's preferences and feelings about sex is the key to a good sex life."

"What's the most important thing you've learned from your research about sex?" Alexandra Penney, author of *Great Sex*, was asked. Answer: "Before all else, communication is the vital, critical, crucial, essential ingredient in sex. 'Communication' is so widely overused and overexplained that I'm sick of the word. But the fact remains that one of the greatest problems in most relationships is the inability of the partners to ask for what they want and need."

Sex experts and authorities are in agreement that couples should talk about their sexual problems. Yet few, if any, give more than a hint or two about how to accomplish this lofty goal.

Why is it that the most fascinating subject known to humankind is the most difficult for a couple to talk about? Why is it that the same couple who can pore over house plans by the hour fall silent when faced with talking about their sex lives?

Some people believe sex is as natural as breathing, and therefore you don't need to discuss it. After all, anything as natural as sex should occur spontaneously without planning or discussion. This belief works well as long as everything functions as it should. But what will happen to such a couple should they encounter a problem?

Others believe your partner should be sensitive enough to meet your desires without having to be told. This is one of the worst traps couples fall into. Unless your partner excels in mind reading, there is no way he or she can "just know" what you like and want.

One woman said, "I don't want to have to tell Harv what I want. We've been married for twelve years. If he doesn't know by now, he never will. And if I have to *tell* him to do something, it wouldn't be the same. I want him to do it because he loves me." Poor Harv is left in the dark regarding his wife's sexual preferences because of her belief in his mind-reading capabilities. And if Harv fails to mind-read correctly, she will label him an unloving and inconsiderate husband. Unfair!

There are those who feel it isn't necessary to talk about sex and instead rely on nonverbal cues to communicate what is and isn't desired. By pulling away, moving a hand, or changing positions, it is possible to convey what is and isn't desired. Early in relationships, most couples do rely on nonverbals. Through touch and the guiding of hands, a message is delivered and received. Such nonverbal methods work—up to a point—but such signals can easily be misread.

Still others are conflict avoiders. When a problem of any kind, including a sexual problem, surfaces, their heads go in the sand. Some people do not sense the need for talking about sex, or they are uncomfortable, or they think it isn't romantic to have to talk about it. Others are afraid.

The most difficult communication lesson is how to communicate sexually. People can revert to the most childish ways of sending indirect messages when sex is involved. "My husband never asks for sex," a class participant told me. "All he does is drag around the house with a hangdog expression on his face. When I ask him what's wrong, he says, 'What's wrong? We haven't had sex in a week and you ask me what's wrong!'"

So-called communication methods such as tantrums, silence, pouting, irritability, name-calling, and threats are some tactics used in dealing with sexual issues. It seems anything but open, honest talking and listening will suffice.

Participants in the Communication Inventory revealed the same reluctance to discuss sex openly. About 30 percent of both sexes said they could definitely discuss their sexual relationship often with their partners. The remaining 70 percent were either unsure about whether they could or definitely could not. A whopping 72 percent clearly indicated they wanted their partners to be more open in discussing sexual feelings with them.

Those who can't open up and talk about what feels good and what doesn't, what they want or don't want, are likely candidates for feelings of frustration, anger, and resentment. Such feelings are hardly conducive to superior sex. Marriage counselors report even severe marriage problems can be solved quickly when couples can talk openly.

"When we don't take the time to talk our problems through, I feel so tense and irritable. But after we talk about things, I immediately feel closer to my husband. It's almost as if he has caressed me physically. Then I often feel like making love," a woman who had learned the value of open communication at a Compleat Marriage seminar confided.

In the end, those who want superior sex are going to have to make known, inform, discuss, tell, reveal, disclose, divulge, state, declare, say—in other words, TALK with each other about—what is wanted or needed.

Intimate Encounters

Radio commentator Paul Harvey tells the story of a young husband who went to the hospital nursery to see his newborn son. After he had a brief visit with his child, a nurse asked if the new father wouldn't like to talk with his wife. "Why should I talk with her now?" he snapped. "We haven't talked to each other in two years." It is a pathetic state of affairs when a couple opens up to each other sexually but not emotionally.

The use of sex to relieve tension, prove love still exists, or confirm masculinity or femininity may create the illusion of intimacy but eventually leads to emptiness as well as boring and routine sex. Unless a relationship possesses openness and trust, along with a sense of freedom, sex is not a genuine expression of love. A couple rushing to genital intimacy while neglecting emotional intimacy may think that to save their marriage they must learn what buttons to push for maximum success. In such cases, even the most ingenious techniques lead to unsatisfactory routine experiences. The search for intimacy may continue: new partners, novel methods, proficient techniques, a just-read book, intensive therapy, a seminar, or the latest film.

Nothing works.

One can learn to become orgasmic and how to help others achieve the experience. But genuine intimacy must first be achieved outside the bedroom before it can be achieved inside. Lifetime passion stems from intimacy, not from expert manipulation of the genitals.

It is only as a couple learn the meaning of genuine love, as they practice accepting each other at face value, as they learn the principles of effective communication, as they unravel individual differences and preferences, as they practice mutual respect and trust, that they can expect a mutually satisfying sexual experience. Healthy sexual satisfaction results from harmony in the other areas of the relationship. Likewise, negative feelings in any of these areas often show up first in a couple's sex life.

The sexual union or "becoming one" is the culmination of working toward a healthy adjustment in each of these areas. When one (or several) of these essential total-relationship ingredients is missing, simply talking about the problem will not assist the couple in achieving superior sex. The sexual relationship cannot be separated from the rest of the relationship. Instead, a strong exciting sexual relationship serves as a barometer of the total relationship.

Whenever a couple confides to me that they have "a sex problem," I look first within the context of the total relationship. Is he meeting her emotional needs for love and security? Is she meeting his needs for appreciation and respect? Does this couple accept one another or is their relationship dominated by nagging and criticism, causing each to avoid and resent the other? Has this couple mastered basic communication skills? Can each state what he or she means and listen caringly? Do they understand their differing needs and attempt to satisfy those needs? Is there an equal distribution of power and authority or is one controlling the other? Only as each of these questions is satisfactorily settled is it possible to discuss a sex problem.

Leave any of these relationship questions unanswered and they will color and distort discussion of sex. Any unsettled problem, hurt, resentment, power struggle, or misunderstanding will be carried into the bedroom. Long-lasting sexual harmony and superior sex are results of building a mutually satisfying relationship.

Covers for Lovers: Anger and Fear

Much trouble in the bedroom is the result of unresolved anger. It begins with little hurts that never get settled. These hurts build into resentments. In my collection of cartoons is a classic that shows a wife with trowel in hand building a solid brick wall down the middle of the bed. Her husband enters the room, sees the wheelbarrow and mortar, sizes up the situation, and says, "You still mad?"

Who can get into bed and embrace someone toward whom you have feelings of resentment and anger? The dutiful wife may allow her husband to use her body but punish him by cutting herself off from any sign of enjoyment. She'll teach him! Physical closeness is next to impossible because they are not close emotionally.

The bedroom is used to act out many problems in other areas of a couple's relationship. A woman may feel totally controlled by her husband, unable to make decisions or move on her own. As a result, her self-worth suffers badly. She rejects his sexual advances, inventing one excuse after another. Probably she is unaware of how she is attempting "to win," by getting back at him so she can control something in her life.

Sexual withholding can be a nonverbal way of punishing each other or expressing anger. A full 20 percent of the CI respondents admitted to withholding sexual privileges as punishment. Withholding sex is essentially a power struggle.

Our nonverbals are always at work, even when we are asleep. Feelings of hostility can be conveyed by staking out one's territory, turning one's back, moving as far away as possible. Rejection is signaled through such nonverbals.

In another situation, a husband becomes verbally abusive, calling his wife "stupid," "inadequate," and a "fat slob." He attacks her, but in reality he's concerned about some recent bouts he's had with erection failure. His masculine ego is too threatened to admit that *he* may have a problem, so he blames his wife.

The impotent husband generally harbors a great deal of unresolved anger against his wife. Over the years his hostility builds. Unable to express his anger directly, he gets back at her by not being able to have sex. The impotent husband needs to learn how to get his anger out through his mouth rather than through his genitals. Expressing anger directly is a frightening thought to many, but authorities testify that once it happens, increased interest and arousal returns. Hostility is an inhibitor of the desire phase of sexual response. When hostility, whether open or repressed, enters the bedroom, it can short-circuit the desire, excitement, or orgasmic phase.

Another roadblock to talking over sexual concerns is fear of being laughed at, made fun of, criticized, or thought of as weird. In other words, the big fear is *rejection*. Whenever we sense a lack of total acceptance, fear stops us from opening up.

As liberated as women are today, they are not without a complete set of fears over aspects of their sexuality. Women probably suffer more anxiety about their weight than any other factor. Excessive poundage, in many women's minds, takes them out of the "most desirable" league and puts them into the least-desirable category, regardless of other redeeming attributes. Since one's sexual nature is forever hooked up with the psychological nature, if a woman feels her body is ugly or undesirable, she will be unable to respond sexually without embarrassment or fear. If her husband teases her— even in jest—about small breasts, skinny legs, or extra pounds, she will probably become self-conscious and uncomfortable during sexual encounters.

Women also worry about what is normal. Is it normal not to achieve orgasm every time? Is it normal to reach orgasm through manual stimulation of the clitoris only? How many times per week is it normal to have sex? Is it normal to want to be held after intercourse?

Fear of not having an orgasm is another sexual inhibitor for women, and being worried or fearful of not having one could foreclose the possibility. Others fear enjoyment because they have been reared in uptight homes where it was either implied or taught that sex is dirty or bad: "Nice girls don't . . ." "All boys want the same thing. . ." "All men think about is. . . ." Depending on the severity of the Victorian upbringing, such attitudes leave their mark. Still others are fearful of assuming a sexually aggressive role because they do not want their husbands to think of them as being too forward.

Males have their own set of fears, although they are less likely to admit or verbalize them. Though the concerns are different, men can experience as much anxiety over them, if not more, than women.

Whereas women are more vulnerable regarding appearance than men, men are not without their own set of hang-ups regarding their body build. Some men consider themselves "less than" because their bodies lack hairy chests or bulging muscles. Being short of stature, having baby-smooth skin or a deformity can cripple a man's performance in bed and greatly complicate his marriage.

Since a man cannot hide the fact that he either is or is not ready for intercourse, performance worries dominate the scene for him. If his wife fails to achieve orgasm, he may feel he has failed her in some way, that he lacks skills and abilities an expert lover should acquire. If she is unresponsive, it imparts serious questions in his mind about his sexual prowess.

As a man moves into his mid-life, he may fear a sexual slowdown. If a younger man has erection fears, they only intensify in the aging male. Will he be able to get an erection? Can he maintain it throughout intercourse? Will he be able to ejaculate? What if he fails?

Although a man may be enjoying the sexual experience immensely, he may have serious questions about his ability to satisfy his wife. Some men might even wonder how they stack up against other men. Men also wonder if what they want sexually is normal. Is what they secretly desire something that might be considered "kinky"?

These are some of the major fears men and women have. Once you face your fears in an open manner, you are better equipped to voice them and work toward a solution. The more closed you are to facing, revealing, or discussing them, the more difficult it will be. Open communication about deep fears brings you a giant step closer to breaking down barriers that stand in the way of deeper love and sexual intimacy, but these fears will not be verbalized in an atmosphere of criticism or rejection.

How to Respond When Fears Are Verbalized

In the past few months, there have been several times when John, age forty-three, failed to maintain an erection. He fears impotence and at the right time communicates this to his wife, Angie. When Angie hears his anxieties, she can respond in one of several ways.

Angie can mind-read. In spite of an honest message from John, she discounts what he said and reads into it her own interpretation. She believes John's impotence is directly related to her weight gain and thinks John no longer finds her attractive or sexually interesting. If she verbalizes her interpretation to him, he may attempt to correct her thinking and reassure her. But when this occurs she draws attention away from his problem to hers. In order to get attention back on his fears, now he'll have to restate them. This was probably an extremely painful admission in the first place. Reopening the subject now presents new complications. Angie didn't appear to hear him the first time. He fears she may not hear him again and instead focus on herself.

Angie might also deny his fear. "Honey, there's nothing to worry about. It happens to all men sometime or other. Don't worry about it. It won't happen again." This becomes a nagging question: "What if it does?" In attempting to reassure him, she has denied the problem. A denied problem is infinitely more difficult to solve.

Angie might avoid discussing the possibility of impotence with John lest she appear to be accusing him of failure or inadequacy. She fears drawing attention to the problem, so she avoids saying anything. But avoidance of the subject leaves both partners open to misleading assumptions.

How, then, should one respond when fears are verbalized? Fears and feelings should be accepted as legitimate concerns. John's fear of impotence should not be denied, discounted, or avoided. Instead, a comfortable, nonthreatening atmosphere should be created where he can share what is behind his fears. All the techniques of active listening should be employed. This will allow him to open up and receive some of the acceptance and reassurance he so desperately needs.

"You seem concerned over this problem. Let's talk about it," or "I hear your frustration over what has been happening in our sex life. Tell me more about what you think is behind it," or "You are worried over what's happening to you sexually. I am happy that you feel comfortable in discussing it with me. Tell me what you are feeling right now." Such lead-ins lay a foundation for John to share.

At a later time, now that Angie is aware of John's fears, they can work together toward a solution. In the meantime, their lovemaking may center less on the genitals and focus more on holding, hugging, and stroking nonsexual areas of the body. Sharing warmth, tenderness, and affection now becomes more important than genital contact. Such sharing may lead to further intimacy and eventually lovemaking. Both are now winners and sharing in the results of their victory. Should these attempts at self-help fail, they are in a better position to seek professional advice because they created an atmosphere in which they can talk about it.

A sexual problem, difficulty, or crisis can separate a couple or it can bond them together, depending on their response to it. If they are willing to trust each other and share their fears, they can more firmly cement their relationship. Sex is like that: It can rip a couple apart or bond them together more securely.

Unclogging the Lines

Bud complained to Elaine that their sex life was really in a rut and suggested they go to a motel for the weekend and try some new things. Elaine froze. *What new things?* she asked herself. In her opinion, their sex life was fine the way it was. She brought with her to marriage many shoulds and should nots from a strict religious upbringing. Bud had tried to discuss sex with her before and she always avoided it by changing the subject or making a quick escape.

Alice finds Ron's touch too rough. In an effort not to hurt his feelings, she avoids sex as much as possible. When they do have sex, she endures the discomfort with much effort, afraid to clue him in on what would be more pleasing to her.

Several years ago Ted asked Ann for a sexual preference he would greatly enjoy. Ann refused and they have never discussed it since. Ted never says anything about it but secretly harbors resentment against Ann for not wanting to please him. He feels sexually frustrated.

Gloria doesn't want sex as frequently as Vern does. She thinks there is something wrong with Vern because all he wants is sex, sex, sex. Vern despises her unwilling, unresponsive nature. Bitter words have been exchanged over the matter, and now it has become such a sensitive issue that neither dares bring it up.

These couples reflect multitudes who have ongoing problems which are never fully discussed between partners. They are typical of the types of problems that result from a failure to verbalize thoughts, feelings, and wishes openly and honestly. Nonverbal cues can be misinterpreted or missed entirely. The advances made and approved by one can threaten or hurt the other. Efforts to communicate are sometimes refused.

Many of these attitudes were reflected in the CI. Only 29 percent of the males and 36 percent of the females would discuss a sexual problem with their mates if they encountered one. When asked if they had discussed their own sexual preferences with their partners, 35 percent of the males and 39 percent of the females said "definitely yes." Almost equal numbers said their partners had discussed their sexual preferences with them. When asked what they would most like to discuss with a partner, both sexes ranked their choices in similar fashion. In descending order, they listed techniques, frequency, and who should initiate sex. This is in line with a *Redbook* survey that identified the number of times a couple have sex as "the topic most argued about."

"It's too late for us," one woman said as she sighed deeply. "We've been married for years and never talked openly yet. I'm too embarrassed to bring up anything and if I did, my husband would die of shock. Our sex life isn't that bad. . .of course it isn't that good, either. . . . " Her voice trailed off. Unless a man and wife learn to communicate openly about sex, they will never enjoy sex at its best.

Maybe you have attempted to discuss sexual matters with your mate and received such negative responses that you vowed you would never try it again. Maybe you've never said anything out of fear of turning your partner off and creating an awkward, unpleasant situation. Maybe you've been laughed at or told your ideas were perverted. Thus you fear making yourself vulnerable to rejection again.

Yes, the risks are high, but in order to make progress in a clouded sexual situation, you have to unclog the communication lines and talk about it. Failure to state your needs and openly discuss problems can cost you the best in sexual pleasure.

Talk or silence? Both have a price. You decide, but the long-term rewards of clear communication are well worth the risk.

Baring Your Soul: Is Total Honesty Necessary?

Openness becomes a force for good by clarifying feelings and avoiding misunderstandings—in certain situations. In others, total frankness can be destructive. This holds true in all areas of a relationship, but it is particularly significant when our sexuality is involved.

Complete and total frankness can be brutal and selfish. Some people engage in it to seek forgiveness for their own actions. When confronted about the choice, the person may say, "Well, he [she] wanted to know everything." It is not always good to disclose "everything," even when it is true or asked for. It can be a need to relieve guilt by dumping it on another person, or it can be a way of venting hostility or obtaining revenge.

A woman teasingly pressured her husband to tell her how he felt about her excess weight. He wisely skirted the questions with creative responses like, "There's more of you to love," or "I love you just the way you are." She eventually pushed him too far and heard what she really didn't want to hear. It hurt.

Another husband admired large breasts, noticing and commenting on them whenever he saw some that pleased him. His wife, feeling she could never measure up to these beauties, asked if her breasts were too small. "To be honest, I wish your breasts were bigger, but I love you anyway," he answered. His wife suffered such a loss of self-worth that she lost all desire for sex.

Each of these responses was "open and honest," but each was also hurtful and detrimental to the relationship. To criticize a partner for something that can't be changed (like breast size) is needlessly cruel.

One man continually encouraged his wife to talk about her relationships prior to their marriage. She held back at first, fearing he might not take it well. Eventually she gave in and he became furiously jealous. His constant suspicion of her led to unending arguments.

Sexually Speaking: The When, the Where, the How

Before launching a discussion about something you do or do not want during lovemaking, build a platform of trust and respect. This means you must like your partner as he is and will respect his right to be different from you. It means you will allow him to possess his own feelings about matters, separate likes and dislikes, regardless of how different they may be from yours. Such a trust level builds a platform so you can talk about emotionally charged, potentially embarrassing topics with ease.

You may also wish to rehearse the entire scene in your mind in advance. Where and how will you approach your partner? Clearly visualize the setting. Now rehearse the script. What will you use for openers? How can you best state the problem and your needs? Practice an imaginary conversation with your mate. State the problem, using the words you will actually say. You may not be comfortable saying aloud some sex terms. Practice allows you to become more at ease using them.

How will you respond if your partner becomes defensive? In what manner will you meet objections? In detail, thoroughly plan out everything you can imagine happening. This prepares you for the event and yields a high rate of success.

The when   When is the best time to start an open, honest discussion about sex with your partner? "You have to watch your timing," wrote one wise respondent on the CI. "For us, it wouldn't work during lovemaking. That would be the worst possible time for me to talk to Sid about not pleasing me."

Most experts agree that except for compliments and positives about what you like, during sex is not the right moment to discuss anything sexual. However, *before* and *after* lovemaking are two excellent possibilities. "Discussion before sex," the same woman added, "can even become part of foreplay. Prior to making love, Sid and I sometimes share with each other some of our likes and dislikes. It becomes a real turn-on for both of us as we tell what we like best and are going to do for each other."

After making love may also be a good time to talk. "It is for us," Sally continued. "Sometimes Sid and I just lie in the darkness holding each other. It seems only natural to talk about what we just enjoyed. I can tell him how much I like what he did and even what I might like to have him do more of. Our conversations are a natural outgrowth of what we just experienced together. This way we don't have to plan what we're going to say." Others detest the instant-replay concept.

When you talk about it isn't as important as agreeing that a time to talk is needed. So whenever you become aware of an unfilled need or when you sense a problem brewing, that is the time to broach the subject. Even when problems have been simmering for years, it is not too late if sensitivity is used.

The where   Look for neutral comfortable ground where you can easily achieve an intimate level of communication. Do you have a special place where you usually talk problems through? The kitchen table? The sofa in the family room?

Generally speaking, bed is not the best place to discuss a sexual problem. Even the entire bedroom may be off-limits for discussion, as it frequently puts people on the defensive. Defensiveness must be eliminated before open communication can take place.

Wherever you decide to talk, make sure you are alone and free of all interruptions. Farm out the children, take the phone off the hook, and turn off the TV. If you find it difficult to achieve such privacy, you may need to schedule a night or weekend away where you can focus on each other without distraction.

Exception: Talking in bed, in the middle of the night, might work for some couples. Where big problems exist or embarrassed feelings run high, it may actually be easier to talk it out in total darkness. Darkness eliminates eye contact, which is difficult to maintain in troubled relationships. The darkness and privacy provided by the bedroom can work to advantage in such cases. Remember, however, that when communicating in darkness, you forfeit observing nonverbals. Fifty-five percent of the message is missing. A perception check or two might fill in the gap.

The how   Dan and Vickie have been married for eight years. Dan is an accountant for a large business firm. Vickie is a nurse who works part-time at a local hospital. They live in a charming, country-style home, which Vickie has decorated with antiques and country crafts. They share a passion for gardening and spend much of their spare time with their two young children outdoors on a friend's property, experimenting with growing various vegetables. They are both church leaders and are active in community affairs.

Scratch the surface of what appears to be "the perfect couple" and you will find a sexual problem. Dan is a premature ejaculator who doesn't know where or how to find help for his problem. He feels ashamed and guilty about not being able to extend the act of intercourse, but he feels it is too late, after all these years, to say anything to Vickie about the problem. Vickie doesn't want to hurt her husband so she fakes a quick release during lovemaking so he will think she is enjoying it also. She is afraid to tell him (or anyone) that she gets next to nothing from her quick encounters with Dan. During foreplay, she avoids touching his genitals at all for fear of exciting him further and making matters worse. Even though she is sexually unfulfilled, she tries to maintain a positive attitude by focusing on Dan's strengths.

If Dan and Vickie could have faced the problem in the early stages of their marriage, much of the frustration and hurt they both feel over the situation could have been avoided. Their problem worsened and intensified as they pushed it aside and ignored it. The longer a couple puts off talking about a problem, the more difficult finding a solution becomes. The prognosis for most sexual problems is good when a couple risks open discussion and demonstrates a willingness to face rather than ignore them.

Let's risk it with Dan and Vickie.

(1) *The opener.*   Sensitively initiate the discussion by stating you sense a problem, and ask if this is a good time to discuss it. Vickie could initiate a discussion with Dan about his

premature ejaculation this way:

"Dan, I've been reading a book about sex that has made me aware of something about our sex life. I think we are missing something special in our lovemaking. Is this a good time for you to discuss this with me?"

If Dan indicates the timing is okay, Vickie can carry on. If not, she would be wise to put off discussing the problem until he is more receptive.

(2) State the problem.   As clearly as possible, state the problem as you see it. State your feelings about it openly, clearly, and gently. Convey your message in I-message form, defining the effect of the problem on you in a nonblameful manner.

A word of warning: In spite of the fact that direct expression of feelings through I-messages has been emphasized throughout this book, think through the purpose of an I-message and the effect of an I-message on your partner at this time. The main purpose of an I-message is to vent your own feelings, not to change your mate's behavior. I-messages in the form of dumping what you don't like may further complicate the situation. Therefore, use the I-message format and style but without expression of irritation or anger. The timing is wrong for that.

Incorrect example: "You are a lousy lover. You never satisfy me. You ejaculate too fast. All you're concerned about is yourself, and I never get anything out of it." This statement name-calls, blames, makes judgments, and sets the stage for a major defensive reaction.

Correct example: "Although I very much enjoy making love with you, there is something I feel we need to talk about. I feel I am missing something during lovemaking. It's all over too fast for me. I need more foreplay. Sometimes our lovemaking is over in five minutes or less. This isn't enough time for me. Things are just beginning for me when they are finished for you. When this happens, it leaves me feeling frustrated, hurt, and yes, sometimes even angry. I've been doing some reading about sex in *The Compleat Marriage* and it says that if a man ejaculates in two minutes or less, he could have a problem with premature ejaculation.[1] Do you think this could be our problem? Can we search for a solution?"

(3) Check the response.   After getting this far, check your

partner's response. Listen carefully to any feedback. If he hasn't totally tuned you out, move on.

(4) Brainstorm solutions. You will want to employ many of the same tactics used in general problem solving but with more sensitivity.

VICKIE: Do you have any ideas for solutions?

DAN: The obvious answer is to give you more foreplay. But I get so excited I ejaculate even faster. So that won't work.

VICKIE: Remember, the book said if a man ejaculates in two minutes or less after intercourse begins, he might be a premature ejaculator. Could this be what we are dealing with?

DAN: Two minutes or less . . . it hurts to admit it, but it could be . . . what can be done for that?

While brainstorming, remember to remain open to all suggestions, which are evaluated in the next step.

(5) Solving the problem. The problem was brought up. Vickie stated her feelings and the effects on her. Possible solutions have been suggested. Now comes evaluation.

VICKIE: If I understand premature ejaculation, there are several methods of changing things. *The Compleat Marriage* suggests one method called the Stop Start method.[2] Can I read to you how it works?

DAN: I don't know. How do we know this method is best or even that it works? Maybe I need to go to Dr. Worley for a checkup and ask him. . . .

VICKIE: You can if you like. But why not try the Stop Start method first and then go to Dr. Worley if it doesn't work. Could we at least read about it? It's a program for both of us, not just you.

DAN: I guess so.

Through open discussion and by avoiding blaming and judging, Vickie negotiates, with Dan's help, a satisfactory method of searching for a solution. It may not always go this smoothly or be as easy as it looks on paper. If this method doesn't work, try something else.

Whatever the problem is, it can only be solved if you are each willing to open up. Because of your love and respect for each other, resolve to work together on a solution. You may both feel uncomfortable or embarrassed, but go ahead anyway. Nothing can change until discussion takes place.

Theoretically, husband and wife share equal responsibility for bringing up problems, negotiation, and finding a solution. However, women who attend our seminars confirm that if change is going to occur in the relationship, usually they must take the initiative.

One lady put it this way: "He won't fight or resist me, but if I want something between us changed, I have to initiate it. It's the same in the bedroom, but when we're talking about our sex life all his defenses go up and my approach must be velvet soft."

One more thing: Years of pretense and not talking about a problem may render some couples incapable of talking about it to each other. A third party who can assist with the communication process may ease the tension. A counselor can help a couple negotiate concerns. So if the two of you are not able to solve the problem on your own, or your mate refuses to admit there is a problem, refuses to discuss it with you, or no change takes place, seek professional help immediately. Problems that result in actual sexual dysfunction, such as loss of all sexual desire, impotency, inability to achieve orgasm, retarded ejaculation, and other problems need professional therapy. Ask your pastor for a referral or search the Yellow Pages for a well-qualified Christian sex counselor.

The biggest deterrent to solving sexual problems is *time*. The longer you put off talking to someone about the problem, the bigger it becomes and the less chance you will have of solving it. Unresolved sexual problems have a way of multiplying through the years, resulting in feelings of bitterness and anger. Seek help NOW!

How Not to Speak Sexually

The following scenario is an example of what to avoid when endeavoring to discuss your sexual relationship:

CASSIE: You never want to make love to me anymore. (*you-message*)

DICK: Get off it. You're the one who never wants it. (*counters with you-message*)

CASSIE: What are you talking about? You are the one who stays up so late that I'm asleep before you ever get to bed. You do that deliberately to avoid me. (*blaming and judging*)

DICK: Don't tell me what I'm doing. (*defensive response*)

CASSIE: Look, we've been over this before. You don't care about me anymore. The only thing you're interested in is your stereo rack system. You expect me to work full-time, take care of the kids, fix all the meals. You never help with anything. (*blaming, judging, put-downs, and a loss of focus on the issue*)

DICK: Here we go again. Nag, nag, nag. It wouldn't matter what I did for you. You wouldn't be happy. (*defense*)

Cassie storms out of the room.

Both Cassie and Dick lose in this scene. Rather than focusing on the issue and each really listening to what the other was saying, they busily engaged in attack and defend, which resulted in isolation and resentment for both.

How to Speak Sexually

There is a better way. Notice the different manner in which Cassie approaches Dick this time and how much more approachable he is:

CASSIE: I'd like to talk with you about our sex life—something is bothering me. Is this a good time?

DICK: As good as any.

CASSIE: Our sex life has always been good. I enjoy sex with you and you are a great lover. But we haven't been having sex frequently enough for me lately. When this happens, I feel lonely and isolated from you. I feel unloved, as if you don't care about me the way you used to. I'd like sex at least twice a week. Now I've told you my feelings about the problem as I see it. Before we discuss it further, I'd like to hear what you have heard me say so far. (*a compliment, I-message, and a perception check*)

DICK: Come on, Cass. Is all this necessary? (*attempt to sidetrack*)

CASSIE: Yes. I presented myself poorly the first time I

brought it up and I'm trying a new way. I need to know what you heard me say.

DICK: Well, you said you wanted more sex.

CASSIE: That's only part of what I said. What else did you hear?

DICK: You said I was a good lover.

CASSIE: And . . .

DICK: . . . that you felt isolated from me when we don't have sex.

CASSIE: And . . .

DICK: . . . that you'd like sex at least twice a week.

CASSIE: Perfect! That's exactly what I said. Is this request reasonable to you?

DICK: It sounds reasonable, Cass. But my new job takes more time than I anticipated. The stress is getting to me. I am just not as interested in sex as I used to be. I'm tired all the time.

CASSIE: I'm concerned over the stress of your new job too. But if we neglect our sex life we could lose our marriage, which would only add to the stress. In order to lessen the stress and take time for us, I'd like to get away overnight once a month. Now what did you hear me say? (*proposed solution and a perception check*)

DICK: I heard you say you are concerned over my stress and would like us to go away for a night once a month. We can't afford it, Cass! Spending more money right now will add to my stress.

CASSIE: I'll work on the details. If my mom won't take the. kids, I'll ask Lois to trade baby-sitting with me. And Gene has this place on the coast. We could afford to rent that for one night. And we'll plan just one meal out and—

DICK: It might work. If I could just get away from the pressure here. Maybe I could relax and be myself again.

CASSIE: Let's agree to try this plan for three months. Maybe with less stress, your sex drive will perk up and I'll feel important to you again. If it doesn't work, I'll want to talk to you again and look for a new plan. Okay?

DICK: It's a deal.

This time both Cassie and Dick end up winners rather than losers. It became possible when each was allowed to verbalize feelings openly rather than defending themselves and getting hostile. Each stated reasons and explored trial solutions. All this was accomplished without blaming, judging, or put-downs.

Caution: Guard against overtalk about a sexual problem. Differentiate between an isolated minor problem and an ongoing one that could prove to be disastrous if left unattended. There is a big difference between being turned off by something one night and the failure to achieve orgasm for months. Constantly dwelling on and emphasizing a partner's failure to meet your needs is likely to stir up resentment and embed the difficulty more deeply.

When Your Partner Refuses Discussion

You braved it and tried to discuss a topic. You did so in the best way you knew how, but your partner refuses to talk about it. What now? Rather than giving up in despair, never to approach the subject again, you might try exploring what lies behind your partner's refusal. The culprit behind a refusal to talk about a sex problem is usually either anger or fear. If your partner's anger or fear could be expressed and addressed, you might get someplace.

Reg and Connie have been married eighteen years and have two teenagers. Connie has reached a time in life when she feels sexually freer than ever before. In fact, she desires sex more frequently than Reg. When she approaches Reg about having sex more frequently, he doesn't want to talk about it. This time, rather than giving up, Connie presses through his resistance:

CONNIE: I understand your desire not to talk about this, but I need to talk about it. We've always had a good sex life and I find you more appealing to me now than ever. I really desire making love to you. I'm pressing you for more sex and you tend to avoid it. Does this pretty well sum up what's going on between us right now?

REG: I guess so.

CONNIE: There must be something that's holding you back. Tell me about it.

REG: I'm too tired. The long hours . . . the kids . . . I just don't feel like it.

CONNIE: You have been working long hours, I agree. Is there anything else that might be bothering you?

REG: I don't want to get into it.

CONNIE: If we don't get into it, this is only going to get worse.

REG: You're not going to like it . . . but you asked. You have been so passive when we make love. You hardly respond. Making love to you is like making love to a mannequin.

CONNIE: It sounds as if you have some strong feelings that have been stored up for a while.

REG: You bet! And furthermore . . . (*anger*).

Note that Connie does not defend herself against Reg's attack, but instead uses her active listening skills and presses on.

CONNIE: You sound really upset by all this. Is there anything else that's bothering you about our sex life?

REG: Yeah . . . well . . . when you pressure me for sex the way you have been lately, it makes me feel as if I have to perform. I'm not as young as I used to be and I don't want any pressure put on me about "performing." Sometimes I avoid sex because it's easier . . . I've worried over this . . . I knew I wasn't being fair to you . . . and I worried about losing you . . . I was afraid to talk with you about it. But I already feel better about it (*fear*).

CONNIE: I had no idea what was going on. I thought it was my fault . . . that you didn't care about me anymore . . . I am so relieved. Thank you for talking with me about this. I want to do all I can to make sex good for both of us again.

Don't expect overnight success. If you have been wandering in a sexual wilderness for eleven years, not talking about your problems or what you desire, it may take time to effect a change. Be patient.

When Your Partner Denies a Problem

Some people follow all the suggestions and still encounter a brick-wall response: "I don't see any problem," or "It's your problem, not mine," or "Nothing is bothering me," or "It's all in your head." How should one respond when there is total denial of a problem?

If you know or suspect a problem but are met with denial when you attempt to discuss it, back off. If you press, you'll only block further communication about it. Rest the subject—but do bring it up again. If your partner continues to deny the problem, try this: "Okay, you may not see a problem, but I do. I'd like to discuss it with you from my point of view." And proceed.

If your partner denies being upset or angry over a problem but you are certain he is, accept what is said at face value rather than arguing about it. It might be better to say, "I accept that you are not angry with me. But if you ever do get angry with me, please tell me so we can discuss it and deal with it."

Should you not break through his or her defenses after several attempts, seek professional help.

How to Talk About . . . Answers to Special Problems

My partner wants to do something I don't want to do. I don't know how to say no.

Be honest and gentle: "Honey, that makes me very uncomfortable," or "I just can't handle that tonight," or "I'm not comfortable with that. It makes me very anxious." A loving partner will be sensitive to an honest admission of anxiety.

What do you do when your partner wants you to do something you can never participate in with a clear conscience?

Again, total honesty is the best policy. "I just can't do that. It is wrong for me;" or "I was brought up in a very strict home and taught that was wrong. I can't participate with you in that activity." Avoid any blameful statements that imply your partner is a pervert.

I've been faking orgasms for years to build my husband's ego. I'm exhausted but don't know how to tell him.

Blurting this out to an unsuspecting husband probably could create more problems than it would solve. The real question is this: "Why are you faking?" Most likely, this question can only be answered with the help of a professional therapist. Faking an orgasm is a form of dishonesty and is destructive to intimacy.

My wife always expects me to be the initiator. Just once I'd like to have her make the first move.

If you want her to know, tell her so: "I'd like to have you take the lead tonight and initiate what you would enjoy. How do you feel about that?" She may be reluctant to lead, fearing you will think her too aggressive. A lead-in from you could alleviate this fear.

We have been married for years and my husband is always an eager, aggressive lover. I have never been able to initiate anything. How can I tell him I'd like to lead without scaring him?

Most men appreciate it when their wives take the lead some of the time, but not all of the time. Try something like this: "I'm in a real sexy mood tonight and would like to initiate some things with you. Are you comfortable with this?" Few men will turn down such an offer. If you are terribly shy and fear your man will think you too aggressive you might say, "I read in a book that men like their wives to initiate new things and take the lead more in sex. Would you enjoy that if I did it for you?"

My husband cannot accept no to sex without feeling totally rejected and unloved. He will be extremely cold, rejecting, and critical the next day, even when I still touch, hug, and compliment him. This causes a lack of desire on my part, and a cycle has begun which can last for weeks. We have tried to talk about it, but he says if I say no even because of fatigue or menstruation, I am totally rejecting him and I cause the problem. I feel the problem is his reaction to me and rejection of me as a person. Is there a better way of saying no?

In a loving relationship, either partner should be able to say no to sex occasionally when not in the mood. But even in the best of relationships, it can be tricky. We are very sensitive about our sexuality.

Most people avoid saying no. Instead, they use a wide variety of avoidance techniques to skirt the issue. Starting an argument is probably the most common. If you are angry with each other, there is little chance of sex. Other tactics involve faking sleep or tiredness, being too busy to go to bed, or not noticing your mate's advances. Such evasive measures don't work and lead to feelings of resentment.

Again, honesty is the best policy. If you are too tired, say so: "I'm too exhausted tonight to be a good sex partner." Then make a date for sex with your partner within forty-eight hours when you won't be too tired. "Give me a rain check and I'll meet you here tomorrow at seven o'clock. I'll get a good rest and make it worth your while." The promise of something great to come within forty-eight hours makes feelings of rejection less likely.

Our sex life is pretty good, but there are some things I'd like my partner to do more of. I just don't know how to ask him.

When asking for something you want or need, frame it in a positive, nondemanding way. "It feels really good to me when you . . . and I'd love to have more of it," or "I like it when you . . . and wonder if you would do that again for me." It is amazing how accommodating lovers can be once they know what is desired and it is asked for in the right way.

Sometimes my husband touches me in places that don't feel good to me. How can I tell him not to touch me there without hurting his feelings?

This is where an I-message would work best. Instead of saying, "I don't like it when you touch me there," try "I get uncomfortable when you touch me there too soon because I'm not ready for that yet."

Six Easy Ways to Talk About Sex

Some people are direct and comfortable when discussing sex. Others are extremely embarrassed or uncomfortable. Whatever your style, here are some easy ways to help you initiate sexual conversations with your mate:

(1) Refer to a book or article. One of the easiest lead-ins is to tell your partner something new you have learned from an article or book that you consider provocative or interesting. Tim and Beverly LaHaye's book *The Act of Marriage* and Ed Wheat's book *Love Life for Every Married Couple* touch on many areas vital to a sexual relationship. The chapter "Sexually Fulfill Your Mate" in my book *The Compleat Marriage* would also provide an excellent takeoff point for discussing a

wide array of topics on a man's or a woman's needs. If your partner balks at reading on his own, read some portion aloud.

(2) *Voice your fears.* Another approach for someone extremely shy or inhibited is total honesty about how difficult it is for you to talk about sex. Say something like this: "This is really hard for me to talk about . . . I want to talk with you about something in our sex life but I'm not good at words and this makes me so nervous. . . . " Leads such as these usually gain attention and empathy.

(3) *Introduce a startling fact.* Another way of initiating a sexual conversation is to introduce a startling fact: "It says here that as many as fifty percent of all married people have sexual problems that they can't talk about. What do you think about that?" or "Did you know that one survey says religious women make better lovers—they are the most sexually satisfied, sexually active, and orgasmic women in the country."

(4) *Ask questions.* Asking questions about what your partner does or doesn't like is another way to begin talking about sex. Frequently, couples don't know what their partners really want or like because they have never asked. A six-point agenda isn't necessary, but subtle questions about preferences can give you much-needed information that can go a long way in increasing your pleasure as well as your partner's.

For a beginner who wants to break the sexual silence barrier, a yes-or-no technique might work well. "Do you like it when I do this? Do you like that? Would you like more of this?" Yes-or-no responses are the simplest for all of us to give and will be especially easy for a man. If this is your first try at discussing sex and all you get are yes-and-no responses, don't despair! For a beginner that is good. You don't have to ask all your questions or get all your answers at one time.

Avoid asking general questions such as, "What do you like best about sex?" or "What turns you on?" You probably will get an "everything" and learn nothing. Specific questions designed to obtain specific information are best.

(5) *Open-ended sentences.* Open-ended sentences can be useful in helping individuals get started talking about sexual topics. Here are some sentence starters: "A funny thing I learned about sex when I was a child was . . . The type of

foreplay I enjoy most is . . . When I talk to you about sex I feel . . . The best sexual experience I ever had with you was when. . . ."

(6) A sex test.   Taking a "sex test" is yet another way of opening communication channels. One of the best is the "Intimate Hours Program" developed by Dr. Robert F. Kaufman. In a totally nonthreatening manner, husband and wife respond in writing to a series of questions with multiple answers. For example: Do you prefer making love: (a) in bright light; (b) in soft light; (c) in shadowy light; (d) in total darkness; (e) regardless of lighting conditions? After completing all questions, the couple share their responses aloud. Thus, many topics are introduced for discussion that might be difficult for them to bring up on their own. The "Intimate Hours" test and other sex tests and methods of evaluating your sexual relationship are available in the *Compleat Marriage Workbook.*

Yet another suggestion is to start a conversation about a topic on which you know you agree—for example, how much you both enjoy kissing, or positions you enjoy. Once you have opened the topic of sex at this level, it makes it easier to move to another level. Eventually, you should be able to move on to potentially embarrassing or emotionally charged subjects.

Expect some anxiety. As you attempt to open up and discuss things never or rarely expressed aloud, you probably will experience increased feelings of tension and fear. Whenever a person attempts something new, whether it is marriage, a new job, or driving a car, there will be stress. Anticipate such feelings and forge ahead anyway. Tension can produce positive reactions when you use it constructively rather than allowing it to create roadblocks.

Keep Sexual Compliments Flowing

Avoid getting so lost in discussing problem areas and things you don't like that you forget to tell your partner what you do like. Give compliments when they are appropriate. Remember that negatives are easier to take on a four-to-one ratio. In other words, offer four compliments to every negative. Herein lies a dilemma: When dealing with a Big Sexual Problem we tend to focus on The Problem while forgetting many pleasant or enjoyable experiences.

Feelings of worth are never more at stake than in the bedroom. Many opportunities to make a partner feel adequate, lovable, and attractive lie behind closed doors. Words such as, "You were terrific last night," or "You are great in bed," or "On a scale of one to ten you rate eleven as a lover," cause one to take pride in his or her sexuality. Sexual compliments work to your advantage, since they encourage your partner to live up to your views of his or her performance. This promotes more love, passion, and giving for the next encounter.

The sexual bond between you and your mate can grow stronger every year when you keep the communication channels open.

From Computer Sex to Loving Sex

As the months, years, and decades of marriage pass, it is only natural that a couple will begin to take each other for granted—and this attitude invades the bedroom too. Such an attitude leads directly to boredom, the desire for something new, and sometimes infidelity. A new partner or technique may temporarily revive sexual pleasure, but the fact remains that sex will not renew itself. The body chemistry that once drew the couple together and lit a fire that could not be quenched must constantly be rekindled and lit by stimuli within the relationship.

Yet "computer sex" still dominates many bedrooms. This is a term for couples who are motivated by a control key: They select the program marked "sex" and it activates—kissing, mounting, moving, climaxing, and falling asleep, according to the prescribed pattern dictated by the prewritten program on the disk. All of this is without personal, caring, passionate involvement. It is essential that routine or computer sex be avoided and that a couple's sexual bond be filled with warmth and mutual admiration.

One of the simplest ways of renewing the sexual bond is to let your partner know how much you enjoy looking at him or her. Reinitiate the habit of watching your partner undress, communicating with your eyes as well as verbally how much you like what you see. For instance, a man could let out a low whistle as he tells his wife how much he enjoys seeing her breasts swing. Words are aphrodisiacs, and these words need not be four-letter words or crude. A woman can communicate to her husband how his physical prowess enriches her sexual desire. This verbal appreciation for each other not only increases sexual desire but also motivates each partner to keep his or her body in good shape.

Successful long-term sex also includes creative lighting, music, and a new setting from time to time. Making love by the light of one tiny candle in a totally dark room can be a turn-on. Soft romantic music, classical baroque, or a Rachmaninoff concerto can set the right mood for some. Even though the bed may be the most comfortable place to make love, experiment with a new setting: your backyard spa, the living-room couch, the car, or the family-room floor. A change of pace or a new place can add interest to old love.

Marriages that are weak sexually tend to disintegrate totally over time, and studies indicate that sexual frequency among married couples is declining in America. A couple who are well bonded sexually and take the time to climb the ladder of bonding frequently will find a vital, rewarding relationship that is impregnable to outside temptation.

8 How to Get the One You Love Talking to You

What can be done in a situation where one wants to talk and the other doesn't?

Dear Van Pelts:

I really have a problem. My husband hardly talks to me. If I ask him a question, there is frequently no reply at all. I don't even know if he heard me speaking. Sometimes I'll wait a few minutes and repeat myself or ask if he heard what I said. Then he gets irritated and says I'm nagging him. This hurts me because I meant nothing bad at all. All I want to do is communicate with my husband and there is little response or a negative one. Sometimes he'll snarl, "Oh, be quiet." How can a husband and wife communicate when one wants to talk and is more outgoing and the other doesn't want to talk?

A Talkative Wife

You are married to an introvert, someone who does not have a high drive to communicate. You must realize that such an individual is less verbal and simply does not feel the need to initiate conversation or even to respond when conversation is initiated. What can be done in a situation where one wants to talk and the other doesn't? There are several things you might do in order to promote more conversation with a quiet partner.

Some general tips:

1. *Make it easy for your partner to talk with you by offering focused attention.* Sit attentively, act interested, and maintain good eye contact. Really listen when your partner does share thoughts and feelings.

2. *When talking with your partner, beware of placing blame or speaking in an accusing or superior manner.* This immediately places the other person on the defensive.

3. *Do not repeat to others thoughts or feelings your partner has shared in confidence.* If your partner gets the idea that nothing

213

is safe with you and that you might tell someone else what was shared in confidence, he may never open up. If you want a quiet person to open up, you must learn to keep confidences private.

4. *Refrain from leaping to wild conclusions about what is being said.* Instead of listening defensively, listen with an open mind and a closed mouth.

5. *Restrain yourself from interrupting to close the silence gap, even if a few seconds of silence elapse.* And just when you think you are through listening, listen thirty seconds longer.

6. *Even when you disagree with your partner, acknowledge that you have heard and understand his or her feelings on the matter.* If your partner is grappling with a problem, put your new active listening skills to work, allowing him or her to get it out of the system. Restrain the urge to offer solutions. Instead, give complete understanding and acceptance. Solutions can come later. Establish an atmosphere of acceptance and trust first.

7. *Reestablish touch.* Verbal communication is easier if preceded by physical touching. Look for occasions when your partner has accomplished something special or received a special commendation. A verbal affirmation plus a hug or a pat on the back is a beginning. Sharing a laugh over a funny story can also yield a favorable time to squeeze a hand or touch a knee. Even sickness offers opportunities for touch through a back rub or a cool hand to a warm forehead.

8. *Look for opportunities to draw your partner out.* Watching a movie together can open the emotional side of a person. A film can bring out feelings that might otherwise be suppressed. Emotions elicited through films are considered "safer." Since the people aren't real, the emotions displayed can be explained more easily. Discussion of the movie at a later time can provide an opening to explore feelings and what is behind them in a discreet and protected manner.

A good conversationalist tries in a thousand ways to draw his or her partner out, to learn about the other's likes and dislikes and what makes them tick. Good conversation involves offering the other person an opening to speak, bringing him or her into the conversation with you. It means you will prepare yourself with tidbits of information beyond your interests—information that will be interesting to your partner.

Techniques for Getting the Not-So-Verbal Person Talking

The right atmosphere has been set so the person can talk. Are there any special techniques that can be used to get the not-so-verbal person to open up? I have no magic potion to transform a quiet partner into an outgoing, warmhearted talk machine. But there are a few techniques to which a cooperative partner may respond.[1]

Skillful questioning   Questions can either open the door for discussion or slam it, depending on the type of question asked and how it is asked. Golden opportunities to communicate are frequently lost because we do not know how to ask questions skillfully.

Here is an easy rule to remember: Avoid *why* questions. *Why* questions are accusatory. Questions such as, "*Why* did you say that?" or "*Why* do you feel that way?" or "*Why* did you do that?" immediately place the other person in a position of having to defend what was just done or said. Accusations arouse defensive behavior. Only use *why* questions when specific information is needed, not when attempting to get a less-verbal person to open up.

Instead, try *what* questions. Instead of asking, "*Why* can't we talk about it now?" try, "*What* will be different about a later time if we put off talking about it until then?" Instead of "*Why* do you like tennis so much?" try, "Tell me *what* it is about tennis that you enjoy so much." Instead of "*Why* can't I buy it?" try, "*What* about spending money on this item bothers you so much?"

Direct questioning   Asking direct questions about specific topics may also help by making it easier for a less-verbal person to open up. Rather than saying, "What happened at work today?" and hearing, "The same old rat race," try, "Tell me about the most interesting thing that happened at work this week." Rather than, "You never tell me anything about your childhood," try, "I'd be interested in hearing something about your childhood. Tell me about the most fun birthday you can remember." Rather than, "You never tell me how you feel about your work," try, "I know very little about your job. I'd like to hear what you enjoy most about your work."

Specific requests for information relieve the pressure on a less-communicative person to formulate original replies. Couple this insight with the tell-me-more techniques learned earlier. Some questions are easier than others. Begin with the easy ones and move on to the more difficult ones.

Sentence starters   A person can be helped to express feelings more adeptly through sentence starters. If you sense something is bothering your partner and he or she is having difficulty talking about it, you could help your partner express himself or herself through the following examples:

> Something that is bothering me right now that I'm
>   having difficulty talking about is. . . .
> Something that really makes me angry is. . . .
> I really get upset when you. . . .

It doesn't matter whether your partner's responses to these sentence starters make sense, contradict one another, or are invalid from your point of view. The point is to get your partner talking, not to evaluate the rightness or wrongness of the response.

Once your partner has gone this far, his or her thoughts and feelings can be expanded by continuing to respond to such open-ended statements as these:

> By telling you this I have become aware that. . . .
> Talking about this makes me wonder if. . . .
> Sharing this with you makes it obvious that. . . .

Now it is your turn to respond. Open-ended sharing isn't complete until you respond with empathy to what has been said:

> Through listening to you I have heard you say that. . . .
> I heard you say today that one thing you would like
>   from me is. . . .
> Through listening to you right now it has become
>   obvious to me that. . . .

Open-ended sharing will break down in a hurry when acceptance is missing. If a woman should get her husband talking about his job and he says, "It's a dead-end street and I'm going to quit," and she screams, "You can't! What about me and the kids? We'll starve and lose the house," he'll probably never open up again. You don't have to agree with a partner's feelings but you can accept how he is feeling today.

The ABC method   One woman wrote on the CI, "My husband is a nothing-but-the-facts man. Though married thirty years, I cannot count him as a real friend. I talk, share feelings, and verbalize easily. Often I stop talking and ask him to tell me his thoughts and feelings. He knows more one-word and one-sentence responses than anyone in history. I still hold out hope that he might change! Have you got any suggestions for me?"

If you are married to a person who is used to giving one-word or one-sentence replies, before giving up in despair, try the ABC Method. Maybe your partner can be moved from the condensed version to the whole story as simple as ABC.

The ABC method includes three parts: (1) a report of the event or experience witnessed; (2) feelings about what happened; (3) the consequences or results of the event. A simple pattern for remembering these three parts is:

What happened is ____(1)____; I feel ____(2)____ about it; as a result of this experience I ____(3)____.

The next time your partner casually announces that he bought a new power tool, help him along by asking him to describe what prompted him to buy the new tool and his feelings about it. Then ask what he will be able to accomplish as a result of having this new tool.

Provide encouragement   Once your partner has opened up and shared with you, let him know how much it means for you to share a portion of his world. Even if it wasn't the level of intimacy you dreamed of, encouragement will pave the way for more sharing and spur his willingness to loosen up in the future. You might also ask if there is anything you can do to make sharing easier for him. Give your partner a hug, a pat on the hand, or a kiss, and thank him for sharing. This provides an incentive to share again.

9 How to Communicate With a Difficult Partner

There are some individuals who actually resist any attempts of caring or communication on an intimate level. Is there any way to reach such people?

Dear Van Pelts:

My husband and I live together separately—a relationship he insists we maintain for the benefit of our children. He works little and contributes almost nothing to our needs. I have no desire to talk with him as he seems to take great pleasure in intimidating me. When we are home alone together for the day, he often follows me from one room to another, seeing if he can top the last ugly thing he said to me. I spend the day going from one room to another, trying to get away from him. I try to find a place to hide until I can get my shaken body together again. Finally, in desperation I'll lash out at him in sobs, and only then will he leave me alone. Communicate with this man? No, he's beyond it, and somehow I've lost all desire for it.

Is it possible that some people are so handicapped when it comes to relating in a normal manner that it is impossible to communicate with them? Is there any way to reach such people? What does one partner do when the other refuses to put any effort toward maintaining the health and vitality of the relationship?

Yes, there are some individuals who actually resist any attempts of caring or communication on an intimate level. What we might consider normal brings anger, silence, or hostility from them.

One thing must be understood at this point: This person has feelings and experiences emotions. The distance he creates through hostility may be only an uncaring front. Your continued attempts at closeness might result in a hostile display only because you are disturbing the equilibrium of buried feelings and emotions. When you attempt to break through the cocoon of hostility he has wrapped around himself, it shakes him to the core.

This throws you into a dilemma. Your partner needs your caring, yet when you attempt to give it, you get a negative response. You feel as if you are beating your head against a brick wall. What should you do when the relationship deteriorates to this degree and you feel you can take it no longer?

Many people, particulary women, reach this point in their marriages. They become obsessed with attaining deep, intimate, and personal communication. A search for the perfect marriage, intimacy, or to get their husbands to open up compels them to read books, attend seminars, listen to tapes, go to counselors, dream up schemes, and exhaust all possibilities to attain their goal. All too frequently their efforts result in more silence, combativeness, and hostility. Nothing works. Their husbands either can't or won't communicate.

This desperate search to get through to a difficult partner affects some women physically, mentally, and spiritually. Some become irritable and hostile in return. Others suffer from severe depression. Still others become physically ill, complain of sleep problems, or shut off all desire for sex. Visits to physicians, psychiatrists, and counselors, along with prescribed medications, all prove fruitless.

If you are married to a difficult partner, there are four options you can consider:

1. You can change partners, hoping another partner will offer what you want.
2. You can run away.
3. You can continue doing what you are doing, experience no change, and hope you live through it.
4. You can change your behavior and expectations so that you do not feel so disappointed, cheated, or continually resentful.

The first two options are the most immature of all the choices. Running away from problems takes on many forms. It can be a literal flight from one place to another. It can be an adulterous relationship, withdrawal into silence, alcohol or drugs, television, or depression. But we can never really run away from ourselves. Running from our problems is very much like trying to run away from God. The Psalmist says to God, "Where can I flee from Thy presence?" (Psalm 139:7 NAS). Try as we may, it is impossible to hide ourselves from ourselves. There is no way around problems—we must work through them.

Choosing the third alternative means you tough it out, grin and bear it. The world will never know how terrible things are at home if you never tell. So you playact in front of others while enduring a rotten relationship. Millions have chosen this route rather than facing personal inadequacies and doing something about them.

The fourth option, changing your expectations and your behavior, may not be easy, but it is by far the most mature of the four choices. Yes, if you want the relationship changed, you will have to be the one to initiate change and do all the work that goes with it. Some women resent having to be the ones to work on relationship building and initiate change, but women are usually ten steps ahead of men when it comes to building a relationship. Resist wasting time and energy in being angry over having to do it alone. Proverbs 14:1 reminds us that a wise woman builds her house while a foolish woman tears hers down by her own efforts.

Here are some survival tips for desperate women (or men):

Give your communication problems to God.   Go to God with a prayer similar to this: "Lord, You know how much I want to be able to communicate with my partner. He, however, does not wish to communicate with me. This has been tearing me apart. I simply can't handle it alone anymore. But You can handle it. I now give our communication problems to You, asking You to handle them however You see fit." Getting through to your partner now becomes God's problem, not yours. This will not alleviate the problem, but it should lessen your stress if you trust Him for the results.

Don't take his negative response personally.   In most cases, a man's silence, anger, or hostility is not directed only at his wife. He would probably respond the same way if he were married to someone else. In other words, his problems stem from his background, something inside himself, not from you. This insight into the problem, while not changing anything directly, can change your feelings about the problem. He treats you the way he does because of some handicap from his childhood, or a previous relationship. See him as a victim of circumstances—a victim with a handicap.

Give up trying to force your husband to communicate with you.   Forced communication is so unrewarding that it is worse than no communication at all. Furthermore, you can't *force* anyone who does not wish to communicate with you to share on an intimate level. That only makes a person more defensive and resistant to change. But you can create a comfortable atmosphere so he could share should he ever wish to.

Accept your partner the way he is.   If your partner, through an accident or birth defect, were missing an arm or a leg, you would accept his handicap and love him anyway. Your partner has a handicap—an emotional one. He cannot understand your emotional needs and at present is unwilling to meet them. Rather than playing mind games, accept the reality of the situation, resolving to love him anyway. Accept him as a noncommunicator and a quiet or angry person. Your responsibility as a marriage partner is not to convince your partner of the wrongness of his ways and the rightness of your position but to accept him where he is today—with all his faults. Continual unacceptance will only entrench him more deeply in resisting change.

Focus on his good qualities.   Rather than focusing on his inability to meet your needs and the massive problems the two of you face, look at his good side. Is he a good provider? A faithful husband? A good father? Focus on his strengths.

Discipline your reactions.   Your reactions to his silence, combativeness, or hostility may be every bit as bad or wrong as his silence! Your depression, fretting, stewing, worrying, nagging, and resentment are hardly admirable amidst an existing problem. Take responsibility for your reactions. Resolve to respond more positively.

Keep a diary.   If you have to get your thoughts and feelings out into the open, write them out in diary form. Writing out thoughts and feelings gets them out of your system and relieves pressure buildup. No one is hurt by words on paper, and if you don't like what you have written you can always burn it later on.

Develop a support system.   Develop supportive relationships with other women. Fulfill your need to communicate by developing friendships with interesting women. This will fulfill some of your needs and lessen demands placed on your husband.

Pursue a hobby.   Put your energy into a hobby you especially enjoy or develop a new and enjoyable interest. This diversion of attention from unfulfilled needs will get your mind off your problems and increase your feelings of self-worth.

Develop an interest in his interests.   Women demand depth from their relationships. Discussing baseball scores, the stock market, politics, jobs, or fishing are usually not on their preferred list of discussion topics. However, if baseball scores, the stock market, politics, his job, or fishing are what interests him, you can get interested! When questioned on this point, women admit that their husbands will talk about some of these subjects, but they fail to respond because they aren't interested or don't want to talk about such trivial matters. But women expect their men to be interested in and want to talk about what men consider trivial. Get interested in some of his favorite subjects so you can share on his level. Read a book, attend a class, join a team. Communication isn't a one-way street.

Exercise daily.   Many studies have proved that exercise reduces depression. Begin a half hour of walking three to four times per week. Think positive thoughts while walking, and you will reap tremendous benefits physically, emotionally, and spiritually.

If you are one who has practiced acceptance, patience, long-suffering, forgiveness, and kindness to a fault, you might feel guilty because you see no change. You may wonder why the more you give, the worse things get. The more love you lavish on your man, the more selfish, demanding, and controlling he becomes.

If this is a rough description of what has been happening to you, it is time to recognize that some personality disorders exist which do not respond to ordinary methods of interaction. Some disorders or handicaps need professional treatment.

The Ultimate Ultimatum

If you have followed all of the previous suggestions with no breakthrough in sight, you may wish to risk *the ultimate ultimatum*. This involves making a list of the behaviors you will no longer accept and stating precisely what changes you must have if the relationship is to continue. Write this out in note or letter form and leave it for your husband to find. If after reading it he berates you, go to another room where you do not have to listen to his attack. If he follows you, leave the house for a short period of time. If he calls you on the phone, ranting and raving about the stupidity of the note and your demands, hang up on him. Disregard how scared you are, how weak your knees are, or how much you are shaking. Every time he challenges one of the changes you have requested, your response is always the same: You leave for a short period of time. But be sure he knows you are not leaving permanently.

Do not fail to leave or hang up even once. Continue responding in this manner for as long as necessary, until he recognizes that you mean business. When you begin to take yourself seriously and stand up for your rights in the marriage, he is much more likely to take you seriously too.

One woman clearly outlined the changes she had to have in her marriage. In addition to the changes, she insisted that she and her husband go for counseling. He had one week to make his decision. She prayed every day while sticking to her guns—walking out on him every time he berated her. Within the week, he agreed to go with her for counseling. Their marriage now had a chance.

Parting Words

I write these words following a visit from our children, who are now married but have been to our home with their children. This has been a very special time for all of us. We were together once again. Our house was full of children, love, and laughter. Our family was "compleat" again. Yesterday the house was hustling and bustling with activities, meals, babies, and wonder. Today it is very quiet. Everyone is gone.

I wander through the house. It isn't as clean as it usually is. There are fingerprints all over the sliding glass door, Cheerios on the kitchen floor, and a small teddy bear that got left behind in the last-minute shuffle of leaving. I smile. This is good for me—to have my extremely neat home messed up a little. I walk to the sofa and straighten the pillows.

How much I love our kids and each of their partners and their children. I'm proud of them. I am also concerned about them. Have their father and I set a good example? Are they prepared to meet the complexities and crises that a lifetime of living together will bring?

I walk to my office and sit down at my word processor. This book is almost finished. I will give birth to another "child." In solitude I shed a few tears, partly from the emotional exhaustion of the last few days and partly from the labor pangs of "this child."

So much of me is wrapped up in these pages. I've tried to lead you, step-by-step, to a closer relationship with your mate. Have I accomplished my goal? Can you now communicate with your partner better as a result of what I have written? Will you be able to relate to your partner in a more meaningful way because of this book? Have you found intimacy or purposed to find it?

Someone has said we must learn to remarry a different and changing person several times during our married life. During these transitional changes, we can choose divorce and seek a new partner who matches our current changes, or we can adapt ourselves to the changes. Experiencing and surviving change in a relationship can be as interesting as it is difficult, but it is much easier and less painful than the change associated with divorce.

In the end, the one message I want to leave with you is this: Set aside time *now* to talk with your partner about how you want your relationship to work. Don't wait. Talk *now*. Share the experience of this book together.

We tend to put off important things while tending to the urgent. We behave as if we can fix things later, do a better job later—when we have more time, more money. No excuse can change the fact that *now* is the best time to discover intimacy in your marriage. There never will be a better time than *now* to enhance your communication.

Some couples get so busy pursuing life that their marriages are forgotten. Such couples live together but don't love together. They forget to touch each other, listen to each other, or share intimacies with one another.

Don't let this happen to you. Let this book serve as a starting point for a commitment to intimacy. It's so important to me that this happens for you.

Nancy and Harry Van Pelt are co-directors of Better Living Programs, Inc., a ministry dedicated to "making families whole" through

> seminars
> retreats and conferences
> books and workbooks
> radio and television appearances
> cassette tapes
> videos
> articles

For further information contact:
Nancy and Harry Van Pelt
Better Living Programs
366 North Lind Avenue
Fresno, CA 93727

End Notes

Chapter 1 Communication: The Number-One Marriage Problem

1. Quoted by Wayne Rickerson in "Just Us," *Virtue* (July/August 1984), 44.
2. Quoted by Deborah Tannen, Ph.D., in *That's Not What I Meant: How Conversational Style Makes or Breaks Relationships* (New York: William Morrow and Company, Incorporated, 1986), 142.
3. Tim Hackler, "Women vs. Men: Are They Born Different?" *Mainliner* (May 1980), 122–132.
4. Donald M. Joy, Ph.D., *Bonding: Relationships in the Image of God* (Dallas, Texas: WORD Incorporated, 1985), 90.
5. Donald M. Joy, Ph.D., "The Innate Differences Between Males and Females" (cassette CS 099: radio program in which James C. Dobson, Ph.D., interviewed Dr. Joy; Focus on the Family, Box 500, Arcadia, California, 91006, 1982).
6. For a brief description of each temperament type *see* Tim LaHaye, *How to Be Happy Though Married* (Wheaton, Illinois: Tyndale House Publishers, 1968), 11–18.
7. For a full description of all the blends *see* Tim LaHaye, *Your Temperament: Discover Its Potential* (Wheaton, Illinois: Tyndale House Publishers, 1984), 29–43.
8. The Communication Inventory, referred to throughout the book as the CI, is a survey which I developed and administered to over 500 individuals who attended the Compleat Marriage seminars taught by my husband and me. From the 500 anonymous surveys, 149 males and 201 females were tabulated. Those in the survey represent various religions, races, ages, incomes, and educational backgrounds. From the 112 questions on the survey, I derived much pertinent information which has been incorporated into the book. For your interest, the survey is printed at the end of the book.

Chapter 2 Pair Bonding: Pathway to Intimacy

1. Donald M. Joy, Ph.D., *Bonding: Relationships in the Image of God* (Dallas, Texas: WORD Incorporated, 1985), 39.

2. M. H. Klaus and J. H. Kennell, *Parent-Infant Bonding,* second edition (St. Louis: C. V. Mosby Company, 1976).
3. Joy, *Bonding,* 111.
4. Ibid.
5. Donald M. Joy, Ph.D., *Rebonding: Preventing and Restoring Damaged Relationships* (Dallas, Texas: WORD Incorporated, 1986), 24.
6. Joy, *Bonding,* 112.
7. Ibid., 115.
8. Headings in bonding steps from Desmond Morris, *Intimate Behaviour* (London: Jonathan Cape Limited, 1971), 74–78. Published in the United States by Random House, Incorporated.
9. Joy, *Bonding,* 42.
10. Proverbs 6:26–29; 32, 33 RSV.
11. Shere Hite, *The Hite Report: A Nationwide Study of Female Sexuality* (New York: Dell Publishing Company, Incorporated, 1976), 144.
12. Leonard Zunin, M.D., with Natalie Zunin, *Contact: The First Four Minutes* (Los Angeles: Nash Publishing, 1972).

Chapter 3 Heart Listening: A Way to Show You Care

1. Jean Harker Burns, "The Greatest Halloween Prank of Them All," *Reader's Digest* (October 1969), 157 and following.
2. Quoted by Leonard Zunin, M.D., with Natalie Zunin in *Contact: The First Four Minutes* (Los Angeles: Nash Publishing, 1972), 21, 22.
3. Norman Wakefield, *Listening: A Christian's Guide to Loving Relationships* (Dallas, Texas: WORD Incorporated, 1981), 90, 91.
4. Quoted by Brad Greene, Robert Isenberg, Duane Rawlins, and Shayle Uroff in *Intra-Family Communication Training: Parents Manual* (Simi, California: ICT Corporation, 1971), 4, 13.
5. Deborah Tannen, Ph.D., *That's Not What I Meant: How Conversational Style Makes or Breaks Relationships* (New York: William Morrow and Company, Incorporated, 1986), 145.
6. Adapted from John Powell, *The Secret of Staying in Love* (Valencia, California: Tabor Publishing, 1974), 90–93.

Chapter 4 Hearttalk: How to Talk to the One You Love

1. "Streep a Perfect Aussie in A Cry in the Dark," the *Denver Post* (November 13, 1988), 1D.
2. "A Cry in the Dark," the *News Tribune* (November 6, 1988), B7.

3. Ronald B. Adler and Neil Towne, *Looking Out/Looking In*, fifth edition (New York: Holt, Rinehart & Winston, Incorporated, 1987), 253.

4. Jerry Richardson and Joel Margulis, *The Magic Power of Rapport* (San Francisco: Harbor Publishing, 1981), 31.

5. John Powell, *Why Am I Afraid to Tell You Who I Am?* (Valencia, California: Tabor Publishing, 1969), 50–62.

6. Deborah Tannen, Ph.D., *That's Not What I Meant: How Conversational Style Makes or Breaks Relationships* (New York: William Morrow and Company, Incorporated, 1986), 20.

7. Gary Smalley and John Trent, Ph.D., *The Language of Love* (Pomona, California: Focus on the Family Publishing, 1988), 32.

8. Tim Hackler, "Women vs. Men: Are They Born Different?" *Mainliner* (May 1980), 122–132.

9. Smalley and Trent, *Language*, 33.

10. Donald M. Joy, Ph.D., *Bonding: Relationships in the Image of God* (Dallas, Texas: WORD Incorporated, 1985), 93.

11. Smalley and Trent, *Language*, 34.

12. Ibid.

13. W. Robert Goy and Bruce S. McEwen, *Sexual Differentiation of the Brain* (Cambridge, Massachusetts: MIT Press, 1980), 64.

14. Tannen, *Not What I Meant*, 147.

15. Hackler, "Women vs. Men," 122–132.

16. Quoted by Miriam Arond and Samuel L. Pauker, M.D., in "Falling in Love Again . . . With Your Husband," *New Woman* (January 1988), 36.

17. Quoted by Julius and Barbara Fast in *Talking Between the Lines* (New York: Viking Press, 1979), 119.

18. Mary Lou Mullen, "Why Men Don't Hear What Women Say," an interview with Aaron T. Beck, M.D., *Ladies Home Journal* (October 1988), 122–126.

19. Tannen, *Not What I Meant*, 134.

20. Katherine Barrett and Richard Greene, "Why Don't We Talk Anymore?" *Ladies Home Journal* (September 1986), 34.

21. Quoted in Tannen, *Not What I Meant*, 43.

Chapter 5 Anger Workout: Coping With Conflict

1. David R. Mace, *Love and Anger in Marriage* (Grand Rapids, Michigan: Zondervan Publishing House, 1982), 45.

2. Quoted by Jeanette C. Lauer, Ph.D., and Robert H. Lauer, Ph.D., in *Til Death Do Us Part* (Binghamton, New York: The Haworth Press, Incorporated, 1986), 133, 134.

3. Ibid.
4. H. G. Whittington, M.D., "When Men and Women Disagree," *Savvy* (September 1981), 46, 47, 51, 54.
5. George R. Bach and Peter Wyden, *The Intimate Enemy: How to Fight Fair in Love and Marriage* (New York: William Morrow and Company, Incorporated, 1969).

Chapter 6 Best Friends: Secrets of Attaining Intimacy

1. Quoted in "What Keeps a Marriage Going?" *Partnership* (September/October 1985).
2. John Powell, *Why Am I Afraid to Tell You Who I Am?* (Valencia, California: Tabor Publishing, 1969), 62, 63.
3. Quoted by Francine Klagsburn in "Secrets and Pleasures of Long-Lasting Marriages," *Ms* (June 1985), 41–44, 93.
4. Quoted by Catherine Johnson, Ph.D., in "Intimacy in the Eighties: His and Hers," *New Woman* (March 1986).
5. Ibid.
6. Marilyn Elias, "Men's Healthy Need for Intimacy," *USA Today* (November 13, 1985).
7. Deborah Tannen, Ph.D., *That's Not What I Meant: How Conversational Style Makes or Breaks Relationships* (New York: William Morrow and Company, Incorporated, 1986), 142, 143.
8. Miriam Arond and Samuel L. Pauker, M.D., "Falling in Love Again . . . With Your Husband," *New Woman* (January 1988), 36.
9. Joseph Luft, *Of Human Interaction* (Palo Alto, California: National Press Books, 1969), 13.

Chapter 7 Sexually Speaking: Strangers in the Night

1. Nancy Van Pelt, *The Compleat Marriage* (Hagerstown, Maryland: Review and Herald Publishing, 1979).
2. Ibid., 133–138.

Chapter 8 How to Get the One You Love Talking to You

1. These techniques have been adapted from many sources, especially H. Norman Wright, *More Communication Keys for Your Marriage* (Ventura, California: Regal Books, 1983).

Communication Inventory

Dear Friends,

We are excited about the following survey, which addresses various aspects of communication and how they affect the marriage relationship. Most of the survey is multiple choice. Please circle the ONE RESPONSE which most closely reflects your present attitude or feeling, unless the question asks for more than one response. Also included are some completion sentences with space provided for your written responses. All surveys are anonymous and will not be used to embarrass you or your partner in any way. Information derived from this survey will be compiled by the Van Pelts and drawn from in a book Nancy currently has under way on communication and intimacy in marriage. Thanks so much for sharing with us.

Yours for stronger families!
Harry and Nancy Van Pelt

Please begin here.

1. The television is on during mealtimes in our home:
   a. all of the time
   b. most of the time
   c. some of the time
   d. rarely
   e. never

2. I enjoy conversing with my partner:
   a. all of the time
   b. most of the time
   c. some of the time
   d. rarely
   e. never

3. My partner senses how I am feeling:
   a. all of the time
   b. most of the time

      c.   some of the time
      d.   rarely
      e.   never

4. My partner listens attentively to what I have to say:
      a.   all of the time
      b.   most of the time
      c.   some of the time
      d.   rarely
      e.   never

5. My partner accepts my ideas and feelings supportively even though he/she does not agree:
      a.   all of the time
      b.   most of the time
      c.   some of the time
      d.   rarely
      e.   never

6. My partner and I engage in nonsexual touching (hugs, kisses, etc.) that do not signal intercourse:
      a.   all of the time
      b.   most of the time
      c.   some of the time
      d.   rarely
      e.   never

7. I carry on conversations in my mind about life, circumstances, and interactions between myself and others:
      a.   all of the time
      b.   most of the time
      c.   some of the time
      d.   rarely
      e.   never

8. When I am having difficulty with painful memories or unresolved problems from the past, my partner responds supportively:
      a.   all of the time
      b.   most of the time
      c.   some of the time
      d.   rarely
      e.   never

9. My partner reveals his inner self to me:
      a.   all of the time
      b.   most of the time
      c.   some of the time
      d.   rarely
      e.   never

10. My partner has a tendency to say things that would be better left unsaid:
    a. all of the time
    b. most of the time
    c. some of the time
    d. rarely
    e. never

11. I am presently experiencing enough intimacy with my partner to satisfy me:
    a. all of the time
    b. most of the time
    c. some of the time
    d. rarely
    e. never

12. If I could change one thing about the way my mate talks to me (in five words or less) it would be:_____
    _____

13. I am interested in hearing about and discussing my partner's daily life activities:
    a. all of the time
    b. most of the time
    c. some of the time
    d. rarely
    e. never

14. My partner accuses me of not listening to him/her:
    a. all of the time
    b. most of the time
    c. some of the time
    d. rarely
    e. never

15. My partner seems to understand the emotions behind what I am saying:
    a. all of the time
    b. most of the time
    c. some of the time
    d. rarely
    e. never

16. My partner responds to my expressed emotions appropriately:
    a. all of the time
    b. most of the time
    c. some of the time
    d. rarely
    e. never

17. My partner is easily distracted and acts uninterested while we are talking:
    a. all of the time
    b. most of the time
    c. some of the time
    d. rarely
    e. never

18. My partner avoids looking at me while we converse:
    a. all of the time
    b. most of the time
    c. some of the time
    d. rarely
    e. never

19. I censure and direct my mind conversations toward positive and constructive thoughts:
    a. all of the time
    b. most of the time
    c. some of the time
    d. rarely
    e. never

20. My partner is willing to put himself/herself out to hear and feel with my problems:
    a. all of the time
    b. most of the time
    c. some of the time
    d. rarely
    e. never

21. I fear emotional closeness:
    a. all of the time
    b. most of the time
    c. some of the time
    d. rarely
    e. never

22. In five words or less, one thing my partner will never listen to is:_____

23. I trust my partner:
    a. all of the time
    b. most of the time
    c. some of the time
    d. rarely
    e. never

24. I feel angry:
    a. all of the time

    b. most of the time
    c. some of the time
    d. rarely
    e. never

25. I express angry feelings:
    a. several times per hour
    b. several times per day
    c. several times per week
    d. several times per month
    e. several times per year
    f. never

You are making great progress! Please hang in there and continue.

26. There is an undercurrent of hostility in our home:
    a. all of the time
    b. most of the time
    c. some of the time
    d. rarely
    e. never

27. When attempting to resolve a conflict, my partner and I stay with one subject until it is resolved:
    a. all of the time
    b. most of the time
    c. some of the time
    d. rarely
    e. never

28. When angry with my partner, I withhold sexual privileges as a punishment:
    a. all of the time
    b. most of the time
    c. some of the time
    d. rarely
    e. never

29. In five words or less, the thing that makes me most angry is:.

_____

30. Our mealtime conversations are pleasant:
    a. all of the time
    b. most of the time
    c. some of the time
    d. rarely
    e. never

31. My mind conversations are negative:
    a. all of the time
    b. most of the time

    c.   some of the time
    d.   rarely
    e.   never

32.   When I am angry with my partner, I am able to ventilate my anger constructively:
    a.   all of the time
    b.   most of the time
    c.   some of the time
    d.   rarely
    e.   never

33.   When negotiating a conflict, my partner and I are able to see the issue from the other's point of view:
    a.   all of the time
    b.   most of the time
    c.   some of the time
    d.   rarely
    e.   never

34.   When my partner and I have sex, I reach a climax:
    a.   all of the time
    b.   most of the time
    c.   some of the time
    d.   rarely
    e.   never

35.   My partner and I have learned to resolve conflicts constructively without one of us "winning" and the other "losing":
    a.   all of the time
    b.   most of the time
    c.   some of the time
    d.   rarely
    e.   never

36.   The biggest problem we encounter when trying to solve a conflict is (in five words or less):_____
_____

37.   My partner and I discuss our sexual relationship:
    a.   definitely yes
    b.   often yes
    c.   unsure
    d.   usually not
    e.   definitely not

38.   My mind conversations help me to reinforce my attitudes, values, and beliefs:
    a.   definitely yes
    b.   often yes

    c.   unsure
    d.   usually not
    e.   definitely not

39.   Painful memories and unresolved problems from the past affect my present:
    a.   definitely yes
    b.   often yes
    c.   unsure
    d.   usually not
    e.   definitely not

40.   In my present marriage, I have disclosed something that would have been better left undisclosed:
    a.   definitely yes
    b.   often yes
    c.   unsure
    d.   usually not
    e.   definitely not

41.   If yes, that something was from:
    a.   my childhood
    b.   a former spouse
    c.   my present relationship
    d.   an extramarital affair
    e.   other_____

42.   Television is a hindrance to satisfying communication in our relationship:
    a.   definitely yes
    b.   often yes
    c.   unsure
    d.   usually not
    e.   definitely not

43.   My mind conversations help me to enhance my self-concept:
    a.   definitely yes
    b.   often yes
    c.   unsure
    d.   usually not
    e.   definitely not

44.   I readily apologize after expressing anger inappropriately:
    a.   definitely yes
    b.   often yes
    c.   unsure
    d.   usually not
    e.   definitely not

45. In five words or less, one thing my partner and I never discuss is:_____

46. My mind conversations help me to develop my behavior patterns:
    a. definitely yes
    b. often yes
    c. unsure
    d. usually not
    e. definitely not

47. On a scale of 1 to 10 with 10 as excellent and 1 as awful, I would rate my partner's listening skills as:
    1 2 3 4 5 6 7 8 9 10 (circle one)

48. On a scale of 1 to 10 with 10 as very close and 1 as distant, I would rate the intimacy of our marriage at:
    1 2 3 4 5 6 7 8 9 10 (circle one)

49. On a scale of 1 to 10 with 10 as high feelings of worth and 1 as low feelings of worth, I would rate my acceptance of self at:
    1 2 3 4 5 6 7 8 9 10 (circle one)

50. On a scale of 1 to 10 with 10 as high acceptance and 1 as low acceptance, I would rate my mate's acceptance of me at:
    1 2 3 4 5 6 7 8 9 10 (circle one)

51. On a scale of 1 to 10 with 10 as high acceptance and 1 as low acceptance, I would rate my acceptance of my mate at:
    1 2 3 4 5 6 7 8 9 10 (circle one)

52. On a scale of 1 to 10 with 10 as very satisfied and 1 as very unhappy, I would describe my overall marital satisfaction as:
    1 2 3 4 5 6 7 8 9 10 (circle one)

You are almost halfway done! Keep moving!

53. On the average, my partner and I spend this amount of time per week talking with each other without TV or other disturbances:
    a. 1–30 minutes per week
    b. 30–60 minutes per week
    c. 1–2 hours per week
    d. 3–5 hours per week
    e. 6–8 hours per week
    f. 9–15 hours per week
    g. more than 15 hours per week

54. My most painful memories and unresolved problems from the past seem to surface most frequently when:
    a. I am alone
    b. I am angry with my partner
    c. we are having serious marriage problems

    d. during stressful periods in my life

    e. other_____

55. I am revealing _____ of my inner self to my mate:

    a. all

    b. most

    c. some

    d. little

    e. none

56. The single most important part of intimacy to me is

    a. mutually satisfying sex

    b. physical closeness

    c. emotional closeness

    d. sharing innermost feelings

    e. other_____

57. If not experiencing sufficient intimacy, the fault lies with:

    a. me

    b. partner

    c. both of us

    d. outside circumstances

58. When my partner talks to me, he speaks to me as if I am:

    a. superior

    b. equal

    c. inferior

59. Most of the conversations I have with my mate revolve around:

    a. our relationship

    b. the children

    c. finances

    d. business (his/hers or yours)

    e. goals and the future

    f. other_____

60. When feeling angry, I usually express it by:

    a. clamming up

    b. suffering in silence to avoid conflict

    c. lashing out at my partner

    d. openly and kindly confronting my partner

    e. not saying anything but feeling resentful

    f. confronting but not attacking my mate

61. When my mate attacks me, I usually:

    a. clam up

    b. defend myself

    c. attack back

    d. tell him/her how much it hurts

62. I am not free to discuss sex as openly as I would like to be due to:
    a. childhood experiences
    b. sexual molestation
    c. painful memories from a past marriage
    d. unresolved problems from my present mate
    e. no problem discussing sex openly
    f. other_____

63. If a problem exists which inhibits me from discussing sex openly with my mate, this problem has been voiced to my partner:
    a. definitely yes
    b. unsure
    c. definitely not

64. We are having intercourse approximately:
    a. 5–7 times per week
    b. 3–4 times per week
    c. 1–2 times per week
    d. 1–2 times per month
    e. 1–2 times per six months
    f. 1–2 times per year
    g. never

65. There are five basic levels of communication. My partner and I spend most of our time on (mark the two used most often)·
    a. cliché or small-talk level
    b. factual information level
    c. idea and opinion level
    d. feeling and emotional level
    e. deep insight (close and intimate level)

66. Communication on these levels is satisfying to me·
    a. all of the time
    b. most of the time
    c. some of the time
    d. rarely
    e. never

67. Most of our conversing takes place:
    a. at the table
    b. in the car
    c. in bed
    d. while engaging in activities together outside the home
    e. while engaging in activities together inside the home
    f. other_____

68. For what reason(s) are you not revealing more of yourself to your mate? (Mark all that apply.)
    a. don't think it is necessary
    b. afraid to
    c. fear of having it used against me
    d. fear of rejection
    e. too painful to discuss
    f. already revealing all of myself
    g. other_____

69. The most irritating thing my partner does while I am talking (in five words or less) is:_____
    _____

70. The person to whom I have revealed most of my inner self during my life is:
    a. parent
    b. mate
    c. sibling
    d. child
    e. close friend
    f. counselor
    g. no one

71. I prefer to discuss problems:
    a. as they occur
    b. during a set time each week
    c. before going to bed each night
    d. problems don't need to be discussed
    e. other_____

72. Conflicts between us sometimes carry on for:
    a. minutes
    b. hours
    c. days
    d. weeks
    e. months
    f. years

73. The source of most strain in our relationship is:
    a. finances
    b. kids
    c. in-laws
    d. sex
    e. communication
    f. other_____

74. What I really want when I get angry is:
    a. attention or sympathy

      b.   understanding
      c.   to get even
      d.   to talk it through
      e.   action to correct the problem
      f.   to be left alone
      g.   other_____

75.   I fear emotional closeness because of:
      a.   painful memories from the past
      b.   unresolved problems from my current relationship
      c.   fear of rejection by my partner
      d.   been hurt too badly to try
      e.   other_____

76.   When my partner and I encounter a problem or conflict situation we:
      a.   talk it out right then
      b.   get hostile and shout it out
      c.   withdraw from discussing it
      d.   defer it until we can discuss it calmly
      e.   don't discuss problems; we bury them

Keep going! You are almost done!

77.   The cause for most of the anger in me is:
      a.   my partner
      b.   my children
      c.   my work situation
      d.   my parents
      e.   myself
      f.   circumstances beyond my control

78.   I would prefer to have sex more frequently than now occurring in our relationship:
      a.   definitely yes
      b.   unsure
      c.   definitely not

79.   If "yes" above, the reason sex is not occurring as frequently as I would like is:
      a.   fatigue and time pressure
      b.   lack of interest by one or the other
      c.   unresolved conflicts and anger
      d.   painful memories of the past
      e.   medical problems
      f.   other_____

80.   The thing I would most like to discuss with my partner about sex is:
      a.   frequency

    b.   techniques
    c.   birth control
    d.   who should initiate sex
    e.   other_____

81. One thing I would never discuss with my partner about sex (in five words or less) is:_____

_____

82. In my opinion the one most overall important ingredient for a happy marriage is:
    a.   sexual satisfaction
    b.   financial security and material possessions
    c.   companionship and friendship with partner
    d.   children
    e.   someone to turn to during trouble times
    f.   other_____

83. I am satisfied with the amount of conversing taking place in our relationship at present:
    a.   definitely yes
    b.   unsure
    c.   definitely not

84. I find sufficient nonsexual touching, caring, and healing in our relationship:
    a.   definitely yes
    b.   unsure
    c.   definitely not

85. When I am angry with my partner I find it very difficult to touch him/her:
    a.   definitely yes
    b.   unsure
    c.   definitely not

86. In my past are unresolved problems or painful memories which I have attempted to bury but which I carry with me:
    a.   definitely yes
    b.   unsure
    c.   definitely not

87. If answer to previous question is yes, I have confided these unresolved problems or painful memories of the past to my partner:
    a.   definitely yes
    b.   unsure
    c.   definitely not

88. I consider my mate and I best friends:

a.   definitely yes
b.   unsure
c.   definitely not

89. My partner and I spend enough time with each other sharing
     feelings and interests to build intimacy:
     a.   definitely yes
     b.   unsure
     c.   definitely not

90. I want to attain an intimate relationship with my partner:
     a.   definitely yes
     b.   unsure
     c.   definitely no

91. Intimacy is next to impossible in our relationship due to the
     many conflicts we have:
     a.   definitely yes
     b.   unsure
     c.   definitely not

92. If my partner and I experienced a sexual problem we would
     discuss it:
     a.   definitely yes
     b.   unsure
     c.   definitely not

93. I have discussed my sexual preferences with my partner:
     a.   definitely yes
     b.   unsure
     c.   definitely not

94. I am interested in learning ways of deepening our communi-
     cation:
     a.   definitely yes
     b.   unsure
     c.   definitely not

95. My partner is interested in learning ways of deepening our
     communication:
     a.   definitely yes
     b.   unsure
     c.   definitely not

96. I tell my partner what pleases me during intercourse:
     a.   definitely yes
     b.   unsure
     c.   definitely not

97. I would like my partner to be more open in discussing sexual
     feelings with me:
     a.   definitely yes

      b.   unsure

      c.   definitely not

98.   When I have enjoyed a particularly good sexual experience I tell my partner:

      a.   definitely yes

      b.   unsure

      c.   definitely not

99.   My partner has discussed his/her sexual preferences with me:

      a.   definitely yes

      b.   unsure

      c.   definitely not

100.   I am:

      a.   male

      b.   female

101.   I am:

      a.   currently married

      b.   single

      c.   separated from spouse

      d.   unmarried but living with a partner

102.   I am in the following age bracket:

      a.   18 to 25

      b.   26 to 35

      c.   36 to 45

      d.   46 to 55

      e.   56 to 65

      f.   over 66

103.   I belong to the following race:

      a.   caucasian

      b.   black

      c.   hispanic

      d.   oriental

      e.   other_____

104.   My spouse belongs to the following race:

      a.   caucasian

      b.   black

      c.   hispanic

      d.   oriental

      e.   other_____

105.   My level of education is:

      a.   grade school

      b.   high school graduate

      c.   vocational training or attended some college

      d.   college degree

      e.   more than a college degree

106. My spouse's level of education is:
     a. grade school
     b. high school graduate
     c. vocational training or attended some college
     d. college degree
     e. more than a college degree
107. Our combined income level is:
     a. less than $10,000 per year
     b. $11,000 to $20,000 per year
     c. $21,000 to $40,000 per year
     d. $41,000 to $60,000 per year
     e. over $60,000 per year
108. Length of present marriage:
     a. 0–5 years
     b. 6–10 years
     c. 11–20 years
     d. 21–30 years
     e. 31–40 years
     f. 41–50 years
     g. over 50 years
109. I have been married _____ times.
110. If previously married, how many marriages ended in death of spouse? _____
111. If previously married, how many marriages ended in divorce? _____
112. We have _____ children.

*THANK YOU! THANK YOU! THANK YOU! THANK YOU!
THANK YOU! THANK YOU! THANK YOU! THANK YOU!*
Please feel free to tell us about any communication problem or success you have experienced. The more specific you are, the easier it will be for us to understand and for you to clarify your own thinking. Please use the back side of this page. Thanks so much!

Bibliography

Adler, Ronald B., and Neil Towne. *Looking Out/Looking In*, fifth edition. New York: Holt, Rinehart & Winston, Incorporated, 1987.

Augsburger, David. *Caring Enough to Confront*. Ventura, California: Regal Books, 1973.

———. *Caring Enough to Hear and Be Heard*. Ventura, California: Regal Books, 1982.

Bach, George R., and Peter Wyden. *The Intimate Enemy: How to Fight Fair in Love and Marriage*. New York: William Morrow and Company, Incorporated, 1969.

Backus, William, Ph.D. *Telling Each Other the Truth*. Minneapolis: Bethany House, 1985.

Bustanoby, Andre. *Just Talk to Me*. Grand Rapids, Michigan: Zondervan Publishing House, 1981.

Carlson, Dwight L., M.D. *Overcoming Hurts and Anger*. Eugene, Oregon: Harvest House, 1981.

Clinebell, Howard J. and Charlotte. *The Intimate Marriage*. New York: Harper & Row Publishers, Incorporated, 1970.

Drakeford, John W. *The Awesome Power of the Listening Heart*. Grand Rapids, Michigan: Zondervan Publishing House, 1982.

Fairfield, James G. T. *When You Don't Agree*. Scottdale, Pennsylvania: Herald Press, 1977.

Fast, Julius and Barbara. *Talking Between the Lines*. New York: Viking Press, 1979.

Goy, Robert W., and Bruce S. McEwen. *Sexual Differentiation of the Brain*. Cambridge, Massachusetts: MIT Press, 1980.

Hocking, David and Carole. *Good Marriages Take Time*. Eugene, Oregon: Harvest House, 1984.

Huggett, Joyce. *Creative Conflict*. Downer's Grove, Illinois: Intervarsity Press, 1984.

Joy, Donald M. *Bonding: Relationships in the Image of God*. Dallas, Texas: WORD Incorporated, 1985.

———. *Rebonding: Restoring Broken and Damaged Bonds*. Dallas, Texas: WORD Incorporated, 1986.

Kassorla, Irene, Ph.D. *Putting It All Together*. New York: Hawthorne Publishing Company, 1973.

Klaus, M. H., and J. H. Kennell. *Parent-Infant Bonding*, second edition. St. Louis: C. V. Mosby Company, 1976.

Konner, Melvin. *The Tangled Wing: Biological Constraints on the Human Spirit*. New York: Holt, Rinehart & Winston, Incorporated, 1982.

LaHaye, Tim. *Your Temperament: Discover Its Potential*. Wheaton, Illinois: Tyndale House Publishers, 1984.

Lasswell, Marcia, and Norman M. Lobsenz. *Equal Time*. Garden City, New York: Doubleday & Company, Incorporated, 1983.

Mace, David R. *Close Companions*. New York: Continuum Publishing Company, 1982.

———. *Love and Anger in Marriage*. Grand Rapids, Michigan: Zondervan Publishing House, 1982.

McGill, Michael E. *The McGill Report on Male Intimacy*. New York: Holt, Rinehart & Winston, Incorporated, 1985.

McKay, Matthew, Martha Davis, Ph.D., and Patrick Fanning. *Messages: The Communication Book*. Oakland, California: New Harbinger Publications, 1983.

Miller, Sherod, Elam W. Nunnally, and Daniel B. Wackman. *Alive and Aware*. Minneapolis: Interpersonal Communication Programs, Incorporated, 1975.

Miller, Sherod, Elam W. Nunnally, Daniel B. Wackman, and Roger Ferris. *Couple Workbook*. Minneapolis: Interpersonal Communication Programs, Incorporated, 1976.

Miller, Sherod, Daniel B. Wackman, Elam W. Nunnally, and Carol Saline. *Straight Talk*. New York: New American Library, 1981.

Missildine, W. Hugh. *Your Inner Conflicts—How to Solve Them*. New York: Simon & Schuster, Incorporated, 1974.

Morris, Desmond. *Intimate Behaviour*. New York: Random House, Incorporated, 1971.

Nierenberg, Gerard I., and Henry N. Calero. *Meta-Talk*. New York: Simon & Schuster, Incorporated, 1973.

Osborne, Cecil. *The Art of Understanding Your Mate*. Grand Rapids, Michigan: Zondervan Publishing House, 1970.

Penney, Alexandra. *Great Sex*. New York: G. P. Putnam's Sons, 1985.

———. *How to Make Love to Each Other*. New York: Berkley Publishing Group, 1982.

Powell, John. *The Secret of Staying in Love*. Valencia, California: Tabor Publishing, 1974.

———. *Why Am I Afraid to Tell You Who I Am?* Valencia, California: Tabor Publishing, 1969.

———. *Will the Real Me Please Stand Up*. Valencia, California: Tabor Publishing, 1985.

Qubein, Nido R. *Communicate Like a Pro*. New York: Berkley Publishing Group, 1983.

Richardson, Jerry, and Joel Margulis. *The Magic Power of Rapport*. San Francisco: Harbor Publishing, 1981.

Rubin, Theodore Isaac. *The Angry Book*. New York: Macmillan Publishing Company, Incorporated, 1969.

Sager, Clifford J., M.D., and Bernice Hunt. *Intimate Partners*. New York: McGraw-Hill Book Company, 1979.

Sell, Dr. Charles M. *Achieving the Impossible: Intimate Marriage*. New York: Ballantine Books, Incorporated, 1982.

Shain, Merle. *When Lovers Are Friends*. New York: Bantam Books, Incorporated, 1978.

Shedd, Charlie W. *Talk to Me*. Garden City, New York: Doubleday & Company, Incorporated, 1983.

Small, Dwight Hervey. *After You've Said I Do*. Old Tappan, New Jersey: Fleming H. Revell Company, 1976.

Smalley, Gary, and John Trent, Ph.D. *The Language of Love*. Pomona, California: Focus on the Family Publishing, 1988.

Smedes, Lewis B. *How Can It Be All Right When Everything Is All Wrong?* New York: Harper & Row Publishers, Incorporated, 1982.

———. *Forgive and Forget*. New York: Pocket Books, Incorporated, 1984.

Tannen, Deborah, Ph.D. *That's Not What I Meant: How Conversational Style Makes or Breaks Relationships*. New York: William Morrow and Company, Incorporated, 1986.

Umphrey, Marjorie. *Getting to Know You*. Irvine, California: Harvest House, 1976.

Van Pelt, Nancy. *The Compleat Marriage*. Hagerstown, Maryland: Review and Herald Publishing, 1979.

———. *The Compleat Marriage Workbook*. Hagerstown, Maryland: Review and Herald Publishing, 1984, revised 1987.

———. *The Compleat Courtship*. Hagerstown, Maryland: Review and Herald Publishing, 1982.

———. *The Compleat Courtship Workbook*. Hagerstown, Maryland: Review and Herald Publishing, 1984, revised 1987.

———. *The Compleat Parent*. Hagerstown, Maryland: Review and Herald Publishing, revised 1985.

———. *The Compleat Parent Workbook*. Hagerstown, Maryland: Review and Herald Publishing, 1984.

Viscott, David. *The Language of Feelings*. New York: Pocket Books, Incorporated, 1976.

Wahlroos, Sven, Ph.D. *Family Communication*. New York: Signet Books, 1974.

Wakefield, Norman. *Listening: A Christian's Guide to Loving Relationships*. Dallas, Texas: WORD Incorporated, 1981.

Wheat, Ed, M.D. *Love Life for Every Married Couple*. Grand Rapids, Michigan: Zondervan Publishing House, 1980.

Wright, H. Norman. *Communication: Key to Your Marriage*. Glendale, California: G/C Publications, 1974.

———. *More Communication Keys for Your Marriage*. Ventura, California: Regal Books, 1983.

———. *Romancing Your Marriage*. Ventura, California: Regal Books, 1987.

Zunin, Leonard, M.D., with Natalie Zunin. *Contact: The First Four Minutes*. Los Angeles: Nash Publishing, 1972.